Beyond Words

Beyond Words presents a range of illuminating approaches to examining every day social interactions, to help the reader understand human movement in new ways.

Carol-Lynne Moore and Kaoru Yamamoto build on the principles that they expertly explored in the first edition of the book, maintaining a focus on the processes of movement as opposed to discussions of static body language. The authors combine textual discussion with a new set of website-hosted video instructions to ensure that readers develop an in-depth understanding of nonverbal communication, as well as the work of its most influential analyst, Rudolf Laban.

This fully revised, extensively illustrated second edition includes a new introduction by the authors. It presents a fascinating insight into this vital field of study, and will be an invaluable resource for scholars and practitioners in many activities, from performing and martial arts, athletics, to therapeutic and spiritual practices, conflict resolution, business interactions, and intercultural relations.

Visual material for Chapters 3, 5, 8 and 9 can be found on the companion website: www.routledge.com/cw/moore.

Carol-Lynne Moore has lectured extensively in the U.S. and Europe on Laban theory, including Movement Pattern Analysis, an assessment of executive decision-making style developed from industrial and managerial movement studies. Her most recent publication is *The Harmonic Structure of Movement, Music and Dance According to Rudolf Laban* (Mellen Press, 2009). She is a founding member and current President of Motus Humanus, a professional organization for movement specialists in the U.S. She currently teaches at Columbia College, Chicago.

Kaoru Yamamoto is Professor Emeritus at the University of Colorado and a Fellow of the American Psychological Association, having taught extensively in the U.S., Canada, Iceland, and China. He has edited scholarly journals on psychology and education, and published widely in both areas, including ten full-length works on human development, creativity, and cultural evolution.

Beyond Words

Movement Observation
and Analysis

Second edition

Carol-Lynne Moore
Kaoru Yamamoto

Routledge
Taylor & Francis Group

LONDON AND NEW YORK

Second edition published 2012
by Routledge
2 Park Square, Milton Park, Abingdon, Oxon OX14 4RN

Simultaneously published in the USA and Canada
by Routledge
711 Third Avenue, New York, NY 10017

Routledge is an imprint of the Taylor & Francis Group, an informa business

First edition published by Gordon & Breach 1988

British Library Cataloguing in Publication Data
A catalogue record for this book is available from the British Library

Library of Congress Cataloging in Publication Data
Moore, Carol-Lynne
  Beyond words: movement observation and analysis/Carol-Lynne
  Moore, Kaoru Yamamoto.—2nd ed.
  p.cm.
  1. Dance. 2. Choreography. 3. Movement, esthetics of
  I. Yamamoto, Kaoru. II. Title.
  GV1595.M59 2011
  792.8'2—dc22
  2011006875

ISBN: 978–0–415–61001–8 (hbk)
ISBN: 978–0–415–61002–5 (pbk)
ISBN: 978–0–203–80607–4 (ebk)

Typeset in Sabon
by Florence Production Ltd, Stoodleigh, Devon

Printed and bound in Great Britain by the MPG Books Group

Contents

Preface   ix
Acknowledgments   xi

Introduction   1

PART I
Module A   3

  1 In search of an elusive phenomenon   5

  2 The perception of human movement   11

  3 Enhancing movement awareness*   28

  4 Body knowledge/body prejudice   32

  5 Deciphering human movements*   58

  6 Movement as metaphor   65

PART II
Module B   85

  7 Functions of movement in human life   87

  8 Movements in context*   127

  9 Basic parameters of movement*   130

10 Observation in practice: process and structure   150

* Visual material for these chapters is hosted on the website: www.routledge.com/cw/moore

Preface

When the first edition of *Beyond Words* appeared two decades ago, it was hailed as "an original, pioneering a category of its own . . ., the discipline of movement observation and analysis"(Warren Lamb writing in the Foreword to the first edition, Moore and Yamamoto 1988). Its appearance coincided with a wave of popular curiosity and scholarly inquiry into nonverbal communication. While the realm of the "nonverbal" incorporates *static* elements of behavior, such as chronic postural alignments, stationary poses, even clothing choices, *Beyond Words* concentrated on *dynamic* dimensions; that is, bodily movements. This was, and remains, a bold choice because "it is indeed difficult to write about how movement can be observed and analyzed. Like a wave that furls and curls and rolls and crashes, then suddenly is no more, how does one pin human movement down?" (ibid).

The original *Beyond Words* was the first movement observation text to take advantage of two twentieth-century innovations—one mechanical and one conceptual. In the first instance, the advent of videotape technology has made it possible to record a variety of movement-events for study and review. In the second instance, the work of polymath Rudolf Laban (1879–1958) has provided a conceptual framework for movement analysis. As a theorist, Laban was one of the first individuals to conceive human movement as a *psychophysical* phenomenon of enormous social and cultural significance. His notation system and taxonomy of human movement provide additional tools for recording, describing, and analyzing nonverbal behavior. Drawing on both innovations, the authors combined written material with "video chapters," linking theoretical discussion of human movement with practical observation and analysis exercises in the first edition.

Readers familiar with the original version of *Beyond Words* will find much unchanged in this revision. Chapter structures and the sequence of presentation of material follow the pattern of the first edition. Movement analysis is still discussed in the context of human perception, endeavors of many sorts, and the ever-present need to understand the movement behavior of other people in real-life settings. However, certain discussions have been streamlined. Many sections of the book have been updated to incorporate current findings, notably in neuroscience, that impact understanding of movement. The referential basis of the text has been expanded, augmenting original sources with contemporary material in an extensive bibliography. Because bodily movement is an ever-present dimension of human endeavor, a wide range of topics are included to encourage students of movement to appreciate the comprehensive nature of this psychophysical, social, and cultural phenomenon.

An exciting new dimension of this edition of *Beyond Words* is the hosting of video chapters (Chapters 3, 5, 8, and 9) on a website. This innovation makes the visual material more accessible for individual study. The website not only hosts sections for student review, it also incorporates an Instructor's Guide. In this section, instructors can find suggestions for tapping into the *Beyond Words* materials in many ways. Guidance includes classroom exercises, structured projects, and practical advice for helping students develop movement observation and analysis skills.

Many things have changed since *Beyond Words* first appeared, yet human movement remains a topic of perennial interest. Since everyone agrees that actions speak louder than words, understanding nonverbal dimensions of behavior remains a critical element in human relations. Movement observation and analysis pave the way for deeper comprehension of the nonverbal aspects of human life in all its diversity. It is hoped that this revised edition of *Beyond Words* will continue to help students and teachers alike reflect on what they see and how they make sense of the most dynamic dimension of human life, namely, bodily movement.

Acknowledgments

Since initial publication in 1988, many students and instructors in various disciplines have utilized *Beyond Words*. The fact that the text and video-tapes continue to prove useful encouraged us to undertake an updated version. The revised edition would not have come into being without the editorial guidance of Mr. Ben Piggott. We wish to express our appreciation for his vision and for the expertise of the whole Taylor and Francis staff. Thanks to them, we could take advantage of new technology that was not available when the book first appeared—to host the video portions of the text, along with the Instructor's Guide, on the World Wide Web. We also want to acknowledge Mrs. Vivian Heggie, who provided superior graphic and technical support when needed, and often at short notice.

The original version of the *Beyond Words* text and videotape was created with the support of several organizations and many people. Since this revised edition builds upon the foundation of the original, we wish to express gratitude for the initial support of the project provided by the Fund for the Improvement of Postsecondary Education (U.S. Department of Education), the Laban/Bartenieff Institute of Movement Studies, and the Video Consortium of Phoenix, Arizona. We extend special thanks to our original project staff members, Dr. Jan Stanley and Mrs. Jody Zacharias. In addition, though too numerous to name individually, we gratefully acknowledge the contributions of the many people who appear in the video examples and photographs, as well as the instructors at various American colleges and universities who tested the text and visual materials while they were being developed.

Introduction

"You see, Watson, but you do not observe."

Sherlock Holmes

The famous fictional English detective, Sherlock Holmes was constantly amazing his colleague, Dr. Watson, with his phenomenal powers of deduction. Yet, according to Holmes himself, it was quite simple. While others merely *watched* life go by, he carefully *observed* the passing human parade, taking note of the many details of individual behavior. According to Holmes, his greatness as a detective lay in these powers of observation.

Watching life go by is, of course, every human being's birthright. We have all been onlookers, people watchers, and spectators since the day we came into the world. Many of life's most fundamental lessons have been absorbed early on by *seeing* and experiencing the world surrounding us. However, few of us have stopped to reflect upon the even more vital function of *observing*.

Indeed, *observation* is critical since, as noted by H.L. Mencken, "What really teaches man is not experience but observation. It is observation that enables him to make use of the vastly greater experiences of other men" (quoted in Carpenter 1970, n.p.). Aldous Huxley characterized the same process in a slightly different manner: "Experience is not what happens to a man, it's what a man does with what happens to him" (Huxley 1932: 5).

How do we actually go about perceiving life around us, then fitting what we see into some sort of scheme that makes sense? That is the question, and observation plays an essential role in the response. Are we keen observers, penetrating to the heart of the matter to learn from what has happened to us and others? Or, are we merely casual onlookers, skimming the surface of passing events?

This book is about learning to observe human life more deeply through the medium of movement. Body movement has been chosen as the focus because it is omnipresent. "Nearly every human activity—talking, walking, working, etc.—involves a complex medley of breathing patterns, eye movements, postures, limb actions, facial expressions, orientations in space"

(Davis 1975: 7). Yet this very ubiquity causes movement to be taken for granted. It is widely recognized by now that nonverbal communication plays a central role in human behavior, but "even though we use nonverbal cues every time we meet or talk with someone, we are generally unable to describe the cues we employ" (Rosenthal et al. 1979: 1).

Beyond Words aims to awaken awareness of movement, to provide analytic tools for accurate movement description, and to encourage conscious reflection on the meaning of this silent dimension of behavior. What is presented in two modules is an integrative approach to making sense of human movement. Because it is not possible to enhance powers of observation by merely reading a book, four chapters are visual, with videotaped examples of movement behavior for study. These chapters, which are hosted on a website, incorporate exercises to increase movement awareness, develop analytic skills, and link enhanced movement perception to reflective interpretations of behavior.

The first module consists of six chapters. Chapter 1 opens with a brief discussion of the salience of movement in human life and difficulties inherent in studying this ephemeral phenomenon. Chapter 2 moves this discussion forward by elucidating sensory processes involved in the perception of human movement. Chapter 3 is a visual chapter, introducing multi-sensory techniques for enhancing movement awareness. Chapter 4 examines cognitive processes involved in making sense of movement, elucidating how these give rise both to understanding and misinterpretations of nonverbal behaviors. Chapter 5 is a visual chapter, introducing techniques for objective descriptions of movement events. Chapter 6 concludes the first module of study, by reflecting on interpretive implications of various metaphors that have been applied to the study of nonverbal behaviors.

The second module of study opens in Chapter 7 with an overview of functions of movement in human life and various approaches to study in these different arenas of activity. Chapter 8 is a visual chapter, in which four different movement events provide material for study. Chapter 9 introduces a system of objective movement description known as Laban Movement Analysis. Basic parameters of movement—body usage, spatial form, and dynamic energies—are discussed in the text. The accompanying, visual Chapter 9 on the website provides examples of these different elements of movement. Chapter 10 discusses observation practice and provides a model for structuring movement study appropriately in order to link movement analysis to behavioral interpretation. Chapter 11 provides examples of how experts employ movement analysis, with reference to study of the events presented in visual Chapter 8. Chapter 12 closes with reflections on emerging trends in movement study and on the challenges and possibilities for further development.

1 In search of an elusive phenomenon

Science tells us that motion is an essential of existence. The stars wandering across the sky are born and die. They wax and wane, some colliding with others, some burning themselves out. Everywhere is change. This ceaseless motion throughout measureless space and endless time has its parallel in the smaller motions of shorter duration that occur on earth. Even inanimate things, crystals, rivers, clouds, islands, grow and dwindle, accumulate and break up, appear and disappear.

Rudolf Laban

Living, the whole body carries its meaning and tells its own story, standing, sitting, walking, awake or asleep. Guilt, craft, vision, meanness, ecstasy, and lure appear in certain arrangements of the arms, hands, shoulders, neck, head, and legs. Thus the stuff of ages goes into man's thinking, is interpreted and comes out in movement and posture again.

Mabel Ellsworth Todd

Movement is everywhere, in the heavens, on earth, in the daily course of human action and interaction. Of all these ceaseless motions, the ones that matter the most are human. And this is not surprising, for movement is an omnipresent accompaniment to human endeavors of all kinds. Not a word is uttered or a thought shaped without an accompanying motion, however subtle, somewhere in the body. "At work or play, everybody emits wordless signals of infinite variety" (Trippett 1981: 71). These motions may be overtly communicative, like smiling warmly, or they can be involuntary reactions, such as widening one's eyes in surprise. Other movements arise spontaneously, as in leaning away to resist a pushy salesperson or swooping down to comfort a hurt child. Whatever the cause, movement is both ubiquitous and expressive.

Indeed, experts contend that human communication depends upon these wordless signals, estimating that 60–65 percent of social meaning is carried by nonverbal behaviors (Guerrero, DeVito, and Hecht 1999). From ancient times onward, the wise have advised that people should be judged, not by what they *say*, but by what they *do*. Contemporary research corroborates

Figure 1.1 The passing parade of social life provides many opportunities for
people watching.

C.L. Moore

this advice, for "nonverbal communication is usually seen as more believable than verbal messages" (ibid: 4). Movement, which is the behavioral
domain beyond words, has been called "the bedrock on which human
relations are built" (F. Davis 1973: 4) and "the provenance of the common
man and the core culture that guides his life" (Hall 1983: 4).

It seems then, that we are all inveterate people watchers. Current studies
of the perception of biological motion suggest that we are particularly
sensitive to *human* movement (I. Thornton 2006b). The human body is a
unique object of perception, unique because we can make use of both inner
and outer sources of information to refine what we perceive. "We each
possess a body; we feel it, see it, and control it. We are also frequently in
close proximity to other bodies, observing, imitating, interacting with, and
predicting their movements" (ibid: 261). As a consequence, "we judge our
fellow man much more by the arrangement and movement of his skeletal
parts that is evident at once" (Todd 1973: 1).

Thus, we can conclude that movement is an omnipresent and particularly
meaningful element of the behavior of *Homo sapiens*. As the bedrock of human
relations, nonverbal behavior needs to be seriously studied and understood.
And yet, it has proven to be an elusive phenomenon for many reasons.

Ever present and constantly disappearing

The ephemeral nature of movement has made it difficult to study. Consider
dance. It is a visual art, tracing lines in space and creating two- and three-

dimensional forms, analogous to the spatial designs created by other visual arts. Yet, in architecture, sculpture, and painting, the artists' drawing and shaping actions remain embedded in the material object they have created, and the trace-lines and forms of these objects endure. In the movements of dance, however, "point after point of the trace-forms vanish into the past" (Laban 1974: 115). As dance critic Marcia Siegel explains, dance exists at a perpetual vanishing point—the moment the dance is performed, it is gone. As a consequence, dance and all the other movement arts are not only ephemeral, but also illusory—"a thing was done; you saw it happen; but a moment later, who could be sure?" (Siegel 1972: 1).

Of course, other performing arts such as music and theatre are also ephemeral. These arts, like dance, exist in time as well as space, and depend upon a sequence of tones and acts that disappear even as they are occurring. Nevertheless, musical compositions can be notated and the playwright's words recorded. These artifacts do not preserve a given performance in all its lively complexity, but they allow compositions and plays to be re-enacted from a score or a script. Consequently, music and theatre have a history and literature extending back many centuries; the other movement arts do not.

Fully functional dance and movement notation systems, such as Benesh (Benesh and Benesh 1969), Eshkol-Wachman (Eshkol and Wachman 1958), and Labanotation (Laban 1928), were not developed until the twentieth century. Earlier attempts had been made to record movement in symbols, but these were not entirely satisfactory. For example, during the Baroque period, European court dances were written down using a system known as Feuillet notation (Feuillet 1968). This mode of recording captured steps and the pattern of progression as the dancer moved across the ballroom floor. The system did not record movements of the arms and upper body in equal detail, however. To draw a musical analogy, this is like having the chords without the melody.

The inherent complexity of movement has contributed to the difficulty of capturing all the relevant details. Every human movement involves activation and coordination of different parts of the body, displacement through space, and use of dynamic energy. Multiple changes in all these elements occur simultaneously as the movement progresses through time and space. At each instant, these configurations are appearing and rapidly disappearing. Recording all these changes proved to be a daunting task.

The development of dance and movement notation systems in the early twentieth century occurred concurrently with the invention of technical recording devices, such as instantaneous photography and cinematography. These inventions have made it possible to capture movements that go by so quickly as to be almost imperceptible to the naked eye. The capability to replay an event has been a great boon to the study of movement, because even highly trained observers make mistakes. This is why football referees, for instance, must sometimes halt the game to review the video recordings of a play from more than one angle, so elusive and illusory is the phenomenon of movement.

Conscious and subliminal

Experts agree that we are particularly sensitive to the *movement* of other humans, in contrast to those of other creatures. Moreover, we tend to take what is *done* more seriously than what is *said*, and base our judgments of fellow humans on the nonverbal dimensions of their behavior (Wainwright 2003). When we watch other people in action, we capture "not only the movement in space and time, but also what may be called their underlying intentional subtext—what they are aiming at" (Prinz 2006: 395). This capacity to read intention from action allows us to discern the meaning in movement. At its most basic level it is a survival skill that allows us to discriminate a friendly action from an unfriendly one.

The importance of being able to make these kinds of judgments regarding the actions of other people would suggest that the perception of movement must occupy a central place in our awareness, a point of conscious focus. And yet, "people watching is not necessarily a conscious activity. It goes on all the time, unconsciously as well. It is part of the omnipresent background to our lives" (Wolfgang 1995: 4).

Polanyi's concepts of subsidiary and focal awareness are useful in understanding this aspect of movement perception. He notes that when we use a hammer to drive in a nail, we attend to the action of hammering and the process of driving in the nail in different ways. We are alert to the feeling of holding and wielding the hammer in our palm and fingers. Yet this is a *"subsidiary awareness,"* which is merged into the *"focal awareness"* of driving in the nail" (Polanyi 1962: 55). Studies in motor control corroborate Polanyi's observation, for experimental evidence shows that "goals come first and only then and thereby can appropriate movements be specified" (Prinz 2006: 407). In other words, "intent organizes the neuromuscular system," enabling the body "to find the motor pattern to fulfill that intent" (Hackney 1998: 43).

While our brains may be sensitive to human movement, our perceptual systems are also designed to "tune out" persistent sensations. This is why we are initially aware of the weight of a jacket or the loud hum of the air conditioner. Yet as these sensations persist, they also fade into the background as our conscious attention is directed elsewhere. Whether we are moving ourselves or observing the actions of others, the very ubiquity of human movement inclines us to tune the attendant sensations out, that is, to relegate them to the background. The goal or intent of the action demands our focal attention, while the particulars of the movement itself elicit only a subsidiary awareness.

If all human movements were straightforward and unambiguous, subsidiary awareness would suffice, for there would be little likelihood of misinterpreting the underlying intention of an action. But this is not the case. It is well established by now that nonverbal behaviors mean different things in different contexts and cultures (Birdwhistell 1970; Morris 1994). While most of us do not see ourselves as biased or prejudiced, "we do observe the world around us through our own cultural blinders and make judgments accordingly" (Wolfgang 1995: 57). This is the paradox of movement perception. It is the basis of empathy, understanding, and compassion for our fellow beings, and yet, it can also be the subliminal source of miscommunication and prejudice.

For this reason, Wolfgang (1995) advocates becoming a *conscious* people watcher. This requires reversing certain habits of mind by actively focusing on our own movements and the movements of others. A switch in the nature of attention focused on movement can be unsettling at first. For example, "if a pianist shifts his attention from the piece he is playing to the observation of what he is doing with his fingers while playing it, he gets confused and may have to stop. This happens generally if we switch our focal attention to particulars of which we had previously been aware only in their subsidiary role" (Polanyi 1962: 56). Nevertheless, movement skills are actually developed through alternate dismemberment and integration; that is to say, observation and analysis of isolated details makes it possible to improve performance as long as these details are subsequently incorporated into the whole action sequence (Polanyi 1969).

Making movement the focus of attention yields unexpected benefits. In addition to the development of physical skills, social intelligence can also be enhanced through focused movement study. Since himself becoming a conscious people watcher, Wolfgang reports becoming much more "focused on working out my feelings, understanding how others respond to the world around them, and getting a better sense of how they respond to me in particular" (1995: 18–19). Because nonverbal communication indicates intention and how people are feeling, it also provides "ways of avoiding conflict" (Hall 1983: 4). "As the global village continues to shrink and cultures collide," writes Axtell, "it becomes more and more important to comprehend the 'silent language' of movement" (1991: 16).

Recapitulation

Movement is an omnipresent feature of the natural and social environments we inhabit. While all our perceptual systems respond to changes in the environment, we are particularly sensitive to the movements of other humans. Studies have shown that nonverbal communication is salient in social life and human intercourse. Actions, rather than words, are seen as more authentic and truthful expressions of what other people are thinking and feeling. Indeed, human-in-motion speaks louder!

Nevertheless, accurately perceiving and decoding nonverbal behavior is difficult for many reasons. First of all, movement is very complex, involving simultaneous changes in body usage, spatial placement, and dynamic energy. Moreover, bodily actions can carry different meanings depending upon culture and context. Difficulty in decoding nonverbal behavior is increased because movement is an ephemeral phenomenon that disappears even as it is occurring. In addition, the very ubiquity of movement inclines us to relegate it to the periphery of conscious attention.

Despite these difficulties, one can become more adept at reading movements. *Conscious* people watching, which puts movements themselves in foreground, can provide information about details of performance. This enhanced awareness of movement can lead to more skillful and insightful understanding of ourselves and others.

2 The perception of human movement

To the five traditional senses—touch, sight, hearing, taste, smell—we must add the sense of movement, or kinesthesia. Its characteristic feature is that it makes use of many receptors, but remarkably it has been forgotten in the count of the senses. By what twist did language suppress the sense most important to survival?

Alain Berthoz

It is understandable that a strong and automatic response to motion should have developed in animal and man. Motion implies a change in the conditions of the environment, and change may require reaction. It may mean the approach of danger, the appearance of a friend or of desirable prey.

Rudolf Arnheim

As noted, human movement is paradoxical. It is an omnipresent accompaniment of almost all human activity. Yet it is an elusive subject to study, because movement disappears even as it is occurring and leaves no artifacts behind. Researchers agree that nonverbal communication is crucial to understanding one another; nevertheless awareness of movement is often relegated to the periphery of consciousness, guiding our actions and reactions subliminally. It is rather unbelievable that the sense of movement, so essential to self and survival, has so often been overlooked.

Contemporary neuroscience research, however, is challenging centuries of neglect. The enhanced ability to study brain and body function is leading to a new understanding of the relationships among sensation, perception, cognition, emotion, and action. A variety of disciplines are now focused on bodily experience as the foundation of thinking and acting, and the long-standing dichotomy of body and mind is dissolving (e.g., Damasio 1994; M. Johnson 2007; Sheets-Johnstone 2009).

Ironically, however, this renewed interest in the sense of movement is also giving rise to new paradoxes, for it seems that the more we learn about movement perception, the more there appears to learn. In everyday experience, the coordinated interplay of the sensory–motor system and the brain is a common occurrence, so simple as to require little conscious effort or control. Lifting a cup of coffee and taking a sip does not require any complex preparation or mental computations; I simply grasp the cup and bring it to my lips. Yet, this seemingly simple coordination of intention and action rests upon sensory, neural, muscular, and cognitive processes that are quite complicated.

Original models described the interaction of body and mind in a mechanical way. Stimuli from the outside world were thought to bombard the sense organs, which faithfully and accurately recorded impressions and sent internal messages, or percepts, to the brain. The neural pathways leading from sense organs were considered to be "hard-wired," that is, each led to a strict location in the brain. The brain itself was thought to be a kind of machine, made up of specialized parts each performing a specific mental function. Hard-wiring and specialization allowed the brain to "read" sensory messages and send a command back to the body, usually for some form of motor action upon the outside world.

The first difficulty with this model arose with the sense organs themselves, for these receptors do not necessarily record external stimuli faithfully and accurately. For example, the image captured by the retina of the eye is distorted. Only the focal center is clear, with acuity diminishing towards the edge of the visual field (Gregory 1972). Moreover, each eye records a slightly different view of an object due to the distance between the two eyes. Yet we perceive a clear and unified image, not the likeness of a Cubist painting with blurry edges. Obviously perception involves more than mechanical recording and transmitting of images.

> We believe in our senses, and we trust that they are providing us with objective, complete, and accurate data about the world around us. We are wrong. Our brains construct our reality, molding every input to what we expect, what we imagine, what we wish for.
>
> (Brynie 2009: xi)

The brain itself is proving to be much less machine-like than it was once conceived to be. The assumption that mental functions are localized in the brain is giving way to evidence that many functions are handled by more than one area. There appears to be a degree of built-in redundancy. This redundancy is useful when a specific area of the brain is injured. In such instances of localized brain damage, an individual usually suffers loss of the function handled by that area of the brain. Yet, this is not always the case. Redundancy makes compensation possible. Moreover, it has been discovered that areas of the brain have the capacity to take on new functions. This "neuroplasticity" means that the brain "is constantly rewiring itself, reshaping its own structure, recruiting new circuits to perform its work when old ones are damaged or lost" (ibid). The brain and nervous system do not appear to be as hard-wired and fixed as they were once believed to be. Thus even the adult brain can change.

It [the brain] can grow new cells. It can change the function of old ones. It can rezone an area that originally executed one function and assign it to another. It can, in short, change the circuitry that weaves neurons into networks that allow us to see and hear, into the networks that remember, feel, suffer, think, imagine, and dream.

(Schwartz and Begley 2002: 131)

Contemporary research indicates that sensory information of one type (visual, auditory, etc.) goes to more than one area of the brain—another example of built-in redundancy. Likewise, many areas of the brain receive multiple types of sensory inputs. This suggests that different areas of the brain must work together to interpret any single kind of sensation. In addition, a given area of the brain may have to decode several different types of sensory information simultaneously. Even simple responses, such as suddenly hearing a door open and turning one's head to look in the direction of the sound, require the rapid coordination of sense impressions (hearing, vision, kinesthesia, etc.) with motoric signals.

Exactly how coherent perception and coordinated action are facilitated by the brain remains to be explained fully (Berthoz 2000). Nevertheless, as more becomes known about the complex interrelations of sense organs, the neuro-muscular system, and brain physiology and function, the body assumes a new importance. Thus we begin our study with an examination of the body itself.

The body as object and subject

We rely on the five traditional senses and more to perceive ourselves and other objects in the world. Whereas we must always regard other objects from a third-person perspective, we can combine objective and subjective perspectives when we consider our own bodies. This unique capacity for self-perception is due to "dedicated sensory systems, in particular the tactile and kinesthetic senses," that provide information about one's own body not directly available for other objects (Knoblich et al. 2006: 7). When it comes to the human body, we are "equally capable of being internally self-aware as well as externally aware" (Hanna 1995: 341).

Information about the outer and inner worlds is carried by three types of sensory nerves: interoceptors, exteroceptors, and proprioceptors. Interoceptors, which are located in organs and soft tissue, receive sensory stimulation from internal, visceral processes. As an organism, the human body is equipped with multiple systems (circulatory, digestive, neuromuscular, respiratory, etc.) that function together to maintain an inner physiological balance known as homeostasis. In order to do so, mechanisms must exist to track the moment-to-moment fluctuations in the state of the body. This is the role of the interoceptors. "All your innards have receptors that send information up to your brain for mapping your 'gut' feelings of hunger, thirst, air hunger, and other visceral sensations" (Blakeslee and Blakeslee 2007: 182).

Much remains to be known about these nerves and their connections with brain, mind, and emotion. For over a century, however, psychologists such as William James have theorized that "emotion arises when you perceive changes in your body" (ibid: 190). At this writing, it appears that the interoceptors not only control purely physiological processes such as breathing, body temperature, and blood pressure, but also serve as a "source of information about the state and function of the body that could influence so-called higher mental functions and behavior" (Cameron 2001: 268). Awareness of the body is basic to awareness of the self, and the interoceptors provide a constant stream of visceral sensation that is now implicated in the manifestation of emotion and even judgment. As Damasio notes, "our most refined thoughts and best actions, our greatest joys and deepest sorrows, use the body as a yardstick" (1994: xviii).

On the other hand, exteroceptors receive stimuli from the external environment. These receptors include the five well known senses: vision, hearing, smell, taste, and touch. Vision, hearing, and smell are sometimes referred to as the "distance senses" (Arnheim 1969: 17). Due to the fact that sound and light waves as well as scents radiate through space from their point of emanation, our capacity to perceive these physical phenomena allows us to receive information about events sometimes occurring very far away. On the other hand, the senses of taste and touch have a limited range of function. Indeed, for taste and touch, the stimuli must actually be in contact with the body itself if perception is to occur.

Proprioceptors are found in joints, muscles, and the vestibular apparatus of the inner ear. These senses "record information about the position of the body in space, its movement, and the relationship of body parts" (Hartley 1995: 122). Kinesthesia, the so-called sixth sense or sense of movement, draws upon many of these receptors, melding sensory data from exteroceptors (vision, hearing, and touch) and proprioceptors. Let us examine how each of these sensory modes contributes to the perception of movement.

Kinesthesia and touch in the perception of movement

Although kinesthesia does not yield distinct perceptions (like hearing a sharp sound or seeing a bright light), it constantly provides us with a substratum of knowledge of the body's position and posture, as well as knowledge of the direction of the movement of our limbs. Without any difficulty we know where the body is, and where it is going, at any moment, with eyes shut.

There are several physiological mechanisms involved in kinesthesia. For example, muscle spindles, a specialized type of muscle fibers, are interspersed among the fibers in most muscles of the body. These spindles contain sensory end organs that quickly and precisely signal changes, such as muscle length and the speed with which that length is changing, to the central nervous system. In addition, Golgi tendon organs are located at the junction of muscle and tendon. These receptors signal variations in tension, gauging the force that a muscle exerts on the bone to which it is attached (Juhan 1998). These sensations are significant.

> One may be said to "own" or "possess" one's body—at least its limbs and movable parts—by virtue of a constant flow of incoming information, arising ceaselessly, throughout life, from the muscles, joints, and tendons. One has oneself, one *is* oneself, because the body knows itself, confirms itself, at all times, by this sixth sense.
>
> (Sacks 1984: 71)

While these muscle and tendon receptors are probably the primary mechanisms used in kinesthesia, the vestibular apparatus located in the inner ear is also important to movement sensitivity. The vestibular apparatus consists of three tubes filled with viscous fluid and encased in a bony labyrinth. The tubes lie in three planes and are lined with hair cells and calcium particles known as otoliths. When the head or body shifts its position in relation to gravity, movement of the viscous fluid and otoliths transmits the displacement to the central nervous system. Thus the vestibular apparatus plays a major role in signaling when the body is tilted off its vertical axis. This apparatus also telegraphs changes in acceleration of motion and indicates when the body is turning around one of its axes. While the vestibular

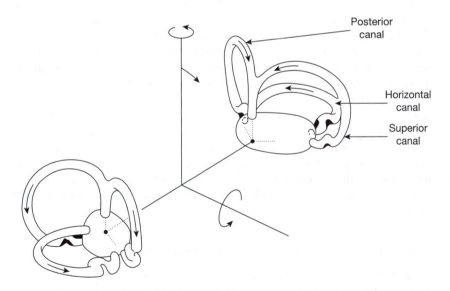

Figure 2.1 The vestibular canals signal bodily motion and shifting relationships to gravity.

Reprinted by permission of John Wiley & Sons, from I.P. Howard and W.B. Templeton, *Human Spatial Orientation*, © 1966 John Wiley & Sons

system is significantly involved in maintaining balance and establishing spatial orientation as the body moves, "these sensors also have a basic discharge whose lack of variation is interpreted by the brain as immobility" (Berthoz 2000: 41). Thus the vestibular system not only senses movement, it also signals stillness.

In addition to these mechanisms, the sense of touch plays a role in movement perception. The skin, which is one of our largest organs, contains many different types of touch receptors. In addition to detecting heat, cold, and painful stimuli, there are receptors that respond to friction, light contact, pressure, and variations in pressure (Brynie 2009). One type of pressure sensor known as Ruffini's end organ is abundant in joint capsules. Since the bones' changing angular relations cause pressure changes in these capsules, the Ruffini organs provide information about the location and movement of the limbs (Juhan 1998). Thus contact and pressure sensations received through the skin and joint capsules are used along with proprioceptive information to discern body position. For example, if one is reclining on a sofa, the areas where the body is touching the sofa help to establish body position. Although proprioception and touch utilize different anatomical receptors, they appear to act in conjunction with each other, yielding a synthetic sense impression of both self and the adjacent environment. For as Juhan observes, "Every time that I touch something, I am as aware of the part of me that is touched as I am of the thing I touch" (ibid: 34).

As Juhan notes, touch yields two streams of information: "information about an object, announced by my senses, and information about my body announced by the interaction with the object" (ibid). Research has found that the near sense of touch can be extended through the use of tools. In essence, all tools amplify bodily functions (Yamamoto 2007). For example, we can hit harder with a hammer than with a bare fist, and when an apple is too high for us to reach, we can knock it from the tree with a stick. Tools expand the reach of the body into the space immediately surrounding the body, which is now known as "peripersonal space." Skillful use of the tool involves sensory monitoring of its motion. This has been hypothesized to be multi-modal, in that visual stimuli presented at the tip of the tool are simultaneously associated with sensations of the hand that holds the tool (Holmes and Spence 2006). While touch is a near sense, we are capable of extending the sense of touch from the body itself to the space around the body.

Hearing and vision in the perception of movement

We move on now to consider the role of the far senses, hearing and vision, in perceiving movement. We will start with sound. Natural sounds in the environment provide spatial information that leads to their location. Because the distance and direction of sound-emitting stimuli can be perceived, hearing yields valuable clues about movement in the environment.

The intensity of a sound is often used to judge its distance from the hearer. Just as a larger object will be perceived as nearer than a smaller one, a more intense or loud sound will be perceived as closer. If the intensity of the sound gradually changes, the listener will perceive it as moving; sounds growing louder signal approaching persons and things; sound growing fainter indicate their drawing away. Moreover, changes in pitch emitted by a sound source can also be used to judge relative movement.

The ability to judge the direction of a sound depends upon the use of both ears. Sound waves emanating directly in front of a hearer will reach both ears simultaneously, while a sound emanation to the left of the listener will reach the right ear slightly later than the left and will be slightly softer in volume. The difference is minimal, but it is sufficient to locate the source (Jourdain 2002). Sound emitted from certain areas around the body can be relatively hard to locate if the hearer remains stationary. But by moving the head, gradations between the two ears can be sensed and help the listener locate the sound. In this instance, the brain must integrate both proprioceptive and auditory sensations in order to detect the direction from which the sound is emanating accurately.

Sound also appears to play a subtle but profound role in the coordination of body movements. William Condon was among the first to discover this through frame-by-frame analysis of films of people engaged in conversation. He recounts, "I began to see that body motions occur in bundles; that, as a person is talking, there's a changing and moving together of the body parts which are precisely synchronized with the articulatory structure of his or her speech" (1982: 54). Condon called this self-synchrony.

Further intensive study led Condon to discover that "listeners move synchronously (entrain) with the articulatory structure of the speaker's speech" (ibid). In fact, film studies of infants have revealed that a normal baby already exhibits interactional synchrony shortly after birth (Leonard 1978). Since the human auditory system becomes active three or four months before birth, the infant can hear in the womb. Researchers surmise that we may become entrained to speech patterns in utero, and this suggests that the tendency to synchronize movement with surrounding voices is innate (Hall 1983). This has led Condon to assert that "the oneness and unity between speech and body motion in normal behavior is truly awesome" (quoted, ibid: 166).

Consequently, hearing plays both a functional and social role in the perception of movement. Functionally, hearing allows us to detect where a sound is coming from and whether it is moving towards or away from us. Socially, the seemingly innate capacity to synchronize movement with spoken rhythms seems to play a critical role in human interaction.

Like hearing, vision also plays a central role in the perception of movement of self as well as other people and objects in the environment. While vision has been one of the most studied senses, its function is quite complex. The visual discernment of movement is also complicated due to the varied contexts in which movement can be observed. First, human beings must be able to discern movement in the environment when they themselves are stationary, picking out the moving object against a stable visual background. Second, individuals must be able to differentiate actual movements from illusory motions. Third, people must be able to recognize stationary versus mobile objects while moving through the environment themselves. How does the visual system keep track of what is moving and what is not?

Let us consider the first situation: discerning movement in the environment when the observer is stationary. As an object moves across the visual field, there is a sequential firing of retinal receptors that is correctly perceived as movement. We also perceive motion when the eyes follow a moving object. There is no reason why we should see motion in this case, however, since the image remains more or less stationary upon the retinas due to the movements of the eyes themselves. The perception of movement when the eyes are tracking an object is thought to involve other sensory data, such as vestibular information about movement of the head and motor neuron information about voluntary movement of the eyes. Presumably this combination of sensory data allows the brain to compare visual signals with other sensory information and decode movement appropriately (Gregory 1972; Heeger 2006).

The capacity of the brain to integrate several types of sensory information also appears to be critical in differentiating actual and apparent motion. For example, one can rapidly sweep one's eyes across the landscape, yet the countryside will appear stable. Seemingly this is due to the fact that the movement of the eyes is voluntary. In contrast, if one gently joggles the eyeball with a finger, the visual field will oscillate and appear to be in motion. This difference in visual perception is due to the brain's capacity to differentiate voluntary and involuntary eye movements.

The brain can be fooled, however, and there are many visual illusions that demonstrate this. For example, if people are sitting on a stationary train and another train alongside starts to move, the passengers on the stationary train may mistakenly feel that they are moving—an illusion of apparent motion. This misperception is thought to arise because only vision is involved. Separating illusory motion from the real thing requires more modes of sensory inputs.

> To make sense of what you're seeing . . . you sometimes need to know what the eyes register, what you're touching, your relation to gravity and motion, and the position of your joints. What we call "seeing" involves all this, and dramatically illustrates the relationship between perception and the whole body.
>
> (Leonard 1978: 41)

Discerning movement is even more complex when one is in motion and there is also motion in the environment. Alas, such situations are commonplace: playing sports, maneuvering through a crowd, driving in traffic, etc. In these instances one experiences what is known as optical flow. As Berthoz explains, "when people move about in the real world, the image of the environment on their retinas is displaced and becomes distorted in a very complex way" (2000: 60). This distortion is known as optical flow. For example, if you are jogging through the park, a visual flow emerges from a focal point in front of you, and "expands out from that point and streams toward you, and then envelops and flows past you" (M. Johnson 2007: 50). This visual flow provides a perception of the relative motion of self through the environment as well as the direction of that motion. Again, this appears to be accomplished by the brain, where visual signals from the retina and proprioceptive signals from the vestibular system are combined and compared with motor information from the eyes to compute motion.

By now it should be clear that what we think of as the perception of motion depends upon a dense interrelationship of proprioceptive and exteroceptive signals, along with a brain somehow capable of melding, comparing, and interpreting sensorimotor information of many kinds. Despite 150 years of scientific scrutiny, the structure and function of human perception remains mind-bogglingly complex. Nevertheless, recent discoveries indicate that when it comes to perceiving and making sense of human movement, we are aided by some very special neurological structures. Not only is the human body a special object of perception, human movement is as well. As mentioned before, we all manifest a heightened sensitivity to human motion, and seemingly we also possess innate abilities to read meaning into the nonverbal actions of other people.

Sensitivity to human movement and the mirror neuron system

Research on so-called biological movement has focused on the visual perception of human movement by human observers. The majority of studies done over the past several decades have worked with a type of visual display known as the "Johansson point-light walker." This display depicts a human in which "the head and each of the major joints (specifically, the shoulders, elbows, wrists, hips, knees, and ankles) have been replaced by single points of light" (I. Thornton 2006a: 262). When filmed in total darkness, the human figure itself is made invisible and transformed into a mere configuration of points of light. When shown as a static array, these points of light are hard to interpret. But when placed in motion, the lights trace the actions of joints, and observers can readily perceive the reduced visual display as human beings in motion.

By now hundreds of experiments have been run to demonstrate convincingly that adult observers can discern the type of action, the gender, and even the emotional state of the mover from point-light displays (Pinto 2006). Additional studies show that four- to six-month-old infants can differentiate

Figure 2.2 The Johansson point-light walker places small lights at major joints to test visual perception of human movement.

V.J. Heggie

between point-light displays of human actions, random motions, and animal movements (Shiffrar 2010). All this experiential evidence indicates a special sensitivity to human movement. Various theories have been proposed to explain this heightened sensitivity. For example, adult observers have had vast experience watching other people move. In addition, human subjects of all ages move themselves, and this motor experience is also believed to contribute to heightened sensitivity. But by far the most convincing explanation comes from the discovery of the mirror neuron system.

Mirror neurons were discovered by a team of Italian neuroscientists led by Giacomo Rizzolatti, Vittorio Gallese, and Leonardo Fogassi. In the course of studying neural activity in primates, they discovered a distinctive class of neurons that fired both when the monkey executed an action and when it observed a similar action being executed. The Italian team named these special receptors "mirror neurons." In order to be triggered by visual stimuli, mirror neurons require interaction between the mover (either a human being or a monkey) and an object. The mere sight of a mover or an object is not sufficient to elicit a response, and the mirror neurons are not triggered by mimetic actions in which no object is visible. Interestingly, however, mirror neurons do fire at the sound of someone doing something, like cracking open a peanut (Dobbs 2006). This is another example of how sound contributes to the perception of movement.

Subsequent studies have found that human beings possess mirror-neuron systems more robust and numerous than those found in monkeys. These systems simulate observed movements.

> Whenever we are looking at someone performing an action, besides the activation of various visual areas, there is a concurrent activation of the motor circuits that are recruited when we ourselves perform that action. Although we do not overtly reproduce the observed action, our motor system nevertheless becomes active *as if* we were executing that very same action that we are observing.
>
> (Gallese 2001: 37)

It may seem odd that observing action activates the motor system of the observer. Still, merely seeing movement gives only visual information without providing information on the intrinsic components of the observed action, what it means to do the action, and how one action is linked to other related actions. By simulating the embodiment of motion, mirror neurons serve many functions. They appear to facilitate understanding the actions of others. They are thought to provide a basic mechanism for imitation and motor learning. Moreover, the mirror neuron system is hypothesized to provide the neurological basis for empathy, which is the capacity to feel the same emotions that others feel (Rizzolatti and Destro 2008).

One of the interesting features of these special visuomotor neurons is that they appear to function automatically, providing a mechanism to directly link the sender of a message and its receiver. Thanks to this mechanism, "actions done by other individuals become messages that are understood by an observer without any cognitive mediation" (Rizzolatti and Craighero 2004: 183). Mirror neurons "allow you to grasp the minds of others, not through conceptual reasoning, but by modeling their actions, intentions, and emotions in the matrix of your own body mandala" (Blakeslee and Blakeslee 2007: 166). This automatic "as if" embodiment has many ramifications.

> It appears we use mirror neurons to learn everything from our first smiles and steps to our most suave expressions and graceful dance moves. Likewise we use them to appreciate these things—to feel the meaning behind a smile or to enjoy, by experiencing it and in a sense doing it at a premotor neural level, the touch of a hand we see laid on someone else's brow.
>
> (Dobbs 2006)

In short, mirror neurons seem to play a beneficial role in helping people get along in complex societies, where recognizing, understanding, and reacting appropriately to the actions of others is critical. Nevertheless, the automatic absorptive capacity of mirror neurons also has a dark side. For example, studies have shown that character-centered video games vigorously engage mirror neurons. Violent video games may reinforce aggression at a basic neuronal level, making it harder to resist (Dobbs 2006). Since mirror neurons operate largely outside of consciousness, they may also play a role in subliminal influence techniques, in which marketers and con men increase social influence by subtly mimicking someone's gestures (Blakeslee and Blakeslee 2007). Many implications of the mirror neuron system remain to be worked out. Nevertheless, these neurological mechanisms help explain why we are all innate people watchers, manifesting a particular fascination with human movement above all other kinds.

Time and memory

In *Remembrance of Things Past*, the French novelist Marcel Proust describes how the simple taste of a morsel of cake dipped in tea surprisingly released a rich stream of childhood memories. This reported incident attests to one of the general properties of the brain, namely, that it is able to identify even a very complex memory without needing every bit of information. The brain has a remarkable capacity for filling in: "by this we mean its ability to reconstruct episodes, shapes, words, and gestures from a few elements among a configuration of signs" (Berthoz 2000: 132). This capacity explains how we are able to "recognize a face in a simple caricature, or a man dancing, as Johansson showed, with only five or six points in motion" (ibid). In other words, movement may be detected from a Johansson point-light walker display because we are able to reconstruct a complex memory from a very slight sensory stimulation.

We remember movements, not merely as discrete actions but as sequences of action that progress through time. Thus there is still another perceptual function that plays a role in movement awareness, and that is the perception of time.

Timing is everything. Catching a ball, modulating tempo when playing the piano, gauging the moment it is safe to cross the street—all these activities depend upon having a sense of timing. Yet the perception of time remains mysterious. As Massad has observed, "the passing of time is a continual *feeling*, but from where does it originate? We continually experience time, yet not by means of the five senses. We cannot taste, see, smell, hear, or touch it" (1979: 3). How, then, is time experienced?

This question has fascinated philosophers, psychologists, and physiologists for many years. Neuroscientists are the latest disciplinary group to become intrigued with the perception of time. Through brain imaging experiments, they are beginning to identify brain systems, such as the basal ganglia, that may be involved in measuring the passing of time (UniSci

2001). Nevertheless, a comprehensive explanation of the neural mechanisms of time perception has not yet been established. Consequently, this discussion focuses less on perceptual mechanisms and more on the nature of the experience of time.

One aspect of temporal experience is the sense of duration. How long an event lasts can be measured quantitatively. A variety of devices, from clocks to metronomes and calendars, have been invented to provide an objective measure of the passing of time. Yet duration also has a subjective side, for time does not move at a steady rate experientially. Some days fly while others drag. Motivation appears to alter the perception of time, for the hour spent waiting in the dentist's office seems much longer than the hour spent playing an exciting video game. Traumatic events, such as having a car spin-out on ice, distort the perception of duration. Such events seem to unfold in slow motion, as mere seconds appear to stretch into minutes (Brynie 2009). On the other hand, aging has been observed to affect the perception of duration. As one grows older, time seems to go faster. Sometimes the amount of information absorbed is thought to determine the perception of time. When many events occur within a given interval, a lot of sensory information is generated. The brain has to work harder to code and store these data. As a result, the interval seems longer to the person experiencing it (Ornstein 1969).

The assessment of duration gets complicated further by the juxtaposition of the "experienced duration" and the "remembered duration." Each of these senses of intervals is misjudged by most people, while the two estimates themselves also tend to diverge one from the other (Block 1990). "They also vary wildly from situation to situation in their degree of inaccuracy, and each individual and culture experiences them very differently" (Levine 1997: 29). Indeed, as a subjective experience, time has a quite elastic quality.

On the other hand, time is also orderly and rhythmic. One manifestation of this temporal rhythm is the internal "circadian" clock that regulates bodily functions across a 24-hour period. Heart rate, metabolism, digestion, breathing, and sleeping all cycle daily (Brynie 2009). This 24-hour cyclical process is so basic from an evolutionary point of view that all plant and animal cells possess it (Orme 1978).

The orderliness of time comes into our awareness in two ways: as a circle and as a line segment. Astronomical or clock time is cyclical and rhythmic, "best represented by symmetrical space" (Tuan 1977: 132). Like the diurnal round of the sun, it is repetitious and has no end.

> We emerge into the theater of consciousness in the rhythm of seconds, hours, days, and years, each following the next and coming full circle with hourly ringing of the bell, nightly prayers, solstices, equinoxes, and one's annual birthday party. We measure the circle of time by the tick marks of actions taken and perceived in repetitive motions: listening to

the heart beat, chewing, walking the dog, dancing, clapping, chanting, rowing a boat, watching the sun set, going to sleep, waking to a new day, and to a new year.

(Freeman 2000: 19)

In contrast, no human life is endless. Recognition of the limits of human life creates awareness of linear time, "a line segment . . . with a beginning in birth and an ending in death" (ibid). Linear time represents one-directional change, for "life is individually experienced as a one-way journey" (Tuan 1978: 9). Thus, human time is "biased in favor of the future," and "like the human body, [it] is asymmetrical: one's back is to the past, one's face to the future" (Tuan 1977: 132). The cause of an event must always precede its effect. What has happened once can never happen again in exactly the same way. The conclusion of an action never loops backward into repetition, but always presses onwards to a new beginning and sequence of events.

Obviously, time and movement are closely related. Movement has duration, for each action passes through time as well as space. The whole duration of an action can be "clocked," i.e., quantitatively measured, as in timing a footrace or a factory worker's operation. Movement can also vary metrically, that is, in relation to the tempo and rhythmic structure. Therefore, time is not merely a measure of the duration of movement; there is also a comparative quality. An action may be prolonged and indulgently drawn out, or it can be compressed suddenly in a staccato burst of energy.

"Suddenly" is basically something both more and other than an interval of time . . . It is a *qualitatively* experienced temporality, just as rushed, prolonged, and creeping are *qualitatively* experienced temporalities. In brief, the distinctive dynamic that defines "suddenly" derives from felt experience.

(Sheets-Johnstone 2009:195)

Movement can be related to both linear and circular time. From a linear perspective, movement is a unique sequence of actions that begins with rest and ends with rest. When we perceive movement, we detect the order of

Figure 2.3 Movements progress through time in unique linear sequences.
R.W. Moore

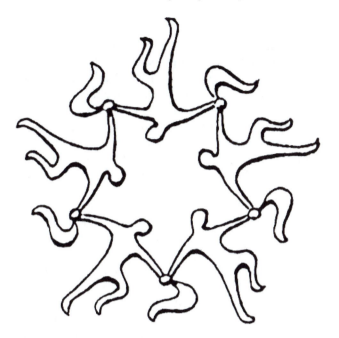

Figure 2.4 Movements also occur and recur in cyclical temporal patterns.
R.W. Moore

different spatial positions of an object or body. As Arnheim notes, during a movement, "we witness an organized sequence in which phases follow one another in a meaningful one-dimensional order" (1974: 375). Art forms such as dance depend on linear sequencing, because "to change the order of events means to change, and probably destroy, the work" (ibid: 376).

On the other hand, the cyclical aspect of time can also be discerned in movement. Through repetition we learn and master physical skills—from walking to playing the piano or executing a broad jump. Moreover, rhythmic repetition underlies our most common activities from dawn until dusk. Arising from bed, bathing, preparing food, commuting, studying, working, and returning home—each day is a circle of repeated actions in which our movement habits are embedded. The cadence of walking, the explosive rhythm of laughter, excited gestures—all these movement patterns become characteristic of an individual.

> A casual world over-emphasizes the face. Memory likes to recall the whole body. It is not our parents' faces that come back to us, but their bodies, in accustomed chairs, eating, sewing, smoking, doing all the familiar things. We remember each as a body in action.
>
> (Todd 1973: 1)

Recapitulation

At one time, sense organs and the brain were thought to interact in a mechanical way, through hard-wired neural circuits that fed into specific areas of the brain, each of which had clearly designated functions. Contemporary research is revising this view, for the peripheral and central nervous systems are now recognized to possess a high degree of plasticity. This means that nerves can regenerate and areas of the brain can change function. Increased understanding of brain anatomy and nervous function reveals complex interrelationships among sensation, perception, cognition, emotion, and action. The human body lies at the center of this dense matrix.

Dedicated sensory systems make the human body unique as an object of self-perception and as a perceiving organism. Interoceptors located in organs and soft tissues monitor visceral function and provide awareness of changes in the state of the body itself. Proprioceptors located in the muscles, joints, and vestibular apparatus provide information about the body's position and movement in space. Exteroceptors receive stimuli from the external environment and include the senses of vision, hearing, smell, taste, and touch. Kinesthesia, the sense of movement, draws upon many of these receptors. Consequently, the perception of movement is multi-modal. It integrates the far and near senses, providing us with awareness of the position and motion of our own bodies and the motion of other organisms and objects in the environment.

Central to the awareness of our own body movements are the proprioceptive sensors. These provide a constant, subliminal knowledge of the arrangement and motion of body parts. This awareness is enhanced by the sense of touch, in which contact and pressure receptors provide additional information about body position.

The distance senses of vision and hearing also play roles in movement awareness. Vision is primarily employed in perceiving motion in the environment beyond the body. However, because we can see parts of our own bodies, vision assists proprioception and also extends the sense of touch into peripersonal space whenever we use tools. Hearing establishes the general location of moving objects in the environment and indicates whether a moving body is approaching or drawing away from the perceiver. Moreover, hearing plays a role in entrainment, the synchronization of body movements with speech that occurs when one is talking as well as when one is listening and interacting with others.

While the perception of movement involves a complicated melding of many different sensory signals, human beings have been found to possess an innate sensitivity to the movement of other members of their species. This has been demonstrated repeatedly through experiments with Johansson point-light walkers. These devices reduce the visual display of human movement to a mere tracery of light, yet adult observers can discern the type of action being performed, the gender of the mover, and the performer's emotional state from these minimal visual signals. Even babies show a preference for human movement over light displays of moving animals or objects.

This special sensitivity to human movement can be explained in part by the discovery of the mirror neuron system. These visuomotor neurons fire not only when we perform an action but also when we observe someone else performing the same action. This internal motor simulation is thought to help us understand the actions and intentions of others, thereby providing an innate foundation for imitative motor learning and social empathy.

Since we are all inveterate people watchers, movement memory also plays a part in helping us decode nonverbal behavior. Movements are recalled not only as discrete actions but as sequences of action that progress through time. In perceiving and performing movement, a sense of timing is critical. Yet, the perception of time does not arise through the known senses. Contemporary brain research is detecting various brain structures that may play a role in discerning temporal duration and regulating circadian biological rhythms, yet much remains to be discovered about temporal awareness.

Time can be perceived as a quantity and also as a quality. Time reveals itself in different ways: as a unidirectional linear progression of unique happenings and as a repeating cycle of predictable events. Because the experience of time cannot be divorced from the perception of movement and change, time-in-motion has quantitative, qualitative, linear, and cyclical aspects. For example, the duration of a movement can be measured quantitatively by a stopwatch or the metric beat of a metronome. Duration can also be experienced in the comparative quality, e.g., in the rushing or prolonging of an action. Movements can be perceived as discrete linear sequences that begin and end, or as rhythmic patterns of action that repeat periodically.

Biological evolution has provided human beings with multiple senses that are attuned to movement and with a brain capable of melding perception, cognition, emotion, and action. Cultural evolution has led to the development of complex human societies. Social life provides not only an ample opportunity to observe human movement, but also the need to understand the actions and intentions of other people. As with all human capacities, the perception of movement can be enhanced. When this occurs, "what was immobile and frozen in our perception is warmed and set in motion. Everything comes to life around us, everything is revivified in us . . . We are more fully alive" (Bergson 1946: 157).

3 Enhancing movement awareness

Introduction

As we discussed in the previous chapter, the perception of human movement is a complex process. It involves the integration of vision and hearing with kinesthesis and touch. Human bodies move through time as well as space, thus the perception of temporal order and duration also play a role in movement perception. Unlike a stationary object, such as a chair or a building, movement does not stand still, giving us time for examination. Rather, movement is elusive, always changing and disappearing. Like catching a glimpse of something out of the corner of one's eye, the perception of motion often leaves us feeling as though the movement vanished just before we could actually pinpoint or identify it. Thus memory must also come into play if we are to comprehend this ephemeral phenomenon.

The processes that underlie our perception of human movement are anything but simple, it seems. Nevertheless, as inveterate people watchers, we get plenty of practice. We know movement from the inside, through our own extensive and continuous bodily experiences. Moreover, we are endowed with mirror neurons, which provide an automatic motor simulation of the actions we see. This neural system is hypothesized to establish an empathic link between observer and mover, albeit a subliminal one.

Indeed, the perception of human movement seems to function just below the level of conscious awareness for many reasons. In everyday life, multiple environmental stimuli compete for our attention. Human motion is only one of many sensations that our minds continuously catalogue and respond to in terms of salience. In social interactions, bodily movement is ubiquitous, and this is problematic. Any environmental stimulus that remains constant tends to be "tuned out"—that is, we simply cease to perceive it after a while. For example, since gesturing normally accompanies speaking, it takes a rather exceptional action to attract our attention. Usually, the on-going flow of motion simply drops below the level of awareness, becoming a kind of perceptual background to the words being spoken. "In physical as well as psychological or social matter, the constant aspects of a situation are most easily overlooked, hardest to be understood"(Arnheim 1969: 21).

Moreover, research on perception demonstrates that "any stimulus pattern tend to be seen in such a way that the resulting structure is as simple as conditions permit" (Arnheim 1974: 63). This, of course, is a paraphrase of the law of *Prägnanz* ("succinctness"/"conciseness" in German), identified close to a century ago by such Gestalt psychologists as Koffka (1922), Köhler (1924) and Wertheimer (1938). For instance, when fleetingly shown an incomplete circle, most observers report having seen a full circle, apparently simplifying their impressions and eliminating details. In the case of movement perception, where most impressions tend to be fleeting, this simplicity principle seems to dominate. The natural tendency for simplification often leads to good results with a better *Gestalt* (form), but not always! The following story serves to illustrate that even those trained in "scientific" observation can fail to discriminate detail in movement events.

> A Manchester physician, while teaching a ward class of students, took a sample of diabetic urine and dipped a finger in to taste it. He then asked all the students to repeat his action. This they reluctantly did, making grimaces, but agreeing that it tasted sweet. "I did this," said the physician with a smile, "to teach you the importance of observing detail. If you had watched me carefully you would have noticed that I put my first finger in the urine but licked my second finger!"
>
> (Beveridge 1950: 133)

In order to develop our power of observation, therefore, we must find ways to overcome the tendency to tune out and simplify the perception of human movement. The visual portion of this chapter provides exercises to refine and augment one's perceptual skills, demonstrating practical ways to increase movement awareness.

Direction for website exercise

The visual portion of Chapter 3 can be accessed on the website. It contains an introduction, followed by six exercises that require your participation. The material is self-explanatory, with directions and an appropriate demonstration preceding each exercise. After experiencing these exercises, the following discussion provides further insight into how the various senses can be used to heighten movement awareness and develop observation skill.

Discussion

Human body movement is an ever-present, complex, and meaningful part of our social lives. Yet, movement awareness usually functions below the level of conscious attention. The first task facing the observer is to increase and refine awareness of movement. The exercises in the visual portion of this chapter were designed to accomplish this task in various ways.

As outlined in Chapter 2, movement perception involves integrating multiple senses—vision, hearing, touch, and kinesthesis. Each of these senses can be called upon as ways of attuning and becoming more sensitive to movement. For example: *Exercise 1 (Mirroring)*, *Exercise 5 (Doodling)*, and *Exercise 6 (Movement Canon)* all utilized vision and kinesthetic embodiment to enhance awareness. *Exercise 2 (Watch, Watch)* and *Exercise 3 (Echoing)* employed vision, hearing, and vocalization to heighten responsiveness to movement as it was occurring. Since motion can be perceived through more than one sensory channel, we encourage you to use all your senses when attuning to bodily actions of others.

Another aspect of movement perception—the role of memory—was introduced in *Exercise 5 (Doodling)* and *Exercise 6 (Movement Canon)*. Since movement is a process of change over time, the first phases of a motion will have disappeared before the action sequence concludes. Often this leaves the observer with a frozen impression of the starting and ending positions of a movement (which are actually moments of stillness), while the transitional phases that make up the action itself drop out of awareness. Consequently, memory must be brought into play if a movement is to retain its lifelike quality in the mind's eye. For example, *Exercise 5 (Doodling)* progressed from a momentary sensory awareness exercise to a memory challenge when the observer was asked to doodle an impression of a motion *after* it had occurred. The role of memory was brought into play more fully in *Exercise 6 (Movement Canon)*. Here, one was asked to observe an on-going movement sequence while kinesthetically repeating increasingly earlier phases of the event. In other words, the observer had to attend simultaneously to what was happening in the moment while remembering what had happened previously. Through exercises such as these, one's ability to recall a movement as it occurred sequentially over time can be developed.

Exercise 4 (Seeing without Words) was meant both to increase visual sensitivity and to serve as a relaxation and recuperation process. We have found that individuals often become tense when they are asked to observe movements closely and continuously, and this tension can interfere with perceptual receptivity. *Seeing without Words* was developed to demonstrate one way to counteract the non-productive tension that may occur while one is analyzing movement.

Initially you may find it necessary to insert relaxation exercises as a special activity in the on-going flow of concentrated movement observation. By all means, whenever you find yourself going blank, becoming tense, or growing sleepy, pause for a while to relax and recuperate by varying your sensory activity or doing something along the lines of *Exercise 4* (*Seeing without Words*). As experience and expertise as an observer increase, relaxation and recuperation will occur more naturally, becoming integrated with the total activity of observing.

To summarize, the visual exercises on the website for this chapter were designed to stimulate movement awareness and to provide a warm-up for the more complex observational and analytical tasks that follow. We will continue to explore movement perception in experiential ways in the visual portions of Chapters 5, 8, and 9. For the moment, however, the conceptual side of movement will be examined in Chapter 4, "Body Knowledge/Body Prejudice."

4   Body knowledge/body prejudice

We are in the world through our body, and the basis of knowledge lies in sensori-motor experience, the most intimate mode of knowing.

Ruth Foster

One thinks not only with the brain but also with the little finger and the big toe.

Rudolf Steiner

The previous chapter introduced exercises designed for sharpening the many senses that are involved in movement perception. Yet, perception is more than mere sensation. Humans are not just sensing organisms, but sense-making beings. The brain and central nervous system play a major role in modifying, correcting, highlighting, or, at times, tuning out movement information pouring in from the environment. The movements we do and do not perceive, the simplicity or complexity of a given movement percept, the judgment as to whether a motion is real or illusory, and the extent to which our perception is swayed by social influence—all these factors underscore our need, not merely to register the occurrence of movement, but also to fit that occurrence into some sort of understandable scheme.

In this chapter we begin examining movement observation as a sense-making operation. Let us start by taking a closer look at the relationships of brain, body, and mind.

Bio-social evolution of the body/mind

According to the ancient Greek myth of creation, the gods delegated the task of making humans and animals to an underling, a Titan named Epimetheus. Unfortunately, Epimetheus was an impulsive and scatterbrained fellow. He chose to make all the animals first, and in the process gave away all the best gifts—great physical strength and swiftness, wings, sharp claws, fur, feathers, shells, and so on. Then when it came to making human beings, there was not a single physical attribute, protective covering, or quality left to make them a match for the beasts of the land, sea, and air. And so

Epimetheus was forced to call on his brother Prometheus, a much more far-sighted fellow, to help the poor, feeble human race prevail. But we shall come to that part of the story a bit later.

In the meantime, this mythological tale of creation succinctly captures the biological destiny of *Homo sapiens*. As a species, we are small, weak, furless, without sharp fangs or claws, and bereft of all but the faintest traces of instinct to direct our behavior. Our solitary biological attribute is an extremely large brain. But even this asset causes problems. Were the brain to reach its maximum size while the human fetus is in the womb, delivery of the baby would become impossible. The head would simply be too large for passage through the mother's birth canal. But a unique solution has been developed; at birth the human brain is only slightly larger than that of a baby gorilla. After this, developmental paths diverge. The gorilla's brain does not continue to grow. For the human baby, however, a growth spurt begins post-partum and continues through adolescence, with three-quarters of the human brain developing outside the womb (Yamamoto 2007). "It is this peculiar leap, unlike anything else we know in the animal world, which gives to man his uniquely human qualities" (Eiseley 1957: 109).

This singular and dramatic growth spurt of the brain profoundly affects human movement patterns, for the parts of the brain and central and peripheral nervous systems that control voluntary movements are among those that develop *after* birth. Unlike many other animals, we do not come into the world "hard-wired," i.e., already programmed for voluntary movement. Rather we emerge from the womb with very "soft" and malleable neuro-muscular wiring—a trait now referred to as neuroplasticity. Initially the newborn's movements are amorphous, aimless, and uncontrolled. A few basic reflex patterns exist to initiate the future development of coordinated voluntary action, and it appears that human infants are somehow bio-logically predisposed to learn to stand, to walk, and to comport themselves as human beings are supposed to do. But it takes an arduous process of imitation, experimentation, and repetition, indeed, one of *learning* how to move, if the infant is to gain mastery of his or her own body and achieve subsequent control of the environment.

As Feldenkrais writes, "the outstanding quality of the human conscious innervations seems to be a unique capacity to form new nervous paths, associations and regroupings of interconnections" (1973: 149). This capacity for learning accounts for the immense variety of human movement behavior, unparalleled by other species.

> When jumping the cat will . . . be relaxed and flexible. A horse or a deer will bound wonderfully in the air, but its body will be tense and concentrated during the jump. Man's body-mind produces many kinds of qualities. He can jump like a deer, and if he wishes, like a cat.
>
> (Laban 1971a: 13)

Figure 4.1 Human beings possess a vast capacity to vary their movement
        behaviors.

Juergen Kuehn

Indeed, the plasticity and complexity of the human brain and nervous systems offer many behavioral possibilities. "The wonderful thing is that man's
movements are not fixed and limited like those of the animals, but he can
decide upon and choose those he will learn" (Montessori 1969: 144).

The biological potential of neuroplasticity carries with it not only the
possibility of learning how to move, but also the *necessity*. Nature has
given humankind a large brain and malleable nervous system, but these
gifts have consequences. Even full-term human births are premature, for all
newborns require care and supportive nurture if they are to survive and
overcome their pronounced helplessness. "The brain's neural building must
continue postpartum, and the provision of proper early experiences by the
family is essential for that" (Yamamoto 2007: 5). There are a few instances
of human infants that have survived in the wild by being cared for by other
animals. Although these feral children survive, they often have difficulty in
mastering human skills such as walking upright and speaking when they are
reunited with their own kind (Lane 1976). Seemingly, these uniquely human
activities not only must be learned after birth, but can only be learned
through interaction with other, older human beings. This social dependence led Eiseley to comment that the newborn "was not whole, was not
made truly human, until, in infancy, the dreams of the group, the social

constellation amidst which his own orbit was cast, had been implanted in the waiting, receptive substance of his brain" (1957: 121).

Initially, the implanting of these "dreams of the group" occurs through actions rather than words. "An infant's initial experience of the world comes from within the protective confines of the primary meeting between infant and parent ... this is communicated and understood by the baby, primarily through implicit nonverbal means" (Tortora 2006: 30). To develop normally within a human group, infants must master three essential and meaningful tasks: they must be able to communicate with their caregivers, they must learn to recognize and manipulate objects, and they must acquire control of bodily action (Gibson and Pick 2000). These tasks all engage the infant's body,

> its perceptual capacities, motor functions, posture, expressions, and ability to experience emotions and desires. Such capacities are at once bodily, affective, and social. *They do not require language in any full-blown sense, and yet they are the very means for making meaning.*
>
> (M. Johnson 2007: 36)

Nonverbal interaction and movement provide meaningful structure in the infant's developing world. The way the baby is handled, the rhythms of adult activities around it, and the kinds of actions it is encouraged to initiate or prohibited from performing—all these exchanges play a role, not only in shaping the movement behavior the infant is learning, but also in helping

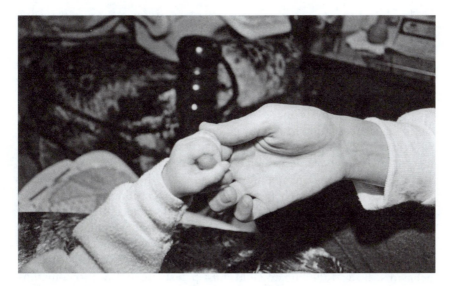

Figure 4.2 The baby's world is structured nonverbally by adult caregivers.
Barry Turner

the infant begin to conceptualize the world as an orderly and understandable place. As Pearce has explained,

> Any bodily involvement by the early child brings about a patterning in his brain system . . . The growth of intelligence rests on a sensorimotor process, a coordination of the child's muscular system with his sensory system and general brain processor.
>
> (1980: 29)

The child's body and mind develop simultaneously and in a closely related fashion. Moreover, sensory stimulation and physical contact with key caregivers have potentially lifelong effects, for these actions and interactions are now known to influence patterns of wiring and firing within the brain itself (Bloom 2006; Hammond 2009). Movement impacts mental development.

> From the earliest stages of development, laying down brain circuits is an active rather than a passive process, directed by the interaction between experience and the environment. The basic principle is this: genetic signals play a large role in the initial structuring of the brain. The ultimate shape of the brain, however, is the outcome of an ongoing active process that occurs where lived experience meets both the inner and the outer environment.
>
> (Schwartz and Begley 2002: 117)

The philosopher Ortega y Gasset has stated that "*man has no nature but, instead, a history*" (1986: 223, italics original). If this is so, our histories are written deep in the neuromuscular patterns of action that we learn from others, according to the time, place, and social conditions of our births. In this sense, even something so seemingly basic as human movement is not an innate manifestation of inherited instinct, but an acquired expression of a given social constellation.

Biological adaptation has endowed human beings with a large brain, one with remarkable properties of neuroplasticity. These biological endowments, however, have necessitated social adaptations. Because the brain and nervous systems are not fully developed at birth, human newborns are extremely helpless. Their physical survival depends upon care from older members of their species. In addition, well-rounded mental and emotional development depends upon socially mediated interactions, for the neural circuitry of brain and body are not hard-wired. Unlike other animal species, *Homo sapiens* is not born with a ready-made set of instinctive behaviors. Instead the human child must painstakingly learn to communicate, to recognize and manipulate objects, and to control bodily movement. In short, we must acquire the skills that grant us membership in the human community. This socialization process begins in infancy when, through movement learning, "the dreams of the group" are implanted in the child's developing body/mind, as the brain itself is being molded.

Cultural evolution—extending the body/mind

According to the earlier-mentioned Greek myth of creation, humankind was placed in a vulnerable position by Epimetheus, who squandered the greatest gifts of physical prowess and protective covering on the other animals. Indeed, helpless at birth, saddled with a prolonged childhood, and even in maturity lacking heavy fur, strong wings, sharp fangs, or various protective assets common to other animals, *Homo sapiens* is not well endowed biologically. But, as the myth goes on to tell, such organic givens are not the only thing that has been assigned to humans, for Epimetheus had pity on humankind and called on his brother Prometheus to help. Prometheus, being much more judicious than his brother, conceived a way to make human beings superior to other beasts. He taught them to stand upright, like the gods, freeing the arms and hands for new tasks. Then he brought fire from the sun, giving humans a better protection than fur, fangs, wings, or any mere biological asset. Having done this, Prometheus exalted, for his gifts to humanity marked the beginnings of culture, and a whole new form of evolution for the human race.

It is now well established that humankind is changing, not so much through adaptation on the biological level as through cultural evolution (Kingdon 1993). From one age to the next, through a series of inventions, humans have literally reshaped the environment to suit their unique needs. These evolutionary "brain children" are known as *extension systems*. For example, clothing and housing extend the protection from the elements that nature has failed to provide biologically for *Homo sapiens*. Similarly, tools and weapons increase the range of human physical capabilities. Spoken and written languages make it possible to store knowledge and pass it on to others. Art, religion, and ritual create symbols that can crystallize the experience of an individual or cultural group and transmit it through the ages. These extensions permit man to evolve and adapt at great speed without changing the basic structure of his body. Thus, the extension systems represent a revolutionary type of evolution (Hall 1976).

> The real evolutionary unit now is not man's mere body; it is "all-mankind's-brains-together-with-all-the-extrabodily-materials-that-come-under-the-manipulation-of-their-hands." Man's very physical ego is expanded to encompass everything within reach of his manipulating hands, within sight of his searching eyes, and within the scope of his restless brain.
>
> (La Barre 1954: 91)

Extension systems fall into two broad categories: external or material extensions and internal or non-material extensions. Material extensions include
the tangible artifacts of human know-how, such as cultivated foodstuff, clothing, shelter, tools, weapons, and objects of art.

> Even a cursory survey of material inventions makes us realize the im-
> mense scope of what we ourselves have created and utilized everywhere
> for hundreds of thousands of years all over the earth. Truly, human
> beings live and die by such extensions.
>
> (Yamamoto 2007: 21)

While these tangible creations are pervasive and immense in their
influence, internal or non-material extensions prove even more dazzling in
scope and effect, "especially in relation to the enhancement of power over
people, including both ourselves and others" (ibid). Non-material inventions
extend the human mind and include such things as language, logic,
metaphor, myth, social conventions, and political structures. These cultural
creations also play a crucial role in human development.

> Man differs from the rest of the animal kingdom not by his biological
> endowments but by the use he has made of them, usually in a conscious
> manner . . . He can thus produce works of art, scientific concepts, moral

Figure 4.3 Cultural evolution proceeds through material extensions—clothing,
shelter, technology—and immaterial extensions—language, tradition,
rituals, etc.

Barry Turner

codes, legal systems and other organizations of experience which constitute the building stones of his psychosocial evolution.

(Dubos 1972: 249–250)

Through the creation of material and non-material extensions, human
beings now live in two worlds—one personal and discrete, the other public
and limitless. The personal domain "is an extremely small world, consisting
only of the continuum of things that we have actually seen, felt, or heard—
the flow of events continually passing before our senses" (Hayakawa 1978:
25). This domain is concrete, specific, and unique; it is a world we, and only
we, can "know in our bones." Consequently, this territory is bound in time
and space by the limits of our own life experience. Meanwhile, the second
domain of human beings is the immensely larger world of extension systems.
This is a public environment in which, through tangible and symbolic
inventions, we all share our personal knowledge and partake of the collective experiences of the whole human race.

Body movement—the original extension system

The definition of extension systems as inventions separate from our bodies
has caused us to overlook movement as one of the primary extension systems
of *Homo sapiens*. Nevertheless, movement arguably was mankind's *first*
extension. Consider the hand. During the course of biological evolution,
our ancestors shifted from locomoting on four legs to standing on two
legs. As the arms were freed from the function of body support, the hand
became "a truly versatile organ, a sort of multi-purpose *tool* or *instrument*"
(Yamamoto 2007: 13). It seems logical to assume that humankind's initial
attempts to extend physical functions included experimentation with other
parts of the body as well. As Mumford muses, "With man's persistent
exploration of his own organic capabilities, nose, eyes, ears, tongue, lips and
sexual organs were given new roles to play" (1967: 7).

It *is* a leap from personal movement exploration, which belongs to the
private world of knowing in one's bones, to the creation of an extension
system where knowledge can be shared and made public. Since body
movement leaves no artifacts or traces behind, reconstructing this leap
requires some imagination. Let us begin with a look at our own movement
experience. Virtually all of us have experienced the pleasure that seems
inherent in moving. Movements spontaneously occurring in the free play of
children—running, skipping, whirling, swinging, tumbling—become more
formal but equally pleasurable in the recreative and sports activities of adults.
Some of these, in fact, are so appealing, so intrinsically satisfying, that we
tend to repeat them again and again.

Repetitive action can induce euphoria. Runners, for example, experience
what is known as the "runners' high" and the whirling Dervish pass into
an ecstatic trance induced by continuous spinning. Feelings of visceral

Figure 4.4 Keeping together in time through rhythmic movement promotes
       muscular bonding and social cohesion.

Jan Stanley

pleasure can be amplified when movements are repeated in unison with
others. For instance, McNeill reports this as an effect of the prolonged
marching drills in which he participated with his fellow army recruits:
"A sense of pervasive well-being is what I recall; more specifically, a strange
sense of personal enlargement, a sort of swelling out, becoming bigger than
life, thanks to participation in collective ritual" (1995: 2). "Muscular bonding" is the term McNeill employs to describe the emotion aroused by moving
together in rhythmic synchrony. Muscular bonding provides "a basis for
social cohesion among any and every group that keeps together in time, moving big muscles together and chanting, singing, or shouting rhythmically"
(ibid).

   In tracing the development of movement as an extension system,
Mumford argues that our prehistoric ancestors must have derived the same
intrinsic pleasure from certain movements that we enjoy today. These
pleasurable movements would tend to be repeated, first for purely private
reasons. But prehistoric man also discovered that such deliberately executed

movements could serve a social function. Through movement the early human being "would call for an audience and demand some answering response, as in the little child's insistent 'Look at me' when it has mastered a new trick" (Mumford 1967: 59). Movements that were repeated often enough, in the same location and in the same context of events, began to acquire communal meaning. In this way, movement became the first form of symbolic communication known to humankind.

As the expressive possibilities of the human body were explored, new functions for human movement came into being.

> Even the hand was no mere horny specialized work-tool: it stroked a lover's body, held a baby close to the breast, made significant gestures, or expressed in shared ritual and ordered dance some otherwise inexpressible sentiment about life or death, a remembered past, or an anxious future.
>
> (Ibid: 7)

Once certain movements became ritualized and socially meaningful, the bridge from the personal to the public, extended world was complete.

McNeill also considers muscular bonding through ritualized group movement to be centrally important in human evolution and history. "Group consolidation through dance was, perhaps, critical in separating our remote ancestors from other protohominid species; and dance certainly operated throughout historic times to maintain village communities and innumerable other human groups" (1995: 11). Laban also has opined that, even today,

> an observer of tribal and national dances can gain information about the states of mind or traits of character cherished and desired within a particular community. Formerly, such dances were one of the main means of schooling the young to adapt themselves to the habits and customs of their forebears.
>
> (1971a: 18)

Mumford seconds this opinion, writing that "it is surely here [in movement ritual] that sharable meanings have their beginnings; for naming, describing, relating, commanding, rationally communicating came as relatively late manifestations. Face-to-face communal expression through bodily movements almost surely comes first" (1967: 61).

These authors' speculations draw some degree of support from the gestural theory of language evolution, proposed by some contemporary linguists and neuroscientists (Armstrong, Stokoe, and Wilcox 1995). According to this theory, "the initial communicative system in primate precursors of modern humans was based on simple, elementary gesturing. Sounds were then associated with the gestures and became progressively the dominant way of communication" (Rizzolatti and Destro 2008, under "Language

Evolution"). The discovery of mirror neurons supports this theory. Through these visuomotor neurons, actions performed by one person can be understood by an observer *without cognitive mediation*. This is because the visual perception of the action simultaneously evokes an identical motor representation in the mirror system of the observer. Thanks to this neural mechanism, "what counted for the sender of the message also counted for the receiver. No arbitrary symbols were required. The comprehension was inherent in the neural organization of the two individuals" (ibid). This has led Sheets-Johnstone to declare that "verbal language is . . . most properly conceived as *post-kinetic*"(2009: 239). Accordingly, movement can be most properly conceived as humankind's first extension system.

Ontogeny recapitulates phylogeny in cultural evolution

The gestural theory of language evolution proposes that body movement became humankind's first extension system, providing a means of "muscular bonding" among early hominid groups and acquiring expressive communal meanings. The association of ritualized gestures with vocal sounds gave rise in time to articulated speech. This hypothetical sequence of events in the evolution of human culture is recapitulated in child development today. Close physical contact between the infant and its caregivers requires "keeping together in time" and fosters "muscular bonding." Communication is primarily nonverbal, although the baby augments this with various cries and sounds. The growing child's exploration of physical capabilities is relentless, leading ultimately to standing, walking, and masterful manipulation of objects. These physical developments have cognitive correlates, as the child explores the natural world and surrounding social environment.

Approximately at the age of two, however, an important turning point is reached in cognitive development. The child begins to talk, and the struggle to master another form of communication ensues. The focus shifts away from the mastery of nonverbal action as the child becomes occupied with words and with the mastery and use of other extension systems. From this point onwards, the stream of movement thinking submerges until, in maturity, the most refined and articulate movement-thoughts appear to occur so spontaneously and "naturally" that we are scarcely aware of having them.

One of the most interesting features of movement is its Cheshire cat-like tendency to appear and disappear unexpectedly. For example, movement often seems to dominate our attention at the very moments when it is most halting, clumsy, and effortful. When we are self-conscious, out-of-shape, nervously attempting a new physical feat, or straining to regain full function after an injury—these are the moments when we are most often aware of our movements.

On the other hand, when movement is articulate and effortless it often seems to vanish from awareness. These moments of grace have been called

Figure 4.5 Learning a new skill focuses attention on movement itself.
Juergen Kuehn

"sweet spots in time" by Jerome (1980). The term "sweet spot" is taken from the physical site on a bat or racket that provides a memorably satisfying sensation to the user when it connects flawlessly with the ball. In sports and other physical activities, the "sweet spots in time" are those moments when the balancing of speeds and forces makes the difficult task easy, resulting in a superior performance. As a boy, Jerome experienced these "sweet spots" in a mundane activity—throwing rocks at old bottles set up on the bank of a river.

> I am haunted by the moment when the rock I threw went precisely where I wanted it to go . . . I think I stumbled onto several of the sweet spots in the same throw, and the result was simply a coming together, a moment when what my mind intended was matched by what my body accomplished. A momentary healing of the mind–body split, to over-dignify it. It haunts me still because it was magic—pipsqueak magic, if you will, but magic nonetheless.
>
> (1980: 23)

Not every movement is magical, however. There are occasions in life when we are acutely aware of our body movements, usually because the realization of our intentions is less than ideal. Something comes between the notion and the motion, the impulse and its execution. For example, during his recovery from a severe leg injury, Sacks became unusually conscious of his efforts to move.

> It wasn't "my" leg I was walking with, but a huge, clumsy prosthesis . . . I cannot convey, except in this way, how strange this pseudo-walking was—how lacking in any sense, and conversely, how overloaded with a painstaking mechanical exactitude and caution.
>
> (1984: 145)

As the recovery progressed, the patient's awareness of movement experience also changed.

> All of a sudden I remembered walking's natural rhythm and melody . . . There was an abrupt and absolute leap at this moment . . . from the awkward, artificial, mechanical walking, of which every step had to be consciously counted, projected and undertaken—to an unconscious, natural, graceful, musical movement.
>
> (Ibid: 146)

While we might not characterize our everyday movements as "graceful" or "musical," we usually manage to handle our bodies without excessive conscious effort. Automatic processing is believed to be the basis of all bodily skills, even modest ones. This is because "controlled processes are attention demanding, conscious and inefficient, whereas automatic processes are rapid, smooth, effortless, demand little attentional capacity and are difficult to consciously disrupt" (Yarrow, Brown, and Krakauer 2009: 588).

Automatic processing affects awareness of our own movements. For example, the plasticity of the brain, sensorimotor, and nervous systems allows us to learn new movement behaviors. Initially, this requires conscious attention and control. With sufficient practice, however, these skills become automatic so that we no longer need to think about them—intention is translated into action with seamless fluency. In fact, expert performance can deteriorate when movers are asked to analyze their actions. It seems that there is some truth in the old story of the centipede. He could maneuver all of his 100 legs just fine, until he was asked to *think* about what one of his legs was doing. Then he got himself in a terrible jumble!

Similarly, our special sensitivity to human movement rests upon the mirror neuron system. Since visual perception of human movement simultaneously triggers a motor simulation in the brain of the observer, this mirroring presumably makes it possible to understand the actions, intentions, and even the emotions of other people. Mirror neurons fire automatically, and their action simulations are independent of logic, thinking, or analysis (Blakeslee and Blakeslee 2007). Perception can be translated into understanding with seamless fluency because seeing and grasping the actions of others derives from neural systems that operate without conscious control.

As regards human movement, ontogeny indeed recapitulates phylogeny. Through the persistent exploration of bodily capacities, movement became humankind's original extension system. For human infants today, movement remains the first form of communication available and also the initial means of extending control over self and environment. As greater bodily mastery is achieved, movement recedes to the background of consciousness, becoming a shadowy accompaniment to the more important matters that demand focused attention. Once we attain a modest level of skill, managing our own bodies is largely automatic. Similarly, perceiving and deciphering the actions of other people arises as the natural outcome of the mirror neuron system, requiring only minor conscious attention. Thus, making sense of movement also becomes an automatic process. Movement may have been humankind's first extension system, but it becomes the last thing we think about, and this can be problematic.

Why the mirror neurons are not enough

The discovery of mirror neurons has been hailed as one of the greatest discoveries ever made about the brain, one that is expected to explain a number of mental abilities. The mirror neuron system has been linked hypothetically to capabilities such as perceiving the functional intention behind the action and even empathizing with the emotional tone of gestures and motions. The ability to imitate movement seems to be connected to mirror neurons, and this system is even thought to provide the basic mechanism from which human language evolved. Since the mirror neurons simulate motion automatically, without any cognitive mediation, deciphering the meaning of other people's actions should be easy, natural, and foolproof. Yet, this is not entirely the case for several reasons.

First, motor simulations of observed actions are not all equal. Familiarity with the observed action affects the simulation, for "your mirror neuron system becomes more active the more expert you are at an observed skill" (Blakeslee and Blakeslee 2007: 169). For example, pianists have stronger mirror response to hearing a piece played than non-musicians. Ballet dancers have weaker mirror response when watching the less familiar Brazilian martial art of capoeira, and Brazilian martial artists manifest less mirror response to ballet (Brown and Parsons 2008). Mirror neurons will still trigger to some extent when one observes an unfamiliar physical activity, like skateboarding —for anybody can relate to basic kinetic components such as balancing and moving through space. But the mirror activity of an observer who has no personal experience "will pale next to that of an expert skateboarder watching the same acrobatics" (Blakeslee and Blakeslee 2007: 169).

Comprehension of sensory stimulus always involves an interaction between the nature of the stimulus and the character of the perceiver. Individual differences in perceptual acuity have long been noted. For example, some individuals are tone deaf while others have perfect pitch.

> In precisely the same environment, you and I will neither see, hear, taste, touch, nor smell the same things—nor will we draw the same conclusions about the information our senses have collected. Our personal worlds are constructions built by our brains using the raw materials of the senses—raw materials that are greatly modified during the construction process.
>
> (Brynie 2009: xi)

In addition to such individual differences, researchers now suspect that culture may influence sensory function through perceptual learning. Perceptual learning occurs "whenever the brain learns how to perceive with more acuteness or in a new way" (Doidge 2007: 299). While all humans possess the same perceptual mechanisms, these can be used in diverse, culturally dictated ways. Use alters perceptual powers. For example, perfect pitch, the ability to name the musical note that one has heard, is considered to be a rare ability among western Europeans and Americans regardless of their musical training. However, perfect pitch has been found to be common among native speakers of tonal languages such as Mandarin Chinese and Vietnamese. Early acquisition of languages, in which tone differentiates the meaning of a word, seems to account for this acute sensitivity to pitch (Deutsch, Henthorn, and Dolson 2004).

Another form of culture-based perceptual learning is found among the Burmese Sea Gypsies. These nomads spend most of their lives in boats on the open sea, where they survive by diving for food. This cultural lifestyle has led to the development of new visual powers, for Sea Gypsies can see clearly underwater at great depths without goggles, while most humans cannot, due to the refraction of light as it passes through water (Doidge 2007).

Meanwhile, becoming literate involves perceptual learning of another sort, for the sense of sight must be isolated.

> A child learns to separate the senses when he learns, in class, to read silently. His legs twist, he bites his tongue, but by an enormous *tour de force* he learns to fragment his senses, to turn on one at a time and keep the others in neutral. And so he is indoctrinated into that literate world where readers seek silent solitude, concert goers close their eyes, and gallery guards warn, "Don't touch!"
>
> (Carpenter 1970: n.p.)

In addition to perceptual learning, culture dictates how the body is to be used. How one eats (with fingers or silverware), how one sits (in a chair or squatting on the floor), when one may or may not touch, how close together or far apart people stand, whether or not it is polite to make eye contact— by now it is well documented that these actions differ along cultural lines (Birdwhistell 1970; Hall 1959, 1969; Morris 1977, 1994). Movements, like words, have different meanings depending upon the context in which they occur. Reading context is something the mirror neurons cannot do alone; other human abilities must be brought into play.

Finally, if the mirror neurons make it possible to grasp the minds of others automatically, how do we account for *misunderstanding*? Our social interactions are often less than harmonious, because it is all too easy to mis- interpret the actions of others. Friends surprise us, con artists trick us, and sometimes we see malice where there is none. While mirror neurons provide a neurological foundation of empathy, it takes experience, conscious effort, and thoughtful reflection to truly understand the meaning of nonverbal behaviors within their varied cultural and social contexts.

Making sense of movement

As mentioned earlier, cultural evolution has created two habitats for human life. Like all other animals, we occupy a small locale whose boundaries are defined by the limits of our own sensory experience. Unlike other animals, however, we also inhabit an extended environment that is communal, symbolic, and virtually limitless. Movement is part of our lives in both these habitats. On one hand, we dwell in a concrete world of kinetic experience; this is the indescribable visceral domain that we, and only we, can know in our bones. In addition, we live our lives among others in an extended social realm, in which our bodily actions take on expressive and communicative meanings, and the actions of others become meaningful to us.

The way we typically differentiate these two worlds of movement—one being the concrete domain of embodied experience, the other being the abstract environment of symbolic experience—causes them to appear to be opposites, one material and the other immaterial. According to Western philosophical traditions, "the human body is not capable of thinking. Thinking takes place only in the 'mind'" (Levin 1999: 137). Paradoxically, however, we cannot come to apprehend external reality except through the instrument of the body. Nor can we make sense of this apprehended reality except through the processes of the mind. In practical life, there is no hard divide between these two domains. Rather, the concrete and the abstract are linked, for body and mind work together to help us make sense of the world.

To recapitulate:

> We have become accustomed, through the influence of the Cartesian tradition, to disengage from the object ... The object is an object through and through, and consciousness a consciousness through and

through ... Thus experience of one's own body runs counter to the reflective procedure which detaches subject and object from each other, and which gives us only the thought about the body, or the body as an idea, and not the experience of the body or the body in reality.

(Merleau-Ponty 1962: 198–199)

In reality, however, "my body is the fabric into which all objects are woven, and it is, at least in relation to the perceived world, the general instrument of my 'comprehension'. It is my body which gives significance not only to the natural object, but also to cultural objects like words" (ibid: 235).

Now, sense-making rests upon two processes: categorization and abstraction. Categorization has to do with recognizing the similarities and differences among things. "Our comprehension of the world around us begins with specific and individual cases—a person, a tree, a song—and through experience with the world, these particular objects are almost always dealt with in our brains as members of a category" (Levitin 2007: 146).

Abstraction has to do with leaving many individual characteristics out to establish the general "properties which a number of particular instances have in common" (Arnheim 1969: 157). Categorizing and abstracting allow us to link experiences, so as to move from specific incidents to more general principles.

These two processes can be illustrated with the "Ladder of Abstraction," a model used in the field of general semantics to examine language and meaning (Korzybski 1933; Hayakawa 1978). Let us choose as our starting point the word, "Fifi." In this particular case, Fifi is the name of our neighbor's poodle. In real life, Fifi is a playful, hungry, barking, running, sleeping, tail-wagging phenomenon that is constantly changing. And yet we summarize all these characteristics, totally arbitrarily, in one simple symbol, the word, "Fifi."

Now let us suppose that a four-year-old child is asking us to explain what Fifi is. Our explanatory conversation might go something like this:

"What's that?" the four-year-old inquires, pointing at Fifi.
"That's Fifi," we reply knowingly.
"What's a Fifi?" the four-year-old wonders.
"Fifi is a poodle."
"What's a poodle?"
"A poodle is a dog."
"What's a dog?"
"A dog is an animal."
"What's an animal?" the child queries, by now totally baffled.
"An animal is a living thing," we assert impatiently. "And don't ask so many questions!"

In fact, the way we "answer" the four-year-old's questions is to continue recasting Fifi in increasingly general terms. These various recastings of Fifi

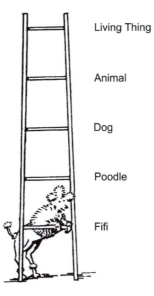

Living Thing

Animal

Dog

Poodle

Fifi

A playful, hungry, barking, running,
sleeping, tailwagging process.

Figure 4.6 "Ladder of Abstraction" (start reading from the bottom).
R.W. Moore

can be visualized as lying along a ladder, shown in Figure 4.6. At the bottom of this "Ladder of Abstraction" is the indescribable creature we know approximately but not completely, because this creature is complex and constantly changing. The nearest approximation to this tail-wagging phenomenon is the lowest rung on the ladder, the name "Fifi." As we ascend the ladder, our representations of Fifi become more abstract and general until the symbol at the top could stand for millions of creatures who are radically different from our beloved pet poodle. Yet, each of these "living things," be they poodles, crabs, or cranberry bushes, have one property in common —they are alive, and by being alive, they differ categorically from those things that are *not* alive.

This process of sense-making was described variously by two philosophers as follows:

> Our merest sense-experience is a process of *formulation*. The world that actually meets our senses is not a world of "things" . . . Out of [the] bedlam of . . . the world of pure sensation . . . so complex, so fluid and full . . . our sense organs must select certain predominant forms . . . their

"categories of understanding" . . . The world of sense is the real world constructed by the abstractions which the sense-organs immediately furnish.

(Langer 1976: 89, 92)

Even the uncivilized man cannot live in the world without a constant effort to understand that world. And for this purpose he has to develop and to use some general forms or categories of thought . . . We find in him the same . . . desire and the need to discern and divide, to order and classify the elements of its environment. There is hardly anything that escapes its constant urge for classification.

(Cassirer 1961: 14)

Body knowledge

We develop understanding of movement behavior, which we shall call *body knowledge*, through similar processes of categorizing, abstracting, and generalizing. Our own physical experiences in the world allow us to discern similarities among different motions. As the linguist Lakoff points out, "whenever we intentionally perform any kind of action, say something as mundane as writing with a pencil, hammering with a hammer, or ironing clothes, we are using categories" (1987: 6). As soon as we begin to identify *kinds* of actions, we are thinking categorically. Writing is a *type* of movement, and this is different from the kind of motions that are made in hammering or in ironing. With time and experience, each of us finds a way to discern related and unrelated movements, and to cluster those that are similar. These schemes will differ from person to person. One person may work with categories of "open and closed movements," while another differentiates "friendly and unfriendly" movements, but clustering, in and of itself, is essential, for "without the ability to categorize, we could not function at all, either in the physical world or in our social and intellectual lives" (ibid).

Here is an example of how these processes of categorization and general-ization might work with movement. The development of body know-ledge begins early in life, so let us imagine that once upon a time when I was a child, my father became angry and threw his arms around in a forceful and abrupt way. After this had occurred several more times, I began to realize that whenever my *father* threw his arms around in a forceful and abrupt way, he was angry. So far, this is a specific association limited to my immediate family.

Then one day I was in a department store with my mother, and I watched a man trying to return some damaged merchandise. When the clerk would not take it back, the man began to gesticulate in a forceful and abrupt manner, more or less like my dad did when he was angry. So now I could

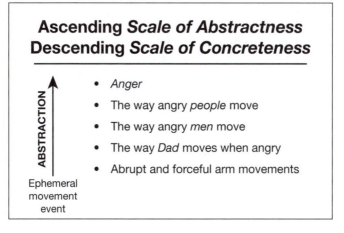

Figure 4.7 "Ladder of Abstraction"—movement example.

make a more general association—when *men* are angry, their gestures become forceful and abrupt.

On another day, I observed a neighbor down the street. She was yelling at the family dog. She was not waving her arms around, but she was tugging on the dog's leash with forceful, abrupt movements, similar to ones I had seen angry men do. So now I began to connect these types of movements, not just with my *father*, or with *men*, but with the way angry *people* move. By gradual increments, my association of forceful and abrupt movements was becoming more generalized. Eventually "forceful and abrupt" movements of any kind will simply become "angry movements" in my personal lexicon of movement meaning. Once this level of generalization has been reached, I will have melded the perception and interpretation of movement into one mental act, so that I can swiftly discern people who are angry from those who are not.

Making sense of movement, then, rests upon categorizing movements and abstracting their properties so as to establish general associations that are intellectually or emotionally meaningful. As Gordon Allport describes, "categories have a close and immediate tie with what we see, how we judge, and what we do. Their whole purpose seems to be to facilitate perception and conduct—to make our adjustment to life speedy, smooth, and consistent" (1958: 21).

Naturally, categorizing is a highly personal process. Each individual has unique movement experiences, and every person will sort, abstract and generalize in a slightly different way. Through these processes, *body knowledge* is built up, becoming a personal lexicon of movement meaning. Once the categories and associations in my body knowledge lexicon have been established, I can perceive a type of movement and fabricate a response rapidly, without having to reflect on the matter very much. So, if I am walking down the sidewalk and I see a man and woman punctuating their conversation with abrupt, forceful gestures, I may cross the street, simply because I do not want to get too close to two angry people.

Of course, the couple might not be angry; they might be simply impatient or excited. Or, they might belong to a cultural group that expresses many different feelings with abrupt, forceful gestures. Like the Roman god Janus, the *meaning* of any given movement is inherently two-faced. First, there is the "import" (Langer 1957: 129), intended or unawares, of the expressed form of the mover and, second, there is the "ascription," again conscious or unconscious, on the part of the observer, interacting or just watching. Thus, it is practically inevitable that our body knowledge sometimes leads us to misjudge the meaning of movement behavior of others. When we misinterpret the meaning of a given movement behavior, and start generalizing, body knowledge becomes body prejudice.

Body prejudice

The following incident, described by management consultant, Pamela Ramsden, illustrates how easily people may be misjudged on the basis of movement behavior. She was sitting in on a job interview with a candidate who was well qualified for the job for which he was applying. Nevertheless, the manager interviewing the applicant came away with the feeling that the fellow was "snobbish," and was prepared to reject him on that basis. When queried about this perceived snobbish attitude, the manager could only murmur that something about the applicant's "manner" had given him this impression. Fortunately, Ramsden was trained to observe movement closely. She recalled that the candidate had a persistent mannerism of raising his head and squinting down his nose. Further questioning revealed that it was indeed this gesture that had led the manager to conclude that the man was a snob. Ramsden pointed out that this movement happened "as if it was just a habit, an unfortunate unconscious expression of nervousness, in no way an expression of anything constant within the man's behavioral pattern" (1973: 77). Her argument was persuasive. The manager overcame his prejudicial impression and hired the candidate, who turned out to be very effective in his job, and not at all snobbish.

Like body knowledge, body prejudice originates from our capacity to categorize and generalize on the basis of personal experience. Over time, a positive or negative meaning comes to be associated with a certain type of movement. If this meaning is automatically projected onto all similar movements, regardless of context and modifying details, an inappropriate and prejudicial reaction may result.

Just because a movement is prejudged does not mean it is judged wrongly, but this is always a possibility. When making sense of movement, the tendency to make prejudicial judgments is magnified because movement is very easily "tuned out" and handled subliminally. This point is quite clear in the job interview anecdote recounted above. In that instance, the interviewing manager was initially unable to identify the action that triggered his negative response. When making sense of movement becomes a subconscious process, as it did in this case, it is all too easy to overlook contextual features that qualify the meaning of a given behavior. Perhaps the interviewer is right in believing that "looking down one's nose" is a hallmark of snobbishness. But his poorly defined powers of movement perception did not allow him to distinguish a movement that was merely a nervous habit from a similar behavior that was a deep character trait. Without the intervention of a more movement-sensitive person, the interviewing manager's body prejudice would have cost his company a fine employee.

No movement has exactly the same meaning twice

There have been quite a few attempts recently to establish fixed meanings for certain movements, thus to simplify the whole process of making sense of movement behavior. So, for instance, wiping the nose with the forefinger is said to indicate disapproval, flashing one's palm is said to reveal flirtation, and crossing one's legs signals a closed or unfriendly attitude. According to certain treatises on "body language" (e.g., Nierenberg, Calero, and Grayson 2010), one need only memorize the meanings of such actions to understand movement thoroughly and to be able to read another person like a book.

Fortunately or unfortunately, settling on any exact and fixed meaning for a given movement is not nearly so simple as such treatises would lead a reader to believe. Instead of a single invariable meaning, a given movement typically has many meanings. In fact, it could be said that *no movement ever has exactly the same meaning twice*. Several features come into play so as to complicate the process of deciphering meaning. First, movement is a dynamic and complex phenomenon and the very process of abstracting results in critical details being left out, details that potentially qualify or even alter the meaning that might be ascribed to the movement. In addition, contextual factors also influence the significance of an action. To return to our earlier example, forceful and abrupt movements may signify anger or excitement or simply be what is needed to push a heavy cart over a bump in the road.

This complex interrelationship of movement and meaning is further illustrated by the following anecdote in which a choreographer describes the reactions of various audiences to one of his dances.

We did the piece called *Winterbranch* some years ago in many different countries. In Sweden they said it was about race riots, in Germany they thought of concentration camps, in London they spoke of bombed cities, in Tokyo they said it was the atom bomb. A lady with us took care of the two children who were on the trip. She was the wife of a sea captain and said it looked like a shipwreck to her. Of course, it's about all of those and not about any of them, because I didn't have any of those experiences, but everybody was drawing on his experience, whereas I had simply made a piece which was involved with *falls*, the idea of bodies falling.

(Cunningham 1985: 105)

If even a basic action like falling lends itself to such diversity of interpretation, imagine how many different meanings a subtle movement may carry. Because the string of associations we develop with a given movement behavior is based on our own bodily experience, our personal history, and our cultural background, each individual will interpret the meaning of a given movement slightly differently. Moreover, even a given individual's body knowledge and body prejudice cannot stay "fixed," for as the person continues to accumulate more movement experience, his or her private lexicon of movement meanings must of necessity change and expand. That is, simply living longer will have an impact on how one makes sense of movement.

As noted above, meaning resides not only in the movement event but also in the eye of the beholder. What one notices about a particular movement (indeed, whether one notices it at all) is highly individualistic in nature. Moreover, how a perceived movement is interpreted depends to a large extent on the observer's past experiences and the inductive generalizations (body knowledge/body prejudice) associated with the behavior. Personal background, bias, and taste greatly influence the interpretation of movement, although these variables are often hidden in the construction of meaning.

Taking all these aspects into account, we can conceptualize the complex process of making sense of human movement as an intersection between the intentions of the mover and the interpretations of the observer, as shown in Figures 4.8 and 4.9. The movement event itself is the concrete point of contact between mover and perceiver. But from this shared contact the two paths of meaning diverge. The extent of divergence is dictated by myriad factors: the clarity with which the mover conveys his or her intentions, the acuity of the observer's perception, the similarity of cultural and social backgrounds between the mover and observer, their personal familiarity with each other, as well as their motivations and needs to understand one another. The clearer the movement expression, the more acute the observer, the more similar the backgrounds, the greater the personal familiarity, and the stronger the urge to understand, then the greater the congruence is likely to be between the mover's intentions and the observer's interpretation. This case is illustrated in Figure 4.8.

On the other hand, if the movement expression is ambiguous (or if the mover purposefully attempts to disguise her or his intentions), if the observer is inattentive or inexact, if the two individuals come from dissimilar backgrounds, if they are also strangers to one another, and if they do not need or want to understand each other, then we may assume that the

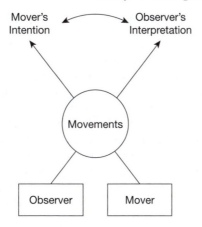
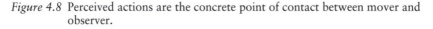

Figure 4.8 Perceived actions are the concrete point of contact between mover and observer.

divergence in their perspectives will be great indeed. This instance is shown in Figure 4.9.

The challenge in understanding movement is to bring these two paths of meaning closer together. It must be borne in mind, of course, that the congruence will never be absolute. There will always be a difference between what a movement event means to the observer and what it means to the person embodying it. We cannot literally slip inside another person's skin. With movement, as with all human experience, there is a limit to what we can know about each other.

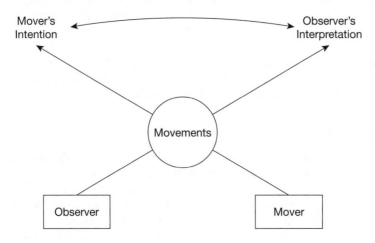

Figure 4.9 Many factors can cause the observer to misinterpret the mover's intentions.

Body knowledge/body prejudice: a two-edged sword

As we mentioned earlier, understanding movement is a paradoxical process. We can only make sense of movement by linking concrete physical experience with more abstract concepts like love, hate, danger, superiority, and so on. If we could not form these links, if we could not draw generalizations based on our movement experience, we would not be able to learn. We would have no *body knowledge*. Each new movement event would be perceived as just that—a totally new event, discrete and unlike any other. Relationships and similarities between events would not be recognized and the range of our response would be greatly reduced, while the *speed of reaction* would become slower. We would have to judge each movement event as if it were being encountered for the first and last time. Experience would serve to teach us very little.

On the other hand, if we did not link concrete physical experience with abstract concepts like love, hate, danger, and so on, we would not be troubled by *body prejudice*. Since we would simply perceive each movement event as a novel happening, we would not observe any and all movement through a thick netting of likes and dislikes or positive and negative associations accumulated in the past. We would be less prone to misjudge the actions of others, for the pre-established categories against which such actions are interpreted would not exist.

And so we come face to face with the central paradox of understanding movement. It is our capacity to abstract that has allowed us to turn the actions of our bodies into an extension system, a form of symbolic communication fraught with social meanings. Since we have transformed our bodies into something other than what they were, we now face the double-edged sword of body knowledge/body prejudice. We cannot enjoy knowledge without having prejudices, for both come from the same source, that is, our capacity to turn a motion into a symbol, to transform an individual action into a class of actions which, based on our past experiences, we have learned to treasure or despise. Body knowledge/body prejudice may be very efficient and also very dangerous. Only by recognizing that it cuts both ways will we be able to harness the power of movement as an extension system and use it as a tool rather than a weapon.

Recapitulation

The greatest biological asset of *Homo sapiens*, developed through eons of evolutionary change, is the very large brain it has. The brain is so large, in fact, that it cannot develop to full size while the baby is in utero, but must grow rapidly *after* birth, tripling in size during the first year of life. Because the brain is incomplete at birth, the human infant is rendered vulnerable in the extreme and is forced to be dependent upon human contact and care for its very survival. Moreover, the baby's emerging mind is molded while it is still forming by the human circle of caregivers into which it is born. As Eiseley has pointed out, this molding in infancy when the "dreams of the group" are implanted in the "waiting, receptive substance" of the brain is crucial if the young *Homo sapiens* is to be made truly human.

With the emergence of the large brain, biological adaptation has become less critical to humankind than cultural evolution. Utilizing increased capacities for thought, human beings have been able to extend biological functions and alter the environment to suit their needs. Language, technology, art, science, religion, and social tradition—it is mostly through these brain-children called "extension systems" that human evolution now proceeds. As a consequence, *Homo sapiens* lives in two worlds—the small, unique, and time-bound world of personal experience and the much larger, timeless, and symbolic world of shared experience, which has been distilled in cultural extension systems.

Because humankind's first attempts to extend their capabilities must have focused on the use of the body itself, movement is assumed to have been the original extension system. Movements that were repeated often enough, in the same location and context of events, began to acquire communal meaning and to pass from the world of private experience into the public world of shared knowledge. Today, movement continues to be a primary, though often overlooked, carrier of socially coded meanings. It is through movement, not through words, that human infants first communicate with their caregivers. And it is through movement that the caregivers respond. This nonverbal interaction shapes the developing brain and central nervous system and lays down patterns for the control of voluntary movement. As physical skills increase, movements become more automatic and require less conscious attention. More refined and articulate movements are executed without notice, whereas we are often painfully aware of movement when it is awkward and halting.

Movement seems to flit in and out of consciousness. The automatic motor simulation of observed actions, which arises through the mirror neurons, provides a basis for grasping and even empathizing with the actions of others. Familiarity with the observed activity, perceptual learning, and cultural patterns of embodiment all impact the mirror system. Despite these admirable biological structures, we still manage to misunderstand one another. Truly comprehending movement necessitates the use of additional human faculties.

Making sense involves categorizing, abstracting, and generalizing. Through these processes, each individual develops *body knowledge*. This private lexicon of movement meaning makes it possible to learn from our experiences so that we can observe a type of movement, judge it, and fashion our own response rapidly, without undue reflection. While this melding of perception and interpretation has many advantages, unreflective flight up the "Ladder of Abstraction" also causes us to misjudge the actions of others based upon our *body prejudice*. Thus body knowledge and body prejudice spring from the same processes; we cannot have one without the other. However, as we will show in the following chapters, there are many ways in which we can make our perception of movement more acute so as to maximize body knowledge and transcend body prejudice.

5 Deciphering human movements

Introduction

The post-partum growth spurt and neuroplasticity of the large human brain are gifts of biological evolution. These gifts in turn have necessitated social adaptation, for human newborns are quite helpless at birth. They need the care and continued support of other human beings, not only to survive but also to acquire the physical and mental traits that characterize *Homo sapiens*. Body movement plays a central role in this process of becoming human. Indeed, our very conception of the world, our reality "is shaped by the patterns of our bodily movement, the contours of our spatial and temporal orientation, and the forms of our interactions with objects" (M. Johnson 1987: xix).

Through acting, interacting, and observing, we come to know ourselves and others. Body and mind work together upon our corporeal experiences, drawing general inferences from specific acts. The result is a personal lexicon of movement meaning. This *body knowledge* allows us to fly through the social world on automatic pilot, so to speak, for we can observe an action, interpret its intent, and react without conscious mediation. Unfortunately, the subliminal melding of perception and interpretation sometimes causes us to crash and burn. Movements, like words, have different meanings to different people and in different contexts. Thus *body knowledge* may also become *body prejudice*.

If we are to enhance body knowledge and overcome body prejudice, we must learn to use our gifts of movement perception more discriminately. Fortunately, this is not so difficult as it may first sound. The initial step is simply to pay more attention to movement. The second step is to focus and hone that attention, teasing out the distinguishing features of movement impressions with greater precision. Just as a painter must refine sensitivity to shape, color, texture, light, and shadow, the keen observer must learn to discern the various properties of human movement. Thus exercises in this chapter invite you to look more closely at movement—at *what* is done, *when* it is done, *where* it is done, and *how* it is done. Through refined discrimination of such properties, the observer gains deeper insight into the "why" of movement, that is, into its expressive meaning.

Direction for website exercise

The visual portion of Chapter 5 can be accessed on the website. It contains an introduction, followed by seven exercises that require your participation. The material is self-explanatory, with directions preceding each exercise. After experiencing these exercises, the following discussion provides further insight into the purpose of each observation task.

Discussion

The observation exercises for this chapter were designed to refine your ability to decipher movement messages correctly. Physical embodiment is one way to begin to make sense of what we see. Imitating movement involves capturing four factors—*what, when, where,* and *how* the action is performed. As you may have discovered in *Exercise 1* (*Learn a Phrase*), even common conversational motions prove to be quite complex when closely studied. Much can be learned about any movement by trying to do it. As demonstrated in *Exercise 2* (*Two Entrances*), even a seemingly simple action such as entering a room and sitting down in a chair can be varied in subtle and complex ways. Teasing out these variations in *how* an action is performed also hones movement perception.

Delineating the properties of any movement event is complicated, because many aspects change simultaneously. Having a point of concentration helps to focus attention. In *Exercises 3, 4,* and *5,* various points of concentration were suggested to aid in deciphering movement events. For example, in *Exercise 3* (*Silly Walks*), you were asked to concentrate on *what* each performer was doing with different parts of the body. Attention was called first to the use of the legs; then, during subsequent viewings, you were asked to focus on other body parts, such as the arms, head, and torso. In *Exercise 4* (*Moving Sculpture*), you were asked to concentrate on describing *where* the movements occurred in the space around the body. In *Exercise 5* (*Dynamics*), you were asked to choose the adjective or adverb that best described *how* the movement was performed dynamically.

Each of these three elements—body, space, and dynamics—can be tapped as a point of focus to help decipher any movement event. Indeed, each of these elements plays a role whenever and wherever motion occurs. That is to say, movement inherently involves the following elements: (1) coordination of actions among the parts of the body; (2) displacement of the body in space; and (3) exertion of dynamic energy.

Movement perception is an interaction between the objective properties of the event itself and the subjective interests of the observer. As noted above, movement events are complex configurations involving progressive changes in the use of body, space, and energy.

Consequently, a single movement event can often convey several meanings, depending upon the point of focus that the observer adopts. This point of focus is often a matter of taste; in other words, one pays attention to the aspect of the movement event that is of greatest personal interest. These individual predilections impact body knowledge/body prejudice and explain why eyewitnesses to the same event so often differ in their accounts of what occurred.

Accordingly, *Exercise 6 (What Are These People Like?)* was designed to provide a chance for you to explore your own body knowledge/body prejudice. You were directed to start at the top of the "Ladder of Abstraction," recording your first impressions of the man and the woman engaged in conversation. You were then asked to track the sources of these impressions, thus descending the "Ladder of Abstraction" to identify increasingly more concrete movement behaviors from which your impressions arose.

Subjectivity can never be eliminated altogether from observation. Still, it is possible to develop a more analytical orientation. This was the purpose of *Exercise 7 (Instant Replay)*. Here you were asked to focus first on the activation of the body, then on the use of space, and finally on the exertion of dynamic energy as the scene viewed in *Exercise 6* was replayed. In the light of these more concentrated and detailed viewings, you were again asked to re-examine your first impressions of the male conversant, and to see how subsequent, close study of his movement behaviors might have altered first impressions.

If you have had the chance to discuss *Exercises 6* and *7* with other observers, you are likely to find that people have formed different opinions about the two conversants. For example, one person might have judged the man to be nervous, while someone else characterized his behavior as "laid back." Moreover, you may discover that the same concrete movement behavior has been interpreted in contrasting ways. For instance, the woman's jiggling foot movements might signal impatience to one person, while another views this rhythmic action as empathic entrainment with the male conversant. It can be unsettling to find that impressions and recollections of a person or an event vary significantly. Yet, discovering that other people interpret nonverbal behavior in quite different ways is the first step towards more conscious reflection on the nature of one's own body knowledge and body prejudice.

To provide further food for thought, you might be interested in learning how the male and female conversants in *Exercise 6* characterize themselves, how they describe each other, and how they are described by a third person who knows them both.

Man's description of self

I am the youngest of four sons. We are approximately five years apart from one another so that my oldest brother is fifteen years older than myself. I was born in my parents' mid-forties. In fact, my arrival was quite a surprise to both of them! My cultural background is Hispanic (Mexican) and my parents are both first-generation Americans.

I was born in the Southwest and have lived there most of my life. Because of my family's religious background (Seventh-Day Adventist), I attended private church schools until my first year in college. All of my social contact centered primarily around this religious community, and I had very little interaction with the outside world. When I did leave the Church, I entered a state university and proceeded to learn as much about the "world" as possible. I finished a Bachelor's degree in humanities, with an emphasis in English literature and art history. I also obtained a teaching certificate.

I taught for approximately two-and-a-half years. During this period I was involved with migrant farm workers' children, primary special education students, and high school English students. It was a vast range of experience, to say the least.

I left teaching to become employed as the director and manager of an art gallery. While working, I began to pursue a Master's degree in counseling, finishing it in two years. Presently I am employed in an employee assistance program that provides counseling services to sixteen different client companies.

I enjoy drawing and painting when the opportunity presents itself. I am a professional organist. I also enjoy cooking, writing, and those other things that are considered to be in the creative realm. I like to travel, but lately this has not been as possible as it was when I was younger. I met my wife-to-be in graduate school, and I have been married less than a year.

Woman's description of self

I was born on the mid-Atlantic coast, the younger child of a middle-aged naval officer and his wife. (I have one brother thirteen years my senior.) When I was five, my father retired from the military, and our family moved to the Southwest so that my brother could attend a state university there. My father secured a position as a school administrator on an Indian reservation. So, I spent my junior high and high school years among Native Americans. In reflecting back on those years I now realize that the culture of the reservation had an impact on my perception as an individual. For example, I believe that I became somewhat shy—very much like my Indian friends.

When I left the reservation, I attended the state university. The transition was difficult in terms of relating to the Anglo culture. I received a Bachelor's degree in education. After graduation I moved to a large city in the Southwest, where I taught a variety of subjects at different grade levels. After five years I returned to graduate school, where I earned a Master's degree in counseling. It was at this time that I met my future husband in class. We have recently married, and now I am a school counselor at the junior high level.

[Note: As you may have surmised, the man and woman in this conversation are married to one another. Their conversation was taped when they were newly-weds, having been married to one another for less than two months!]

Further descriptive information about this couple is summarized in Table 5.1.

Table 5.1 Characteristics of the conversants in *Exercise 6*

	Five adjectives for	
Given by	*Man*	*Woman*
Man	caring	shy
	loyal	caring
	creative	smart
	somewhat honest	stable
	concerned to do best possible job	ambitious
Woman	harried	always trying to work towards something
	attractive	extremely sloppy or extremely neat
	knowledgeable	aggressive
	assertive	shy
	diversified	nags at times
Mutual friend	artistic	assertive
	intelligent	helpful
	friendly	pleasant
	active	purposeful
	involved	catches on quickly

Now you have had a chance to learn more about the man and woman in *Exercise 6*—what they say about themselves, how they characterize each other, and how they are described by a friend. How do you assess the accuracy of your first impressions? What does the experience suggest about your own processes of perceiving movement, what you notice and what you overlook? What have you discovered about your own body knowledge/body prejudice?

Recapitulation

Movement theorist Rudolf Laban has suggested that movement can be perceived from three different perspectives. The first is the view of those who perceive movement subjectively, through the medium of their own bodily experiences. These "biological innocents" are enthusiastic lovers of movement who, according to Laban, "swim more or less contentedly in the same never-ceasing stream" (1974: 7). The second view is a more distanced and objective perspective, taken by those "people who are obliged to practise and observe movement more closely" (ibid: 6). These "scheming mechanics" view movement analytically. Finally there are the intellectuals who seek "living reality in emotions and ideas alone" (ibid). These "emotional dreamers" view movement symbolically.

These viewpoints actually "represent degrees on a scale of temperaments of observers who unavoidably are in the same stream of existence but look at it from different angles" (ibid: 7). These different angles of approach can be related to the "Ladder of Abstraction" discussed in Chapter 4. As shown in Figure 5.1, bodily involvement in movement is the most concrete perspective and lies near the bottom of the ladder. Objective description of concrete actions stands in the middle, while interpretation of movement as a symbolic form of communication hovers at the top.

These three perspectives also suggest different ways to approach the task of deciphering human movement. *Exercise 1* (*Learn a Phrase*) tapped the perspective of bodily experience. *Exercise 2* (*Two Entrances*), *Exercise 3* (*Silly Walks*), *Exercise 4* (*Moving Sculpture*), *Exercise 5* (*Dynamics*), and *Exercise 7* (*Instant Replay*) all utilized the more analytical approach. Finally, the most abstract approach was summoned up in *Exercise 6* (*What Are These People Like?*). In this exercise you were encouraged to make judgments about the individuals solely on the basis of their nonverbal behaviors.

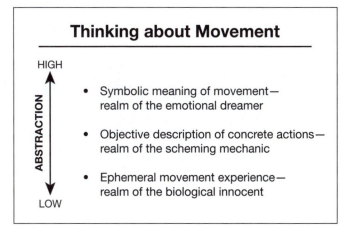

Figure 5.1 The "Ladder of Abstraction" applies to thinking about movement.

Each of these varied perspectives is vital and important as a means for deciphering human movement. As Laban commented, "We are all emotional dreamers, and scheming mechanics, and biological innocents, simultaneously: sometimes we waver between these three mentalities, and sometimes we compress them in a synthesised act of perception and function" (1974: 7). In the chapter that follows we will continue to cultivate an integration of these modes of perception as we investigate the use of metaphor in movement study.

6 Movement as metaphor

The metaphor is probably the most fertile power possessed by man.
José Ortega y Gassett

It has often been noted that cultural evolution has become far more crucial for the human race than biological adaptation. Utilizing increased capacities for thought made possible by the gradual evolution of a large and powerful brain, *Homo sapiens* has gone on to extend biological functions and to alter nature itself to suit its needs (Dubos 1981). Science, language, technology, art, religion, and social tradition—it is through these brain-children called "extension systems" that much of human evolution now continues. As a consequence, human beings live simultaneously in two worlds—the small, unique, time-bound world of concrete, private experience and the much larger, timeless, symbolic world of shared experiences, pooled in cultural extension systems. In that, to borrow Aldous Huxley's expression, humans are "multiple amphibians" (1962).

It is quite likely that movement was the original extension system, since humankind's first attempts to extend their capabilities must have focused on the use of the body itself. Oft-repeated movements in the same space and context could easily acquire communal meaning so as to expand from the realm of private experience into the public world of shared meanings. Today, movement continues to play a vital role in all areas of human endeavor. Movement is a part of our work activities, of our games and contests, of the way we make war, of the way we make love, of how we behave in public, of our attempts to heal and to educate, and of the expressions of our most intangible longings for knowledge, beauty, peace, even immortality.

In this modern era, as in primordial times, movement remains as a primary, though often taken-for-granted, carrier of socially coded meanings. Consequently, the crucial need to understand what movement means persists.

In this chapter we will begin to take a closer look at the meaning of movement. Meaning, of course, is not simply given to us by the world. Rather, we give meaning to the world through the constructions of our minds. One of the chief ways we so give meaning and make sense of our lives, events, and movements is through the development and application of metaphors. And it is to metaphor that we now turn.

What is a metaphor?

A nose is a nose is a nose is a nose . . . perhaps. But as Cyrano de Bergerac points out, this barely begins to cover what one can say about a nose, especially such a large and prominently colored one like his. Indeed, Cyrano once demonstrated to a would-be insulter just how much one *can* say about a nose.

> If one wishes to be descriptive, " 'Tis a rock—a crag—a cape—A cape? Say rather, a peninsula!" Or to be insolent, "Sir, when you smoke your neighbors must suppose your chimney is on fire." A rustic might observe, "That there's a blue cucumber!" Or the poet would say, "Hark—the horn of Roland calls to summon Charlemagne!" To be eloquent or dramatic, one could also say of a large nose, "When it blows, the typhoon howls and the clouds darken," or "When it bleeds—the Red Sea." Or to be familiar, "Well, old torchlight! Hang your hat over that chandelier—it hurts my eyes."
>
> (Rostand 1981: 31)

And such quips only begin to tap the wealth of what one could say about a large nose through the use of metaphor.

Figure 6.1 Cyrano de Bergerac had an extremely prominent nose.
R.W. Moore

Metaphor is usually thought of as a "device of poetic imagination and rhetorical flourish" (Lakoff and Johnson 1980: 3). That is to say, as a matter of words, and special words at that. In fact, however, "metaphor is pervasive in everyday life, not just in language but in thought and action. Our ordinary conceptual system, in terms of which we both think and act, is fundamentally metaphorical in nature" (ibid). But what exactly *is* a metaphor?

Put most simply, a metaphor is a transfer, "a figure of speech by means of which we denote one kind of object, or idea, by means of another, generally because of some analogy existing between the two" (Belth 1977: 75). If we say, as Cyrano did, that a nose is a peninsula, we are implying that the nose, like a peninsula, is long, narrow, and juts out. Or if we say that a nose is a torchlight, we imply that it is bright and shiny. The metaphor rests upon the similarities of one object or idea with another.

So, "metaphor deliberately makes use both of certain similarities in proportions *and* an emphasis on observable differences. This lends to every metaphor a quality of the absurd, for that difference is, in a sense, winked at" (ibid). So when Cyrano smokes, his nose might be similar to a chimney, since smoke comes from both. But it is absurd that anyone would think a nose on fire because of the great amount of smoke pouring from it. Yet this might happen in the case of a chimney.

Metaphors, in essence, reframe the way we think about the world. We take the common and embed it in a new context, whereby the thing or event is given new meaning. "Metaphor is defined in terms of movement," wrote Ricoeur (1977: 17). The interest is "in the transpositional movement as such," and the "process designates change of meaning as such" (ibid). For instance, when Newton opined that the universe was a machine, he provided generations of researchers with new ways of thinking about the motion of the planets and thus opened a whole new era of science. In this sense, through switching the point of focus and creating novel associations, metaphor has the power to lead on to other thoughts and new discoveries.

"Movement is a language" is one such metaphor that has seemingly been quite prevalent and illuminating in relating to movement. Numerous everyday expressions, such as "body language," "nonverbal communication," "decoding silent messages," "how to read a person like a book," or "what is her body saying?" attest to the popularity of this metaphor. Scholars of human movement have also put this same metaphor to use in their attempts to make sense of what they observe. At least three distinctive views, each derived from the language metaphor and purporting to explain how movement means, can be delineated.

Movement is a universal language

Movement is often considered to be the universal language of humankind. All people move, of course, and because motion is silent, it is thought to be

Figure 6.2 Smiling is one physical expression understood around the world.

Jan Stanley

immune from the confusion attendant to the proliferation of spoken tongues among humankind. Yet more than mere commonality is implied in this metaphor. Let us take a closer look at what this metaphor suggests.

Fundamentally, "movement is a universal language" says that everyone, regardless of race, creed, color, sex, age, etc., can understand physical action in the same manner. Unlike languages such as French, Japanese, Russian, or Sanskrit which most of us must study to be able to decipher, no learning is necessary to be able to understand movement. That is, the ability to decipher movement meaning is innate—we are born with it. This natural ability to interpret movement rests upon a biological imperative and an intrinsic identification of the observer with the mover. Consequently, what a given movement means is absolute—the action conveys the same message in China as in South America, in Alaska as in Arabia.

Interestingly, the movements most often used to illustrate this metaphoric view are facial expressions. None other than Darwin eloquently championed this view as follows:

That the chief expressive actions, exhibited by man and by the lower animals, are now innate or inherited,—that is, have not been learnt by the individual,—is admitted by everyone. So little has learning or imitation to do with several of them that they are from the earliest days and throughout life quite beyond our control; for instance, the relaxation of the arteries of the skin in blushing, and the increased action of the heart in anger. We may see children, only two or three years old, and even those born blind, blushing from shame; and the naked scalp of a very young infant reddens from passion. Infants scream from pain directly after birth, and all their features assume the same form as during subsequent years. These facts alone suffice to show that many of our most important expressions have not been learnt.

(1998: 348)

Similarly, Eibl-Eibesfeldt has argued:

The similarities in expressive movements between cultures lie not only in such basic expressions as smiling, laughing, crying and the facial expressions of anger, but in whole syndromes of behavior. For example, one of the expressions people of different cultures may produce when angry is characterized by opening the corners of the mouth in a particular way and by frowning, and also by clenching the fists, stamping on the ground and even by hitting at objects. Furthermore, this whole syndrome can even be observed in those born deaf and blind.

(1972: 299)

Ekman joins the above two by declaring that "our evolution gives us these universal [facial] expressions" (1998: 393). As a strategy for deciphering movement meaning, this "universal language" view has some interesting implications. First, if one believes that "movement is a universal language," very little deciphering is actually necessary. We enter the world programmed biologically, so to speak, *to express* certain feelings in certain ways. Moreover, we are born with the instincts that equip us *to recognize* these feelings in others. Hence, our response to and comprehension of movement is automatic. We do not need to think, reflect, or decipher—we *know*.

This approach to the understanding of movement has sometimes been called the "physiognomic approach" which, as Gombrich puts it,

carries strong and immediate conviction. We all experience this immediacy when we look into a human face. We see its cheerfulness or gloom, its kindliness or harshness, without being aware of reading "signs" ... We all know how easily a similar response is evoked by other creatures, how the penguin will strike us as grave, the camel as supercilious or the bloodhound as sad ... we speak of cheerful colours or melancholy sounds.

(1963: 47)

Indeed, this physiognomic approach holds that not only are we bio-logically programmed to encode and decode feelings in universally fixed ways, but movements themselves, through their inherent qualities, carry intrinsic, expressive meanings that are immediately and viscerally appre-hended. Sad movements sink, while happy movements rise with buoyancy. The defiant stand with arms akimbo, and the meek shrink with elbows held in. The vital, the ecstatic and the passionate are physically expansive, while the frightened, the intellectual, and the sickly are contained.

In other words, the relationship between movement and meaning is one of identity—they are one and the same. This identification of the formal factors of movement with moods can be illustrated by an experiment recounted by Arnheim.

> Members of a college dance group were asked individually to give im-provisations of such subjects as sadness, strength, or night. The dancers' performances showed much agreement. For example, in the representa-tion of sadness the movement was slow and confined to a narrow range. It was mostly curved in shape and showed little tension. The direction was indefinite, changing, wavering; and the body seemed to yield passively to the force of gravity rather than being propelled by its own initiative. It will be admitted that the physical mood of sadness has a similar pattern. In a depressed person the mental processes are slow and rarely go beyond matters closely related to immediate experi-ences and momentary interests. All his thinking and striving displays softness and lack of energy. He shows little determination, and activity is often controlled by outside forces.
>
> (1974: 449)

Arnheim goes on to point out that the understanding of movement expres-sion does not necessitate a "mind." Indeed,

> people normally respond to external behavior itself, rather than thinking of it explicitly as a mere reflection of mental attitudes. People perceive the slow, listless, "droopy" movements of one person as con-trasted to the brisk, straight, vigorous movements of another, but do not necessarily go beyond the appearance to think of psychic weariness or alertness behind it. Weariness and alertness are contained in the physical behavior itself.
>
> (ibid: 451)

More recently, the positive "effects of power embodiment" were reported in a laboratory experiment (Carney, Cuddy, and Yap 2010). Both in men and women, those who took the open, expansive "power" postures under instruc-tion exhibited an increase in the secretion of testosterone (the dominance hormone) and a decrease in cortisol (the stress hormone). They also experienced "increased feelings of power" (by self-reports) and "tolerance for risk" (on a gambling task). Exactly opposite effects were seen among those who took the "low-power," contractive, closed body positions (ibid: 1363–1364), even though both groups held their respective poses of two varieties for a total of only two minutes. According to the authors, "these results suggest that any psychological construct, such as power, with a signature pattern of nonverbal correlates may be embodied" (ibid: 1366).

In short, the universalist or physiognomic world view holds that the medium is the message. Meaning is intrinsic to the movement and thus comprehended immediately by the observer, for this meaning is rooted in universals of physical experience.

Movement is a foreign language

A quite different view is manifested by those who hold with the metaphor, "movement is a foreign language." Here, it is not assumed that the ability to comprehend movement is innate or that the recognition of movement expression is a spontaneous birthright of humankind. Rather, movement is seen as being much more analogous to spoken language; a "sound and fury signifying nothing," *until* we master, through learning, the meaning of the code. Moreover, just as the ability to speak and understand English does not automatically equip one to use and comprehend German, so too the knowledge of movement codes must be specific to cultural and other contexts. Actions that carry one meaning in the United States may convey something entirely different in Italy or China. The meaning of movement is therefore culture-specific.

One of the chief proponents of this view is Birdwhistell. He initially shared Darwin's view that nonverbal expression is universal in its meaning. However, as he began to study smiling, his views started to alter.

> From the outset, the *signal* value of the smile proved debatable. For example, not only did I find that a number of my subjects "smiled" when they were subjected to what seemed to be a positive environment, but some "smiled" in an aversive one . . . As I enlarged my observational survey, it became evident that there was little constancy to the phenomenon. It was almost immediately clear that the frequency of smiling varied from one part of the United States to another. Middle-class individuals from Ohio, Indiana, and Illinois, as counted on the street, smiled more often than did New Englanders with a comparable background . . .
>
> In one part of the country, an unsmiling individual might be queried as to whether he was "angry about something," while in another the smiling individual might be asked, "What's funny?" . . . Except with

Figure 6.3 Interpreting gestures accurately is like learning a foreign language.
C.L. Moore

the most elastic conception of "pleasure," charts of smile frequency were not going to be very reliable as maps for the location of happy Americans.

(Birdwhistell 1970: 30–31)

These studies led Birdwhistell to conclude that, "just as there are no universal words, no sound complexes, which carry the same meaning the world over, there are no body motions, facial expressions, or gestures which provoke *identical* responses the world over" (ibid: 42).

A similar conclusion was reached by Hall in his work as an anthropologist (1969: 154–164). He has found that different cultures have distinctive codes for how they use space and time. Americans, for instance, tend to maintain a large territory of space around themselves and feel uncomfortable when anyone stands too close. In the Arab world, on the other hand, personal space is small, and anyone who stands too far away is likely to give offense.

When movement meaning is seen to be culture-specific, different strategies are needed to decipher significance to those used when movement meaning is thought to be universal. To begin with, one has to learn which movement behaviors are appropriate in a given culture. Scheflen has explained this process in the following way:

> A given tradition has a characteristic repertoire of words, gestures and structural arrangements for the communication of meaning, and the meanings of these behavioral forms are culturally specific . . .
>
> In growing up people have opportunity to observe these hierarchical arrangements in their typical and usual form: they also participate in assembling these behaviors, and are told the meanings of representations when they occur . . .
>
> An individual can experience the contextual referents and learn the system of behaviors which are used to represent these. And he himself keeps performing the traditional activities, so his children and students get a chance to learn them. In this way the customary forms . . . are passed on from generation to generation.
>
> (1973: 45)

While growing up, in other words, a child learns not only what to do and how to do it, but also when and where a given movement behavior is appropriate in his or her culture. Consequently, a narrow range of correspondence is set up between movement and meaning, based heavily upon contextual rules that are gradually acquired through experience and familiarity with a culture.

Rehearsed from earliest childhood, these rules become so taken for granted that, ultimately, ways of handling the body, space, and time, though in fact peculiar to a specific culture, come to be assumed to be natural, even universal. Indeed, if one has mastered the code of one's culture, understanding the nonverbal behavior of other members of the same culture may take on the spontaneous and unambiguous nature that the perception of the so-called "universal" movements is supposed to carry.

However, when this same "master" of movement behavior is plunked down in another culture, or in a very different context even within his or her own culture, what often results is a series of missteps and misunderstandings that may be quite serious in consequence. Consider, for example, the legendary account of the voyages of Captain Cook.

> It is said that when Captain Cook landed on the Fiji islands' beach and walked to meet an oncoming band of natives, he thrust out his hand in token of friendship. It never occurred to him that an offer to shake hands could be interpreted as a threatening gesture, because his countrymen were all conditioned to "read" his gesture as friendly. In the split second of his action, however, the natives, who were *not* so conditioned, interpreted the thrust of hand and arm as an aggressive action, and promptly killed the explorer. Legend has it that before he made his

gesture they were ready to be friendly; they just did not know about the conventional gesture we call a handshake.

(Lamb and Watson 1979: 15)

Even when nonverbal misunderstandings are not fatal, variations in movement code often leave the traveler befuddled and disoriented. For instance, Wolfgang discovered in Rio de Janeiro that another simple hand gesture, *meaning* "A-OK" in the United States, conveys a rude meaning in Brazil (1995: 19–20). Of course, "in a high-context society . . . the meaning of what is communicated depends heavily on the [context]" (ibid: 59). The situation can get serious or hilarious, particularly if the traveler clings to old customs or attempts to interpret the new culture in terms of the old. This form of "culture shock" was recorded also by a member of the first Japanese delegation to the United States in 1860.

> In the evening there was a dance at the hotel. This dance was accompanied by the piano. The sound of the piano resembles the Japanese koto but the shape of the piano is quite different. It is a large square shaped instrument. In the dance the man and woman take each other's hands and step from right to left but do not move their hands. When we saw this it looked to us just like exercise and did not seem a bit interesting.
>
> (Yanagawa 1973: 51–52)

Indeed, as Tocqueville observed;

> Nothing seems at first sight less important than the outward form of human actions, yet there is nothing upon which men set more store; they grow used to everything except to living in a society which has not their own manners.
>
> (1945: vol. 2, 228)

To become fluent in "foreign" manners is just as arduous a process as becoming fluent in another tongue. That is, a person must first set aside the "language of manners" he or she already knows (lest one should wind up like Captain Cook). Then she or he must acquire anew the vocabulary and grammar of the other culture's movement code *and* learn the rules of context—when a given motion is appropriate and when it is not. Only after each of these hurdles has been surmounted will the individual have achieved nonverbal fluency. Until then, the culture-specific school of movement metaphor would claim that understanding movement in another culture is like listening to a foreign language we know only slightly—at best picking out the few words or phrases we think we recognize and trying to use context, often erroneously, to give meaning to the rest.

Movement is a private code

Yet another view is manifested in the metaphor, "movement is a private code." Here, movement is seen to have neither pan-human nor even culture-specific meanings, but only unique and individualistic senses to it. That is, each person uses body movement somewhat idiosyncratically, thus conveying meanings that are unique to him or her. An analogy might be drawn here to the gurgles, coos, and screeches that an infant murmurs. These sounds are almost totally indecipherable to everyone except the doting mother. Through a process of trial and error, and long intimacy and familiarity, the mother comes to distinguish the "I'm hungry" screech from the "I'm lonely" one, or the "I'm about to burp" gurgle from the "Isn't this fun" coo. What is nothing but "one big, blooming, buzzing confusion" (James 1981: vol. 1, 488) to the rest of us is a private code fraught with meaning to a particular child and the mother.

Another analogy parallels the way we have learned to look at modern art. Let us consider, for instance, the significance of the color blue. A proponent of the pan-human school might conclude that blue, because it is a cool color, evokes universal physical sensation of coldness (Itten 1961). A proponent of the culture-specific school might hold that blue represented the aristocracy in medieval coats of arms due to its association with precious gems (Gage 1999). Yet if we wish to understand Picasso's famous "Blue Period," neither of these approaches will get us very far. Instead, we have to ask, "What did the color blue mean to Picasso? How does his 'Blue Period' relate to what he painted before and after, to the subject matter and composition of the paintings? Was Picasso serious or making a joke in the paintings?" In other words, we need to be familiar not only with the world and societal contexts in which Picasso painted blue pictures, but also with Picasso the individual.

The understanding of a private code is hard since it makes a great many demands on the viewer to place what is perceived in proper context. Probably for this reason we find very little movement research from the social sciences that utilizes the "private code" metaphor.

Social sciences, after all, are interested in humankind in general, or in the statistical average, and *not* in the miracle or the exceptional that happens "only once, or even very rarely" (Bertrand Russell, quoted in Langer 1976: 274). In the field of art history and criticism, however, one finds many examples of the deciphering of private codes, whether in the form of painting, writing, music, or dance (e.g., Cunningham 1985; Siegel 1985. Also see, Adshead 1982; Banes 2007; Battcock 1966; Bloom 2006; Copeland 1941; Ewen 1933; Fry 1926; Kirstein 1970; Kozloff 1968; Manning 1993; Martin 1936; McDonaugh 1970; Preston-Dunlop 1998a; Rosenfeld 1972; Tortora 2006).

Furthermore, the "movement is a private code" metaphor plays a prominent, if unobtrusive, role in all intimate human relationships. For example, if my husband unfolds the newspaper and silently studies it in a coldly deliberate manner, I know he is angry—not because all humans are coldly deliberate when angry (they are not), or all husbands in a given culture behave so when mad (they do not), but because that is what *my* husband does. On another day, however, when my husband unfolds the newspaper and silently studies it in a coldly deliberate manner, I know he is worried and preoccupied rather than angry. I understand this because I know not only his private code but also the circumstances of his life. I have come to comprehend his individual movement expressions in addition to the multiple meanings of those expressions as they vary from situation to situation.

Interestingly, the approach to understanding movement based on the "private code" metaphor has a paradoxical effect. On the one hand, the unique movements of a given individual may appear quite ambiguous since they are not limited to either universal or cultural signs or symbols. On the other hand, once a private code has been decoded, the perceived meaning will be accurate most of the time. That is to say, I am far more likely to understand truly my husband's behavior than that of another male from the same cultural background, or that of *any* human male. This is the paradox of the private code—when movement meaning seems most ambiguous it is simultaneously most precisely decipherable.

Contexts high and low

At first glance, the three metaphors—(1) movement is a universal language; (2) movement is a foreign language; and (3) movement is a private code—would appear to represent mutually exclusive views. For instance, if meaning is intrinsic to the movement and all members of *Homo sapiens* are born with understanding, as the first metaphor implies, how can actions have different meanings from culture to culture, which must be painstakingly learned, as the second metaphor asserts? If, likewise, each individual creates his or her own body code, as the third metaphor proposes, how can nonverbal communication function as a cultural extension system, so that all members of a given culture understand one another, as the second metaphor proposes?

What *is* movement after all? Is it a universal language that unites all human beings through bonds of nonverbal understanding, or is it a cultural extension system that reinforces the mores and values of a given group? Or is it an idiosyncratic language, a kind of baby-talk babble understandable only among those who are intimate with each other?

In fact, movement is all of these things. That is, some motions seem to have universal meanings that all people understand, while other physical behaviors vary from culture to culture, thus requiring people to learn the significance of these actions. Finally, individuals must tailor movement to suit themselves if they are to have a personal identity as well as a social one. Naturally, such uniquely personal movements can be deciphered only through a thorough familiarity with a given individual in his or her context.

Consequently, each metaphor can contribute to our understanding of body movement. The difference would seem to lie in the extent to which the sense-making strategy depends upon contexting. Hall has pointed out that messages conveyed through extension systems can be classed according to the extent to which the message must be contexted to be understood. At the low-context end of the continuum are those communications in which "the mass of the information is vested in the explicit code" (1976: 91). At the opposite end of the continuum is the high-context communication in which "most of the information is either in the physical context or internalized in the person, while very little is in the coded, explicit, transmitted part of the message" (ibid).

Due to their variable dependence on context for meaning, each of the three "movement is a language" metaphors may be positioned along this continuum, as shown in Figure 6.4.

At the low-context end of the continuum we find the "movement is a universal language" metaphor. Because meaning is supposed to be intrinsic to the movement itself, contexting is not necessary. All the information needed for understanding the action is explicitly coded in the action itself. The relationship of movement to meaning, as shown in the model, is one of *identity*—the movement *is* the meaning.

At roughly the midpoint of the continuum is the "movement is a foreign language" metaphor. Here a given nonverbal behavior may have multiple meanings from culture to culture, or from situation to situation within a

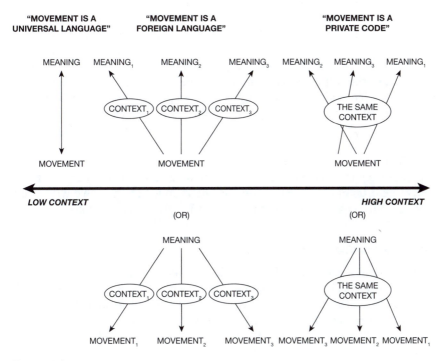

Figure 6.4

culture. To decipher meaning, a one-to-one correspondence must be established between the motion and the specific context in which it occurs, taking
into account both the situational factors and the social conventions. Needless to say, it is also the case that different movements can carry the same
meaning as a function of different contexts.

Finally, a detailed contexting is essential to deciphering the private code
of a given person's movement behavior. Here the relationship of movement to meaning is not one of identity regardless of contexts, or even one-
to-one correspondence as a function of a given context, but a seemingly
more erratic and oblique relationship. A given movement within the same
context may have multiple meanings. Or a given message may be conveyed
through a variety of different physical actions, again within the same context.
Therefore, physical action must be subjected to rival hypotheses—it could
mean x or y or z—and only through contexting the event both externally
(where and when does the behavior occur?) and internally (what is the mover
like? How has he/she behaved in the situation before?) can the meaning be
established.

This process of contexting may actually incorporate the other metaphoric
approaches through generating rival hypotheses. That is, if my Japanese
friend is quiet, I may entertain both universal and culture-specific hypotheses
in my attempt to understand what the behavior means. That is, I might think,
"When people are quiet, they are generally in a serene or contemplative
mood." Or I might reason, "My friend is Japanese, and Japanese are often
quiet." Finally I might reflect, "My friend tends to be quiet as a person, but
he is especially quiet when he worries about something. Therefore, I think
he's worried right now." My interpretations of the observed behavior in
general, of the cultural background of the person, of the situational factors,
and of the particular individual all come into play as part of the contexting
through which the movement may be understood. When movement is seen
as a private code, it demands to be dealt with as high-context communication.

While each of the three "movement is a language" metaphors provides
us with insight into the phenomenon of human action, still other metaphors
provoke different comprehensions. In the following section we will briefly
explore alternative metaphors that are of use in movement study.

Alternative metaphors

The "simplest definition of a metaphor would be that it is treating some
primary event as if it were something else" (Belth 1977: 80). This metaphoric
process provides us with new ways to handle old ideas and thus gives us
the power to restructure creatively the way we perceive the world. The
metaphor "becomes a kind of lens ... by means of which the familiar is
seen in new light, new organization, new interrelationships of meanings"
(ibid: 77). Like a lens, the metaphor sharpens and magnifies that upon which

it is focused. However, whatever lies outside the field of vision is perceived only dimly, if at all. "When we say that a concept is structured by a metaphor, we mean that it is partially structured and that it can be extended in some ways but not others" (Lakoff and Johnson 1980: 13). As with all extensions of human thought, in other words, metaphors both amplify and diminish.

What needs to be remembered is that, "In allowing us to focus on one aspect of a concept . . . a metaphorical concept can keep us from focusing on other aspects of the concept that are inconsistent with that metaphor" (ibid: 10). In the previous sections of this chapter we have discussed the ways in which variations of the metaphor, "movement is a language," have facilitated an understanding of human motion. But we must also ask ourselves, "In what ways is movement *not* like language? What is left out with this metaphor?"

In order to answer this question, of course, we must first say a bit about the nature of human language. This is a vast topic upon which much research has been concentrated. A currently prevalent view is that language consists of a variety of different units that have no meaning in themselves but may be arranged in various ways to build up complex messages that do have meaning (Bronowski 1977: 132–154). Sounds are combined in various sequences to create syllables and words. Words are then arranged in variable orders to create phrases and sentences; sequenced sentences become paragraphs; paragraphs become chapters, books, and so on. To speak or to write, then, the communicator must break an experience or idea down into named parts (words) and then structure these parts sequentially to convey a message.

Speaking or writing is like stringing beads—in principle, we may put any colored bead we choose after any other, but we cannot put two beads of the same color side by side on one string at the same time. Or, as Hall puts it, "It is just that one can talk about only a single aspect of something at any moment" (1976: 89). That is to say, verbal language is inherently linear. It depends upon the one-dimensional progression of sound after sound, word after word, sentence after sentence, to communicate its message.

If movement *is* a language, then it is assumed to have this structure too. In other words, movement must consist of basic acts that have no meaning in themselves but may be arranged in various ways to build up complex sequences of action that do have meaning. The language metaphor has spawned many attempts to delineate the simplest basic action units of which the language of movement is made, as well as to map out the grammar of how these units combine to build meaningful sequences (e.g., Birdwhistell 1970; Condon 1982; Scheflen 1973). This, of course, is not an easy task. But to a certain extent movement has been shown to share the structural makeup of verbal language. Simple actions that follow one another linearly combine sequentially to construct meaningful phrases, sentences, even paragraphs of action.

However, the language metaphor fails to account for certain other aspects of one's understanding of movement. Let us consider, for example, the legendary phenomenon of the "first impression." We all know how striking an initial glimpse can be. Such an immediate, vivid impression cannot be built up through the gradual perception of acts that succeed one another, but must be conveyed by multiple elements perceived and interpreted simultaneously. For example, recently while walking across campus, one of us was struck by a mixed feeling of pity and revulsion for a passer-by who seemed to be a music student. The impression that this musician was troubled and to be avoided was perceived at once. It was only at second glance, in retrospect, that the elements of this global nonverbal impression could be isolated and examined one by one. The person's rigid posture, the tightly closed position of the arms, the wide-eyed, alarmed stare, and the headphones (of a tape player) worn securely on his head all combined to convey the impression that this person was upset and fending off the world. The fact that the individual was listening to a tape player, carrying musical scores, and heading toward the music building all contributed to the sense that here was a music student in all probability.

In vivid first impressions such as the one above, movement has much more in common with a painting than with a sentence. One does not start at the edge of a painting and proceed gradually to take it in—one sees the whole picture at once (Arnheim 1974: 376–377). The more instantaneous, global, and complex a nonverbal impression, the more likely that movement is functioning, not like language, but like visual art.

While visual art provides a metaphor for the simultaneous effects of a movement impression, music suggests yet another approach. Music, of course, combines a sequential melodic line of single notes sounded over time with a simultaneous harmonic structure of many tones being sounded together. Unlike language, where only one meaningful sound may be made at a time, many tones may occur at once in music. But unlike visual art, where the impression of the whole is manifest at once, the cohesion of a musical composition can only be appreciated as the piece sequentially progresses through time to its ending.

By combining successive development with simultaneous effects, music has sometimes been called "time made audible" (Langer 1953: 110). This is, of course, not the strictly measured time of a ticking clock, but a subjective time of lived experience in which "we undergo tensions and their resolutions" (ibid: 112, 113). Music makes the form and continuity of these tensions sensible, for we hear them build, break up, diminish, or merge into larger and greater tensions until a resolution can be reached. While music may be thought of as "nothing but a succession of impulses and repose" (Stravinsky 1970: 36), it is the task of the composer to give a pattern to this succession so that the piece has "a recognizable shape with a beginning and an end, rises and falls in its overall line, and differences in length for variety" (Humphrey 1959: 68).

Figure 6.5 First impressions are often vivid and global.

Juergen Kuehn

At this point some parallels between music and movement may be begin-ning to suggest themselves. For example, the succession of impulse and repose becomes visible in movement as action and stillness. As this succes-sion develops over time, patterns of tension and release begin to emerge. Melodic phrases of spatial design are underscored by rhythmic accents and the delicate interplay between limbs of the body begins to suggest consonant and dissonant harmonies.

In short, when the organization and quality of a succession of actions becomes apparent, we begin to feel the "musicality" of motion. As Sessions has said of music:

> Those of us . . . who listen to music . . . can certainly hear, and be aware of more than one thing at a time. But, as we continue to listen, our ears exercise their coordinating function and unify various sounds into one single if complex impression . . . If the separate strands to which we listen

are to retain their identity for us . . . they must . . . develop, or, to put it in more general terms, move . . . If our attention is to persist, the movement of which I have spoken must assume a pattern, and one which we can eventually apprehend as significant.

(Sessions 1971: 39, 40)

Indeed, if we wish to study the pattern of movement over time, music provides us with many useful concepts, such as harmony, rhythm, dynamics, scales, and chords, to name only a few. This metaphor would seem to offer much scope for discovery beyond the limits of the language metaphor (e.g., Jaques-Dalcroze 1921; Lomax 1982; Steiner 1983; Moore 2009). Between the harmonic components of music and those of dance, there is not only "an outward resemblance, but a structural congruity, which although hidden at first, can be investigated and verified, point by point" (Laban 1974: 122–123).

Language, painting, and music are only some of the metaphors that might be employed to spark further understanding of the meaning of human movements. Many other metaphors can be used to invite new discoveries. However evocative, any single metaphor restricts the growth of knowledge if taken too literally. Movement *is* similar to language, art, and music. But it is also dissimilar. Metaphors highlight, but they do not encompass and exhaust that which they describe. Only movement *is* movement. If the fertile power of metaphor in movement study is to be realized, the distance between the literal and the metaphoric must be kept in mind constantly.

Recapitulation

Through the construction of metaphors, in which one event or idea is treated *as if* it were something else, we are enabled to see the familiar in unfamiliar light, and vice versa. For example, each variety of the metaphor of language, namely, movement is a universal language, a foreign language, or a private code, allows us to perceive the nature of nonverbal communication in a new and different light.

Movement is a universal language. According to this metaphoric view, the significance of nonverbal action is rooted in universals of physical experience and is accessible to all human beings. Consequently, the ability to understand movement behavior is believed to be innate, and meaning is thought to be intrinsic to the motion itself.

Movement is a foreign language. In this view, it is not assumed that the ability to comprehend movement is innate. Rather, one must learn to decipher movement meaning, just as one learns to speak a language. Moreover, a movement may have different meanings in varied situations, while a given intent may be embodied in differing ways from culture to culture. Consequently, some degree of familiarity with a given society is necessary for a correct interpretation of movement behavior.

Movement is a private code. Here, movement is considered to have neither a pan-human nor culture-specific character. Instead, each individual is seen to construct his or her own body codes. Accordingly, only a thorough familiarity with the given person and the situation in which a particular action occurs will allow an appropriate deciphering of the message of the movements.

Each of these metaphors depend to a differing extent on the ability of the observer to put the action in context. If movement is a universal language, innately and identically understood by all human beings, situational factors need not be taken into account. In this case, movement is a low-context communication. However, if movement is seen as a foreign language or a private code, its significance can only be perceived through contexting, since the same action may have entirely dissimilar meanings in different settings. In these cases, movement is a high-context communication.

Because some motions have universal meanings, and others are culture-specific in their significance, while still others have idiosyncratic connotations, each of the ideas drawn from the root metaphor that "movement is a language" can aid in our understanding of nonverbal behavior. However, other metaphors suggest different ways of making sense of motion. Such metaphors as "movement is a visual art," or "human motion is physical music" offer alternative views for movement study.

In the final analysis, of course, any metaphor taken too literally will restrict the generation of knowledge. The distance between the actual movement or act itself and a particular metaphoric view must always be kept in mind. After all, only movement *is* movement.

7 Functions of movement in human life

Man moves in order to satisfy a need. He aims his movement at something of value to him. It is easy to perceive the aim of a person's movement if it is directed to some tangible object. Yet there also exist intangible values that inspire movement.

Rudolf Laban

We have been emphasizing throughout this inquiry that movement is an ever-present feature of human activity. Though so commonplace as to be taken for granted, this vital dimension of life permeates nearly every human endeavor. Movement is a part of our work activities, our games and contests, the way we make war, the way we make love, how we behave in public, our attempts to heal and to help, even the expressions of our most intangible longings for knowledge, beauty, peace, and immortality. In other words, movement is inextricably a part of almost all life experiences.

Because movement is a common denominator in human experience, the study of movement embraces many different disciplines. Accordingly, fields as diverse as socio-behavioral sciences, performing arts, military science, technological design, and athletics, to name just a few, incorporate movement analysis in their inquiry and training today. In an age of increasing specialization of knowledge, movement study provides a means for seeing unifying trends across disciplines and for gaining insight into a variety of human endeavors.

In this chapter we will be tracing the common threads of movement experience as they are woven into the intricate pattern of the fabric of human activity. To follow these common strands is not a simple matter. As we track the function of human movement from one endeavor to another, we discover not only an underlying unity, but also a mind-boggling diversity. That is to say, each discipline seems to generate a unique perspective on movement study. For instance, the spinning and balancing acts of a ballerina appear to be so different in intent and outcome from the motions of a soldier brandishing his weapon that any similarities in the movements of the dancer and the warrior are obscured. The thread we are following leads us into the lair of a many-headed, monstrous Gorgon. We find ourselves staring with fascination at the different faces, some beautiful and some gruesome, forgetting for the moment that all these visages belong to the same creature.

This encounter with the diversity in unity and the unity in diversity brings us to the heart of human creativity. Through our capacity to abstract (the process discussed in Chapter 4) and our ability to think metaphorically (discussed in Chapter 6), we are able to take a given object, event, or behavior and transform it into something else. Consider the simple motion of pounding with a hammer. The hammer is first and foremost a constructive tool used to drive nails into wood. When a hammer is used in this way, we call the experience "work." But a hammer may also be utilized to smash another person's skull. In this instance, we cry out "murder." Then, again, a hammer can be brought into play to drive the last spike of the transcontinental railway. Here the hammering action takes on a symbolic meaning, signifying the connecting of the eastern and western United States. A pagan priest might use the hammer as a religious object, as when the ancient Scandinavians employed it to represent the great god Thor. In this instance, a hammering action is imbued with a magical power.

Through all these varied endeavors, the forceful swing and falling impact of the hammer stays the same, yet the intent and outcome of the action change. Each time the sound of hammering resounds in a new context our Gorgon sprouts another head. However different, nevertheless, all these visages rise from the same source—our basic human needs. So let us begin our trip into the monster's lair with a look at the needs and the role movement plays in satisfying them.

Human needs and the functions of movement

Motivation, the mysterious spark that propels our action, has excited a great deal of study and speculation over the years. Everyone from playwrights to criminologists, historians to worried parents have wondered why we do what we do. Accordingly, theories abound attempting to answer this question. One long-standing model is the so-called "need hierarchy" notion proposed by Maslow (1970).

According to Maslow's model, human needs can be roughly divided into two groups. The first group is comprised of basic, or lower-level motivators, known as *deficit* needs. These motivations address obtaining things that we must have to maintain our lives decently—e.g., food, shelter, safety, love, a sense of belonging, and the esteem and respect of others. If fulfillment of any of these needs is threatened, we find ourselves compelled to act. If we are hungry, our primary motivation is to find food; if unloved, to seek affection; if outcast, to regain our niche; and so on. The second group of needs, the higher-level motivators, are called *being* needs. These needs address the intangible things that make life meaningful and include the urge

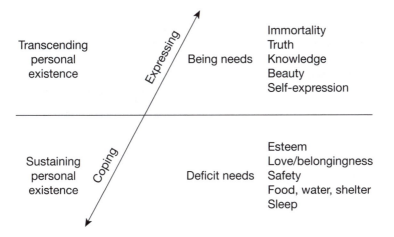

Figure 7.1 Hierarchy of human needs.

for self-expression, the desire for beauty, the yearning to understand nature, and the quest for spiritual realization.

Thus, Maslow's "hierarchy of needs" can be seen to range along a continuum. The *deficit* needs primarily touch upon what must be done to handle the physiological and psychological necessities of existence. In contrast, the *being* needs encompass more expressive functions, touching upon one's pursuit of transcendence over the particular limits of individual existence, through art, science, philosophy, religion, or other abstract endeavors. The whole continuum of needs may be summarized as in Figure 7.1.

This motivational model can be related to the functions of movement in human life. Movement is employed to satisfy human needs in four broad arenas of activity: work, war and contest, social display, and worship. Work serves a *productive* function, allowing us to procure what we need to survive, either by making it ourselves, bartering for it, or purchasing it with the wages we have earned. War and contest serve a *protective* function, providing a means to protect ourselves and safeguard our collective security. Social display serves a *communicative and affiliative* function, confirming one's sense of self, as well as one's membership and status in a given social setting, and satisfying psychological needs for love, belonging, and esteem. Finally, movements made in the context of ritual, meditation, or worship aim to satisfy the need for *self-transcendence* through the identification with enduring values. These four arenas of movement align themselves along the continuum from coping to expressing, as shown in Figure 7.2.

Needless to say, it must be borne in mind that a given arena of activity may fulfill more than one basic human need. A particular movement activity, such as a tribal war dance, may simultaneously serve protective, social, and even religious functions. In fact, few movement activities are discrete

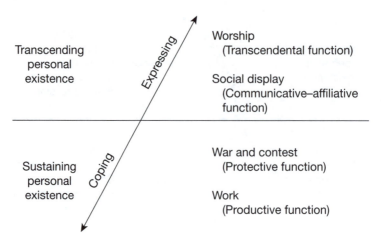

Figure 7.2 Movement functions.

and singular in function. Most serve several needs because, despite our attempts to compartmentalize endeavors, human life remains a whole. For example, in the case of a professional athlete, the chosen sporting activity becomes a job, establishes social identity, and takes on higher values, for, in the heat of play, athletes report experiencing self-transcendence, "altered states, and even ecstatic moments bordering on the mystical" (Murphy 1992: 415). Thus, the four arenas of activity outlined above—work, war and contest, social display, and worship—provide a basic schema for surveying the functions of movement in human life, and it is to that task that we now turn.

Figure 7.3
R.W. Moore

Humans at work

As we noted in Chapter 4, the human species has not evolved specialized bodily equipment suited to a particular environment or mode of life. However, this very lack of evolutionary specialization has resulted in a unique capacity for humankind: the ability to alter the environment to suit its needs. Such an alteration is accomplished mainly through work, defined as "any purposive human effort to modify man's physical environment" (Udy 1970: 3).

The human body itself, of course, was the first means through which work was accomplished. Through the development of an upright, bipedal stance, coupled with a pliant five-fingered grasp, the upper body, arms, and hands were freed to take on new functions. As Laban noted in an unpublished manuscript:

> Hands can break, tear, cut, destroy a material and they can put parts together, join, assemble, press and bind them. Hands can twirl, rub, push, pull, and roll. Hands can shovel and sieve and sort things. Hands can wave, weave, knot, knit and sew. Hands can give shape and form to any material.
>
> (Laban, n.d.)

However, very early in human history these motions of the hands were extended through the development of stick, stone, and bone tools. It is estimated that the use of tools originated as early as two million years ago. Moreover, tool-making marks an important point in the ascent of the species, for it reflects an enormous leap in the powers of the mind. To prepare and store a stone tool for later use implies foresight and the ability to conceptualize the future. As Oakley surmises, the discovery of these prehistoric tools suggests that "even in relatively early stages of culture, man was capable of imagining, deducing from and speculating about observed relationships between things" (1961: 126–127).

About one million years ago, the quality of these primitive stone tools improved. A greater variety of shapes and functions appeared, with accompanying sophistication in how the tools were made. Other advances in human control of the environment also arrived, the use of fire being a salient example. Many thousands of years later, agriculture was developed, animals domesticated, and metal mined and molded into implements. Technological advancement began to accelerate rapidly at that point and in a matter of a mere 10,000 years or so, *Homo sapiens* was able to unleash the power of the atom and propel its kind into outer space.

Technological development and the elaboration of movement behavior

Some have argued that the human ascent results from this persistently accelerating improvement of technology. They believe that tools, power, and productive mechanisms are the primary shapers of human culture. An extreme version of this position is represented by Marx, who claimed that "the mode of production in material life determines the general character of the social, political and spiritual processes of life" (quoted in Freedman 1962: 5). While it is true that changes in technology and new sources of productive power have profoundly affected human lives, such a purely technologically based view of human history overlooks what is occurring in the movement behavior of the human being who operates the tools and technology. For example, the improvement in stone tools, which occurred a million years ago, was not just a material advance but, more importantly, it was a refinement in the manipulative skill of the human hand that shaped and used the tool. As Bronowski points out,

> The development of such refined skills as this and the use of fire is not an isolated phenomenon. On the contrary, we must always remember that the real content of evolution (biological as well as cultural) is in the elaboration of new behavior.
>
> (1981: 26)

Some provocative hypotheses regarding this elaboration of new behavior can be found in the Choreometrics study (Lomax 1968). Choreometrics compared the movement style of work with dance movements found in pre-industrialized societies around the world, using filmed examples from over a hundred cultural groups. Researchers found that there was a marked similarity between the movements utilized in productive work actions and the movements used in dances.

Not surprisingly, "the development of greater manual skills, finer co-ordinations, greater sensitiveness to both outer stimuli and inner prompt-ings, a greater aptitude for learning, a more retentive memory and a more wary forethought" (Mumford 1978: 8) were reflected in more than one realm of human activity.

Thus, as cultures advanced up the technological scale from stick-and-stone to metallurgy and to advanced agricultural economies, the movement behaviors in both work and dance became increasingly more elaborate and complex. For example, in a stick-and-stone culture, one-dimensional linear spatial pathways predominate, supposedly because the use of more circular or twisted paths would be likely to break the fragile stick or bone imple-ments. Once further advances brought metal into life, however, arc-like two-dimensional pathways gained dominance, presumably because metal can stand, without breaking, the twist and torque inherent in this manner of use. Finally, more complex three-dimensional looping and spiraling move-ments came to be found in the high agricultural societies, such as those of the Far East, which utilize irrigation and terracing to restructure the environ-ment (Bartenieff and Paulay 1970). Seemingly, as cultures progressed on, the use of body in space became increasingly more complex, multidimen-sional and adaptive.

Figure 7.4 As tools develop, workers must also adapt their movements.
Jan Stanley

Industrialization and the science of work

While tool development appears to influence both productive and expressive movements in pre-industrial societies, industrialization has also had enormous impact on the physical character of work. The transformation occurred first in Western Europe and the United States. The history of this revolution shows that a variety of problems arose from the mechanization of labor. Conditions for workers in the early factories were appalling, as it is well known. The hours were long, and the factories themselves were often dark, dirty, overcrowded, and unsafe. Attempts to improve conditions occurred first on the social front, through unionization and other reform movements, which aimed to limit the exploitation of human labor for capital gain. By the latter half of the nineteenth century, however, the improvement of factory work aimed to proceed in a more "scientific" manner, and the study of work movement became central. While European and American approaches differed in many particulars,

> each claimed validity as a science of work, each claimed to analyze the worker's task and movements in minute detail, each claimed to improve productivity and efficiency, and each claimed to be able to transcend the constraints of class interest and ideology in the interest of a rational and scientific economic organization.
>
> (Rabinbach 1992: 238)

In the following sections, significant contributions to the science of work study are discussed. This is not merely a matter of historical curiosity, for work study is still critical in industrial societies. Analytical methods developed a century ago continue to be applied today to resolve man–machine problems arising from technological change.

(A) SCIENTIFIC MANAGEMENT

The man who propelled movement study into international acclaim was an American mechanical engineer named Frederick Winslow Taylor (1855–1915). He recognized that the first hundred years of the Industrial Revolution had proceeded by trial and error. "Management as such was in the hand of the shop foremen, who based their approach on experience rather than objective scientific method" (Moore 2005: 10). Taylor went in search of systematic laws to determine how a given factory operation could best be done. Through careful observation and study of isolated elements of a task, assisted by a stopwatch, he sought to establish a definitive method for doing a given task, such as pig iron handling or shoveling. This method was then taught to those workers best suited for the job. The goal was to establish orderly methods uniformly applied by workers, who, in turn, would be paid better wages for the increased productivity that would result. "By enlisting the expertise of engineers in redesigning work processes, Taylor transformed both labor and management" (ibid).

The following excerpt, drawn from Taylor's study of shoveling coal at the Bethlehem Steel Works, illustrates how he went about instituting more "scientific" approaches in the work setting.

> What we did was to call in a number of men to pick from, and from these we selected two first-class shovelers ... These men were then talked to in about this way, "See here, Pat and Mike, you fellows understand your job all right; both of you fellows are first-class men; you know what we think of you; you are all right now; but we want to pay you fellows double wages. We are going to ask you to do a lot of damn fool things, and when you are doing them there is going to be someone out alongside of you all the time, a young chap with a piece of paper

and a stop watch and pencil, and all day long he will tell you to do these fool things, and he will be writing down what you are doing and snapping the watch on you and all that sort of business. Now, we just want to know whether you fellows want to go into that bargain or not?"

(Taylor 1971: 132–133)

Taylor goes on to recount that the two shovelers agreed to be a part of the experiment. They were started to work on a task requiring a very heavy shovel load, with two men appointed to time and study the shoveling. The number of shovel loads that each worker handled was calculated daily and the total tonnage of coal shoveled was computed. At this point Taylor began to tinker with the shovel, cutting it off so that each shovel load weighed less. He discovered that the total tonnage of coal shoveled by each man increased. Taylor kept experimenting with varying the weight of the shovel load until he found that, at 21 or 22 pounds per shovel, the men were doing their largest day's work.

Taylor's unshakable conviction that these newly found methods would improve conditions for workers and managers, as well as his ability to persuade others to try his methods, went a long way to selling his system. "Scientific Management," as Taylor's work came to be known, became enormously influential in the United States and Europe following the turn of the century and, through its incorporation in military practices, during World War I. The popularity of Scientific Management ranged as far as post-Revolutionary Russia, including even Marxists like Lenin among its enthusiasts (Rabinbach 1992). Moreover, Taylor had the good fortune to have several outstanding protégés among his American followers who carried the work forward. Prominent among these was Frank Gilbreth, who made his own unique contribution to work study.

(B) TIME AND MOTION STUDY

Frank Gilbreth (1868–1924), who was a successful contractor before his conversion to Taylorism, is credited with putting the "motion" into the "time and motion" study. Together with his wife, the psychologist Lillian Gilbreth (1878–1972), he developed the concept of the basic unit of work, or "Therblig" (Gilbreth spelled backwards!). The Therbligs essential to a job would be determined through timed observations and the use of photography and cinematography. By eliminating unnecessary motions, the Gilbreths sought to find the "one best way" to do the job. Workers would then be taught this more efficient method. For example, through an exacting analysis of the elements of bricklaying, Gilbreth was able to reduce the motions involved from eighteen to five, thereby increasing production from 120 to 350 bricks per man-hour. He explains the underlying rationale of their motion study approach in the following way.

The great point to be observed is this: Once the variables of motions are determined, and the laws of underlying motions and their efficiency deduced, conformity to these laws will result in standard motions, standard tools, standard conditions, and standard methods of performing the operations of the trades ...

It is also well to recognize the absolute necessity of the trained scientific investigator. The worker cannot, by himself, arrange to do his work in the most economical manner in accordance with the laws of motion study. Oftentimes, in fact nearly always, the worker will believe that the new method takes longer than the old method ... All of which shows that the worker himself cannot tell which are the most advantageous motions. He must judge by the fatigue that he feels, or else by the quantity of output accomplished in a given time. To judge by the quantity of output accomplished in a given time is more a test of effort than a test of motion study, and oftentimes that element that will produce the most output is the one that will cause the least fatigue.

(Gilbreth 1953: 196–197)

Like Taylor, the Gilbreths were supreme rationalists, believing that time and motion efficiency would lead to increased productivity, profits, and higher wages, as well as greater worker satisfaction. In their work study reforms, "they tended to regard the worker as a nondescript productive presence upon which standardized patterns of efficient actions were to be inscribed" (Moore 2005: 14). Interestingly, European work study took a different approach.

(C) ECONOMY OF MOTION

Étienne-Jules Marey (1830–1904) was a French physiologist, known for his studies of blood circulation and animal and human locomotion. In addition to inventing mechanisms to measure physiological functions, Marey devised photographic techniques for recording images of movement that presage the Johansson point-light walker and motion capture technologies used today (see Chapter 2). Known as chronophotography, Marey's recordings were similar to the instantaneous photographs of Muybridge (Moore 2005: 6–8)—both approaches breaking a continuous motion into discrete parts for purposes of scientific study. Marey applied chronophotography to the study of physical labor. Here, his concern differed from that of Taylor and the Gilbreths. While their goal was to maximize production by minimizing the work actions involved, Marey was concerned with the physiological effects of labor on the body of the worker, particularly with minimizing the effects of fatigue. He aimed to find "an efficient deployment of energy" in manual labor, one based upon physiological laws of economy of motion (Rabinbach 1992: 118).

(D) EFFORT ANALYSIS

Yet another approach to work study was developed during World War II in England. Rudolf Laban (1879–1958) had created a movement notation system during the 1920s, which was being used primarily in recording dance. But when war shortages made it impossible to obtain film for studying factory line operations, Laban was recruited by a management consultant, F.C. Lawrence (1895–1982), to notate and analyze workers' movements. "Laban's notation system allowed for a more precise recording of details of work actions than did the Gilbreths' system of 'Therbligs'" (Moore 2005: 22–23). Movements of individual workers could be analyzed more precisely. When these details were compared with output records, Laban and Lawrence did not find that the fewest movements necessarily resulted in the greatest productivity. Instead, they identified rhythm as the key to improving efficiency and reducing fatigue. Their approach involved analyzing the rhythmic features of a task, defined in terms of the flow, weight, time, and spatial factors it required. After this, the unique movement style of each worker was identified, and the worker was either matched with a suitable task or coached to be able to employ the combination of motion factors needed.

For example, Laban was called in to study the manufacturing practices in a British tire factory. Because of the war, the factory was only producing heavy-duty tires and employing women in their fabrication. Difficulties were arising because the manufacturing process required these women to hang the heavy tires on pegs above shoulder height, but the tires weighed more than the officially prescribed lifting limit. By studying and altering the movements used to place the tires on the pegs, Laban discovered that women could easily handle objects almost double the weight of those quoted in the official scales, without undue wear and tear.

> It was, of course, necessary to instruct the operators not to lift but to give the tyre a swing, by which it would be carried by its own momentum to the desired height. It was also necessary to train the operators to support the tyre at the right instant before it had exhausted its momentum, which requires little strength but involves the faculty of suddenly changing the sustained free-flowing effort used during the swinging into a bound flow in order to stop the movement. The presumed lifting operation thus vanished into a rhythmic alteration of the contrasts of flow effort and time effort. The observation of two women painfully pushing the tyre to the desired height engendered the vision of the freely flowing material which needed only a small addition of human energy exerted by one woman.
>
> (Laban and Lawrence 1974: 80)

Unlike Marey, whose movement analysis studies were confined to manual labor, Laban and Lawrence went on to study clerical and managerial functions. They found that, while the movements made in such jobs were more subtle, clerks and managers also used a working rhythm that could be described in terms of effort. This discovery represents a theoretical breakthrough in the science of work study.

> No longer were physical and intellectual labors discrete, nor was one more privileged than the other. Instead, effort rhythm was seen to underlie all human endeavor. The difference between physical and mental labor was not one of kind but merely one of scale. The stage was set for the study of managerial function through the analysis of movement.
>
> (Moore 2005: 32)

(E) MOVEMENT PATTERN ANALYSIS

By the late 1940s, Laban and Lawrence were applying techniques developed for the analysis of physical labor to the study of management action. Managers were observed on the job or in an interview, and movement notations were made to produce a profile that could be compared to job specifications. This pioneering work was carried forward by Laban's protégé, Warren Lamb (1923–). He found that the sorts of movements made in normal conversation occur in a rhythmic pattern that is highly individual. This pattern provides insight into a person's motivations, indicating how a given manager, for example, will go about making decisions and implementing action (Lamb and Turner 1969). Lamb's approach, known as Movement Pattern Analysis, has been used for over fifty years now to select individuals for executive roles and to develop senior management teams (Moore 2005).

(F) ERGONOMICS

The British fighting effort in World War II generated yet another approach to work movement study, which has since been applied to industrial problems in a peacetime economy. During the war the rapid advance in technology was outstripping the human capacity to operate new weapons. In one case, engineers were building fighter planes that were so sophisticated that no human being could fly them! Other challenges, including that of adjusting soldiers, as well as machines of war, to extreme climates from the tropics to the arctic, were also requiring solutions. In order to solve these complex problems, ad hoc teams of scientists from different disciplines were brought together, and a new field known as "ergonomics" was born (Edholm 1967).

The term "ergonomics," derived from Greek, means "the customs, habits, or laws of work." As an area of study, it looks at the human–machine relationship as an interactive system, and draws on the interdisciplinary expertise of physiology, psychology, physics and engineering to improve the functioning of this system. Ergonomics attempts to adapt the job and the machine to the physical needs of the worker. This often involves a redesigning of work space and mechanical control systems, in addition to a better training of the worker.

New technologies generate man–machine interface challenges that demand ergonomic ingenuity. Manned space flight provides a good example. Astronauts must remain healthy, alert, and productive in a weightless and unforgiving environment. In zero gravity, even a small movement continues until physically arrested, and objects float unless anchored. Piloting the craft, conducting scientific experiments, and making repairs necessitate alertness. But sleep often eludes space travelers in low earth orbits, where the sun rises every 90 minutes. Devices of all sorts must be designed to help human beings cope. At the same time, the astronauts must learn how to use these devices and monitor their own behavior and responses in an unusually demanding environment.

Closer home, the invention of the personal computer has given rise to a number of work-related physical problems. Because computer users tend to become engrossed and forget how long they have been sitting in front of the machine, they tend to gain weight and get out of shape. Moreover, other physical problems develop from prolonged computer use. These include eye strain, neck, shoulder, wrist, hand, and back problems. On the machine side, ergonomics experts have been called in to redesign computer controls, monitor screens, keyboard trays, and even office chairs to address these problems. On the human side, "best use practices" have been identified to help workers redress physical stresses that arise from prolonged hours of computer use. These include advice on arranging and adjusting equipment to promote good posture and developing recuperation strategies, such as simple exercises that can be done in conjunction with working and during breaks.

As our tools become more complex and subtle, humans must become increasingly ingenious to use them in the right way. If work is to be productive and not destructive, it seems that we must remember to move! Moreover, we do not yet know whether increasing technological sophistication in industrial societies is leading to reciprocal elaboration in movement behavior, or to more dull, routine, and boring productive activities. However, we do know that the harnessing of ever more powerful technologies is having a major impact on the way humankind conducts its *destructive* activities in the form of warfare, and it is to this area of human endeavor that we now turn.

Humans at war and in contest

As noted in the previous section of this chapter, the invention and development of tools and technology often go hand in hand with the refinement and elaboration of behavior. For example, since stone tools for hunting had to be made in advance, their fabrication induced humans to plan ahead, and led to a greater capacity for abstract thought. Yet, these material and immaterial extensions proved to be both boon and bane. As Turney-High observed, "A tool or a weapon is an abstraction out of total reality, and with this power of abstract thought came the idea of the fellow-man as an abstraction ... who could be killed without compunction" (1981: 22).

Nevertheless, it took time before group aggression was organized and refined into what has come to be known as the art and science of warfare. Between the invention of the first stone tool and the deployment of the atom bomb elapsed countless years of behavioral and social elaboration. This elaboration began with hunting and developed into war's precursor, namely, the raiding party and the limited battle. Finally, it was transformed into what we now call, rather ironically, "civilized warfare." Movement study has been crucial to the conduct of all three activities. Let us take a closer look at how the body knowledge of attack and defense, first utilized in hunting, evolved.

Figure 7.5
R.W. Moore

Origins of battle: hunting and early combat

In primal times, the tools, social organization, and body knowledge of the hunt were all relatively simple. The prey was stalked, cornered, and attacked by a small group of armed hunters, usually on foot. Yet, even this deceptively simple activity required planning, coordination of activities, and a keen sense of timing if the joint attack was to succeed. "The hunt is a communal undertaking of which the climax, but only the climax, is the kill" (Bronowski 1981: 28). Thus, a "critical indicator of cognitive advance might consist in evidence of planning, or thinking many steps ahead of the present situation" (Toth and Schick 1993: 359); in other words, "anticipating a future as only man can do, inferring what is to come from what is here" (Bronowski 1981: 34).

Stories of how the bushmen of the African Kalahari desert hunt antelope today illustrate all these features. "These skilled hunters work silently in small cooperative groups, relying on gestures of the face and hands to chase antelope" (Lonsdale 1982: 65). Knowing this animal to be an inquisitive creature, the Bushmen will imitate antelope sounds, such as the cry of the fawn, to draw the prey into the open, then shoot the animal with poison-tipped arrows.

The tools, social organization, and body knowledge of the hunt are often seen to be closely related to aspects of warfare. Such similarities have been enumerated by Lonsdale in the following way:

> Hunting and war require similar weapons, skills, and inner qualities. A hunting spear doubles as a warring lance; the hunter's ability to plan the strategy of the hunt . . . corresponds in war to the plotting of military tactics, the training and arrangement of troops on the battlefield and the successful capture or routing of enemy forces. And the hunt and warfare are alike in that they require intelligence and sangfroid, courage and fortitude, and a flair for deceit: "outfoxing" your opponent. In one final way war and the hunt are similar: they accomplish the same end, that of robbing an animate being of its life-force.
>
> (1982: 59)

Exactly when or why the skills and social organization of the hunt were turned against human prey is not known. As Dyer has pointed out,

> It is no surprise that a race that lived largely by hunting and that knew effective techniques for killing animals would have the same techniques available for killing its own members. Since conflict is inevitable, it is also not surprising that people sometimes kill people.
>
> (1985: 6)

These early conflicts, however, seldom resulted in huge casualties. Indeed, among the hunting and gathering tribes that exist today, warfare takes one of two relatively benign forms. Most clearly related to hunting is the raiding party, in which a small group of warriors stages a surprise attack on the enemy, snatching whatever they seek and getting away quickly. When face-to-face combat is involved, it is often prearranged and highly ritualistic. Insults may be thrown by both sides, and there might be some shows of bravery in hand-to-hand combat between individual warriors. Often, nevertheless, the fighting stops as soon as one side has exacted a death, as in the fabled confrontation of David and Goliath. "Primitive warfare is not lethal, nor even very destructive to the societies that engage in it." Rather, such battle is "predominantly a rough male sport for underemployed hunters, with the kinds of damage-limiting rules that all competitive sports have" (ibid: 9, 10).

What does it take, then, to transform a ritualized competition between warriors into the mass slaughter of "civilized war"? Undoubtedly, many technical, social, economic, and political factors have changed the nature of armed conflict over the ages, but details of the emergence of full-scale war are lost in time. Consequently,

> It can never be proved, but it is a safe assumption that the first time five thousand male human beings were ever gathered together in one place, they belonged to an army. That event probably occurred around 7000 BC—give or take a thousand years—and it is an equally safe bet that the first truly large-scale slaughter of people in human history happened very soon afterward.
>
> (Dyer 1985: 11)

In this hypothetical first battle, packed formations of well-drilled soldiers, armed with shields and spears, faced off against anonymous strangers in the enemy line. This was no longer the traditional damage-limiting contest between individual warriors. Rather, this clash was impersonal and deadly. The front lines of each army collided, pushed forward by the ranks behind. "The result of such a merciless struggle in a confined space is killing on an unprecedented scale. Hundreds of thousands of men would die in half an hour, in an area no bigger than a couple of football fields" (ibid: 12). To engage willingly in such destructive warfare is a socially conditioned response, for individuals must be trained to stand and fight in situations where any sane being, even the most aggressive, would turn tail and run. This social conditioning is accomplished through basic military training, wherein a disorderly mob of civilians is turned into a disciplined fighting group. Movement study and physical training are essential in effecting this transformation both physically and psychologically.

Uses of movement in military training

Movement plays a crucial role in military training in three ways: (1) instructing the would-be soldier on the rudiments of attack and personal defense, in case he or she should be engaged in hand-to-hand combat; (2) training the recruit to mesh actions with those of the other soldiers in his or her unit, so that they become a cohesive and efficient fighting machine; and (3) preparing the former civilian for combat through psychological indoctrination, conditioning him or her to behave on the battlefield in ways that would be, in peacetime, sociopathic and unthinkable.

Body knowledge provides the basis of training in attack and defense. "Military operations—tactics, strategy, and logistics—almost more than any other cultural construct rest upon the correction of the essential weakness and permeability of the human body, and the exploitation of the enemy's essential feebleness" (Turney-High 1981: 50–51). Tactically speaking, the first function of military training is teaching the soldier to protect his or her own vulnerable areas, e.g., the soft belly, fragile rib cage, the right and left sides, and the back. The second function is training the recruit to inflict damage on the opponent in these same vulnerable areas. This body knowledge is ages old, as the following instructions on the use of the sword in a Roman army training manual demonstrate.

> A slash cut rarely kills, however powerfully delivered, because the vitals are protected by the enemy's weapons, and also by his bones. A thrust going in two inches, however, can be mortal. You must penetrate the vitals to kill a man. Moreover, when a man is slashing, the right arm and side are left exposed. When thrusting, however, the body is covered, and the enemy is wounded before he realizes what has happened.
>
> (quoted in Dyer 1985: 5)

Strategically speaking, parallels with the strengths and weaknesses of the human body must be observed if army troops are to be deployed to maximum effect. The strongest area for offensive action lies to the front of an army while the left and right flanks and the rear are its most vulnerable areas defensively. For almost all human history, a battle "has been an event as stylized and limited in its movement as a classical ballet, and for much the same reasons: the inherent capabilities and limitations of the human body" (ibid: 36).

The body knowledge of attack and defense is transmitted to the modern would-be soldier during basic training. Through physical exercise, repetition, and drill, recruits hone their reflexes until certain offensive and defensive movements become automatic and swift. Such reflex-like reactions are essential in battle, where the proper rapid action can mean the difference between life and death. Moreover, once the soldier has been in combat, these automatic protective reactions become ingrained, as the following story indicates.

> Now you take any individual . . . if he's seen combat, he's different. When I first came back in '69, my mother would not go in the same bedroom with me when I was asleep. I was dangerous. The first night I was back—they had a two bedroom trailer—I slept on the floor because my sister was home at the time. My mother came by and she was going to step over my arm, which was flung out the side, and go turn the air conditioner on. She got within two feet of me—I wasn't even awake—I had her down. I had her by the throat, and my father pulled me off of her. I was not even awake. I just reacted. There was a footstep. I didn't know where I was, and so I reacted.
>
> (Canadian Broadcasting Corporation 1983: 8)

In addition to offense and defense, the movement training of the military drill is also used to mold a group of individuals into a disciplined, obedient, and loyal fighting unit. Consider, for example, the precision, close-order marching that is synonymous for most of us with soldiering itself. Such close order maneuvers have been of no practical use in actual battles for over a century. Yet every army in the world still drills its troops. Marching in synchrony with others generates group cohesion and *esprit de corps*. Troops develop "an unthinking readiness to obey their officers, and an almost complete disregard for competing attachments" (McNeill 1995: 111).

So far we have discussed the functional use of movement in military training; that is to say, teaching the individual soldier how to attack the enemy and defend oneself, to meld a group of individuals into an obedient and efficient fighting machine, and to maneuver troops strategically on the field of battle. But movement is also used ideologically, that is, to inculcate military values in recruits. This psychological conditioning is accomplished both in terms of what the trainees are expected to do, as well as of how they are expected to move while doing it.

To this end, a large part of basic training is designed to immerse the recruit in the rituals of military culture. Myriad details of everyday life must be done "according to the book." From the making of a bed and the care of a rifle, to the proper cadence and tone of voice with which to address an officer, the trainee must absorb and master endless elaborations of movement behavior if he or she is to become a soldier worthy of the uniform. These elaborations make up the tradition, drama, and pageantry of military life and account for much of its appeal. More fundamentally, the careful prescription of how even the simplest actions are to be performed is one of the primary ways of indoctrinating the would-be soldier. With every little motion, the recruit's behavior is reshaped to military specifications, and the soldier becomes less a unique individual with thoughts and will power of his or her own than a standardized part of a great machine, drilled to a finely tuned precision and ready to respond automatically to any command.

Thus through hard physical training, mere civilians are transformed into soldiers, ready to face the rigors of modern warfare, eager to fight and prepared to die for the honor of their uniform and their cause. The movement components of the training, which have been carefully refined through millennia of experience, emphasize the rudiments of attack and defense, the development of group loyalty in the ranks, and the psychological conditioning necessary for combat. In its way, military training represents the perfection and systematization of the older forms of "body knowledge," dating back to the hunting/raiding party. Elements of modern warfare can be discerned in the earlier activities, yet these predecessors were bound by informal rules that limited aggression and damage. Few restraints obtain in warfare today, but fairness and playing by the rules still count in the "virtual battle" of games and sports. Let us take a closer look at this aspect of human life and the function movement plays there.

Virtual battles

There are elements of combat and conquest in many games and sports. Individuals may struggle to establish physical supremacy over their opponents in contact sports like boxing, fencing, and wrestling. Teams may compete to achieve the highest score, as in baseball and basketball. On the other hand, conquest of territory may be the goal of the game. Long jumpers or javelin/discus throwers aim to cover more distance than their opponents. The Japanese game of *go* has everything to do with a territorial conquest. Similarly, in American football, one team can score only by invading the opposing team's territory and pushing the opponents back to their own goal line.

Another parallel between actual and virtual battles is seen in the adoption of military terms to describe sports and games. A few examples from sports page headlines underscore this close association: "Stars shot down in overtime," "Peace breaks out for the Mets," "Baylor turns record into offensive weapon," "Lewis to defend two titles," "Spartans demolish Red Raiders," and so on. Of course, more than just jargon has been borrowed from the military. Many implements of war have been incorporated over time into sporting competitions, e.g., bows and arrows into archery, maneuvers on horseback into the game of polo, swordsmanship into the sports of fencing in Europe and kendo in Japan.

However, one critical attribute separates actual battle from virtual battle—the element of play. Play has been broadly defined by Huizinga as "a free activity standing quite consciously outside 'ordinary' life as being 'not serious,' but at the same time absorbing the player intensely and utterly" (1955: 13). Play can be spontaneous and free, or governed by rules. Even rule-bound play

> remains nonutilitarian and in that sense has its own kind of freedom
> from the need to provide food, shelter, and other material requirements
> of existence; but games symbolize the willing surrender of absolute
> spontaneity for the sake of playful order.
>
> (Guttmann 1978: 4)

Rule-bound games can be cooperative or competitive. Sports belong to the latter type of game and can be defined as "'playful' physical contests" (ibid: 7).

Gaming and sporting activities have a long and varied history. As McLuhan has pointed out, "When cultures change, so do games" (1964: 239). For example, primal and classical games and sports were not, strictly speaking, purposeless play. Our prehistoric ancestors lived by foraging and hunting, and "most sports began as a form of practice for fighting and hunting," suggests Umminger (1963: 113). "Increased skill gave man a better chance for being successful at both, and so, of living longer and better" (ibid).

Figure 7.6 Modern sports such as basketball are virtual battles bound by rules and
a sense of fair play.

Jan Stanley

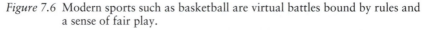

Also, these activities often had magical or sacred functions. Mimetic hunting games and dances, still found among some tribal peoples today, invoke sympathetic magic by association. Imitating the movement of the hunted animal projects the hunter into "the mind and spirit of the enemy prey. On a magical level, preparatory hunting dances attract the desired species" (Lonsdale 1982: 69). The games of Mesoamerica and ancient Greece were also rituals with magical and religious significance. The ball courts of the Mayans and Aztecs were located within the vast temple complexes, while the ball games themselves were under the protection of their gods and goddesses. Likewise, the Greek Olympics were sacred games, staged in a sacred place as a religious act in honor of a deity (Guttmann 1978).

The modern age of sport began ceremonially with the rebirth of the Olympic Games in 1896. Spearheaded by Baron Pierre de Coubertin, the first games since ancient times got off to a rough start, with small teams and limited international representation. Once inaugurated, however, "the games acquired a momentum of their own … Except for the world wars of 1914–1918 and 1939–1945, the Olympics have been held every four years and have grown spectacularly in size and appeal" (Segel 1998: 218). The modern Olympics, nevertheless, are secular games, for "the physical cultism of the late nineteenth and early twentieth centuries was accompanied by a repudiation of organized religion" (ibid: 219). Subsequently, sports have been transformed from a ritual play dedicated to the gods to a contest for records set by men and women.

The secularization of sports has brought with it many other changes. These include an emphasis on equality, that is, the belief that everyone should have the opportunity to compete and that the "conditions of competition should be the same for all contestants" (Guttmann 1978: 26). Since everyone does not have equal physical gifts, however, modern sports have also become highly specialized. Amateur and professional competition alike demand hours of concentrated practice and single-minded dedication on the part of the athletes. Moreover, "modern sports are characterized by the almost inevitable tendency to transform *every* athletic feat into one that can be quantified and measured'" (ibid: 47). When the desire to win is combined with the mania for quantification, "the result is the concept of the record" (ibid: 51). World records have become a "curious institution," one that seemingly defines the ultimate limits of human strength, speed, and endurance (Jerome 1980: 37).

Contemporary world records demonstrate that a revolution in athletic performance is occurring, since previous standards of excellence are continually surpassed. As Murphy explains, "Roger Bannister broke the four-minute barrier for the mile in 1954. By 1990, 595 men had run the mile in under four minutes, and during 1990, 62 men accomplished the feat" (1992: 417). The quest for excellence has generated a host of sports-related sub-disciplines—specialized training and coaching, sports medicine, sports psychology, even sports neuroscience—all studying movement and all aiming to provide the athlete with that winning edge.

The performance revolution has also stimulated the public appetite for sporting events. For example, the 2000 Summer Olympic games in Sydney, Australia, drawing 10,300 athletes from 200 countries, was estimated to have been watched by 3.7 billion people worldwide (Jarvie 2000). "Sport's social and commercial power makes it a potentially potent force in the modern world, for good and for bad" (ibid: 2). The popular power of sports has also made it a subject of many a sociological study, one means of understanding cultural groups and sub-groups.

For example, baseball has been called the national pastime of the United States. This game became popular in the nineteenth century, during the period of rapid industrialization and urbanization. But, as Ross noted, "baseball was old-fashioned from the start," a "pastoral sport" that created "an atmosphere in which everything exists in harmony" (1973: 103). Nowadays, however, football appears to be replacing baseball as the national sport. American football can be traced back to the game of rugby, which was imported from England and first played in Ivy League colleges in the mid-1800s. Yet, in the ensuing years, the original English game has been constantly altered to become distinctly American. Adaptations include

> the mid-field dramatization of line against line, the recurrent starting and stopping of field action around the timed snapping of a ball, the trend to a formalized division of labor between backfield and line, above all, perhaps, the increasingly precise synchronization of men in motion.
>
> (Riesman and Denney 1972: 103)

The rapidly changing and sometimes violent collisions of team against team on the football field contrast the more leisurely pace of baseball, with its dispersion of players on the field. The growing popularity of football suggests that Americans are "slowly relinquishing that unfettered rural version of ourselves that baseball so beautifully mirrors" (Ross 1973: 111–112). Indeed, the national preoccupation with football suggests that "we have come to cast ourselves in a genre more reflective of a nation confronted by constant and unavoidable challenges" (ibid).

Interestingly, while contemporary American football and soccer can both be traced to amateur ball games played for centuries in England, soccer has become "the most popular global sport of the early 21st century" (Maguire et al. 2002: 120). From the players' point of view, soccer requires less specialized equipment and has fewer rules than American football. On the other hand, the fast-paced action and central focus on the player with the ball makes American football the perfect sport for television. Consequently, its popularity worldwide as a spectator sport is growing.

Video games, of course, are the ultimate spectator sports. A variety of devices invented in recent decades have literally put these games at the players' fingertips, since the operation of such devices merely involves pushing a lot of buttons. As Schiesel explains:

> In video games there has traditionally been a button for everything. Press a button to jump. Press a button to punch. Press a button to shoot. Press a button to throw. Press a button to catch. Press a button to run. Even press a button to speak. Along with moving a mouse a few inches or twiddling some thumb sticks, this is what it has meant to play a video game.
>
> (*New York Times*, November 28, 2010)

The visual quality of motion depicted in character-based video games has steadily improved, due to the application of motion capture technology in computer animation. However, "the physical mechanics of play—pressing buttons—have usually had nothing to do with the actions being evoked" (ibid).

This, however, is changing. New video game systems can see and hear the player. This technology allows the players to generate the motion of the object or character on-screen by themselves jumping, kicking, swinging, or speaking basic commands. As the player's body itself becomes the game controller, natural human movement is reintroduced into these virtual contests.

To summarize, hunting, raiding, warring, and gaming are all social inventions. In the changing nature of actual and virtual battles we must inevitably recognize aspects of human nature. In each of these endeavors, movement plays a role, not only in developing the physical skills necessary for attack and defense, but also in socializing individuals to compete, to struggle and, if necessary, even to kill. Movement is a powerful socializer. And it is to the social functions of movement in human life that discussion now turns.

Figure 7.7
R.W. Moore

Human life on display

In Chapter 4, movement was described as one of the prime carriers of social and cultural values. Since voluntary movement patterns are learned after birth rather than genetically inherited, they remain socially malleable. The child's manner of moving will be profoundly influenced by the style of adult movements he or she observes and by the kinds of actions she or he is encouraged by caregivers to make. In even the most seemingly spontaneous motions, as noted by Goffman, individuals "are learning to be objects that have a character, that express this character" (1979: 7). Increasingly social scientists recognize that codes of bodily behavior and movement mores are the dynamic means through which personal and cultural identity, as well as social affiliation, are established and maintained. Scheflen sums up these movement functions as follows:

> Sometimes we hear it said that the purpose of communication is the transmittal of new or novel information or the expression of individual feelings and thoughts. And we must agree, of course, that both language and body movement can be used in this way. But ordinarily the transmittal is of old information and doctrines to new organisms or group members who become indoctrinated by the transmittal.
>
> (1972: 132)

This same socially reinforcing role of nonverbal behavior is termed "style" by Lomax and defined as a summary of models of appropriate behavior within a given culture. "The most important thing for a person to know is just how appropriate a bit of behavior or communication is, and how to respond to it appropriately" (1968: 12). Such insider knowledge guides social judgments by inexplicable means.

> Any culture member can immediately sense that something is stylistically wrong about a greeting, a cooking pot, a song, or a dance, without being able to explain why this is so. Everyone in a culture responds with satisfaction or ecstasy to the apropos and with scorn and resentment to the unseemly.
>
> (Ibid)

Style, in the broad behavioral context where Lomax places it, makes it possible for us to understand, seemingly intuitively, others in our affiliative group. At the same time, style delineates what is different, alien, and incomprehensible about another culture, society, or race. A great deal of style, in the sense in which we are now using the concept, rests upon behaviors that are nonverbal in nature. As Szwed observed, stereotypical folk-notions about different races

> arose out of early historical contacts in which it was found that an alien people not only looked different from oneself, but also performed differently, behaving in exotically stylized, recurring presentations of self. Never mind that another people's institutions . . . might be profoundly different, it was their use of their bodies that had the most impact.
>
> (1975: 258)

In the stylistic sense then, body movement plays a crucial role in establishing the social, cultural, or ethnic group with which one is affiliated and, simultaneously, providing a means for discerning those who do not belong to one's group. Through how we behave bodily we display and reinforce our social and cultural identities. At the same time, we establish who we are *not*. This embodied self is both singular and multiple.

On the one hand, social life is fairly routine, and the nature of most interactions follows a predictable course. Bodily behavior in public places is governed by rules, and "we show through our bodily behaviours that we know the rules" (Thomas 2003: 60). Self-management is required.

> Each person may have a multifaceted personality and a large repertoire of possible performances, but at any given transaction he is supposed to specialize. He is expected to reduce the variability of his activities and take a particular role which he is to carry out in a customary and predictable way.
>
> (Scheflen 1972: 126)

Failure to enact a role appropriately according to this social script carries consequences. Looking too long at a stranger or not adhering to regular patterns of walking in public spaces "is likely to lead to charges of abnormality" and disturb conventional interactions (Thomas 2003: 61).

On the other hand, "the self is not a unified, unique self but one that is constructed through our encounters with others" (Blackman 2008: 23). To a certain extent, we all do play different roles depending upon the audience whom we wish to impress. As William James observed,

> Many a youth who is demure enough before his parents and teachers, swears and swaggers like a pirate among his "tough" young friends. We do not show ourselves to our children as to our club companions, to our customers as to the laborers we employ, to our own masters and employers as to our intimate friends.
>
> (1981: 294)

Shakespeare shrewdly commented long ago, "All the world's a stage and all the men and women merely players." This observation has given rise in the social sciences to the *dramaturgical* model of the self. "This is the 'performing self' that creates and manages its own image" (Blackman 2008: 42). Since bodily communications are social codes acquired in the process of growing up, they become habitual while remaining somewhat malleable. In fact, movement appears to play a dual role in human societies. As a social habit learned from birth, movement behavior helps to stabilize the social order, for individuals are conditioned to play whatever role they have been assigned, however lofty or lowly. "People learn how to present their bodies in everyday life through body techniques, dress and style. As the individual's body comes to be formed it bears the unmistakable marks of his or her social class" (Thomas 2003: 56–57).

On the other hand, as James noted, we are all called upon to play many different roles. In addition to this momentary, situational switching of roles, those who aspire to social mobility may practice a more or less enduring imitation of the group with which they wish to be affiliated. Szwed has described this role switching process in the following way:

> If we can be sure of anything throughout history, it is that two people— regardless of the lines drawn and the barriers between them, whether socially unequal or not—will in the process of everyday close interaction, learn and adopt some aspects of the other group's behavior. And some of each group will become proficient to the point of being capable of assuming the *cultural* if not the racial identity of the other group.
>
> (1975: 261)

It stands to reason, then, that whether we wish to affirm or to alter our social, cultural, or racial identities, we must have not only the *means* but also the *manners*, not only the *substance* but also the *style* of the group with which we desire to be affiliated. Indeed, a great deal of movement study, both formal and informal, has focused upon the acquisition of the proper manners and the social stability or mobility that goes with them. Let us take a closer look at this area of movement study.

Etiquette and deportment

Published instructions outlining conventional rules of personal behavior in polite society emerged in Europe during the Renaissance. The breaking up of medieval feudal societies resulted in increased social mobility and the need for instruction in manners and physical demeanor. Members of the rising merchant class needed to learn how to comport themselves appropriately at Court, and this included learning how to dance. "Dancing was an every-day adjunct to court life in all European Renaissance palaces" (Kirstein 1969: 138). By the mid-1400s, we find the emergence of a professional class of dancing masters, who not only taught dancing but also advised on other aspects of nonverbal behavior. For example, Guglielmo Ebreo of Pesaro advised young ladies on appropriate conduct at a ball:

> Her glance should not be proud or wayward, going here and there as many do. Let her, for the most part, keep her eyes, with decency, on the ground; not however, as some do, with her head sunk on her bosom, but straight up, corresponding to the body, as nature teaches almost of herself . . . And then at the end of the dance, when her partner leaves her, let her, facing squarely, with a sweet regard, make a decent and respectful curtsey in answer to his.
>
> (quoted in Sorell 1986: 42)

An even more detailed description of the proper behavior of the aristocrat is found in *The Book of the Courtier*, written by Baldesar Castiglione in the early 1500s. The virtues of a gentleman include discretion, decorum, nonchalance and gracefulness. In order to create such impressions, the gentleman must attend carefully to his dress, his speech, and his gestures. The following excerpt reveals what an exacting course is set for one who would be a courtier.

> It is also fitting that the courtier should know how to swim, jump, run and cast the stone for, apart from the usefulness of these accomplish-ments in war, one is often required to display one's skill and such sports can help to build up a good reputation, especially with the crowd which the courtier always has to humour. Another noble sport which is very suitable for the courtier to play is tennis, for this shows how well he is built physically, how quick and agile he is in every member, and whether he has all the qualities demonstrated in most other games . . .

Then again, since one cannot always be taking part in such strenuous exercises ... one must always be sure to give variety to the way one lives by doing different things. So I would like the courtier sometimes to descend to calmer and more restful games ... Let him laugh, jest, banter, romp and dance, though in a fashion that always reflects good sense and discretion, and let him say and do everything with grace.

(Castiglione 1981: 63–64)

Ebreo and Castiglione are the great-great-grandfathers of a tradition in etiquette training that extends to the present day. Physical manners reveal the social status of their possessor and the acquisition of the proper manners is often the key to being accepted as a "full member in good standing" of a high-status group. Indeed, in its own peculiar way, a great deal of contemporary research in nonverbal communication appears to focus on the description of appropriate high-status behaviors, since the physical actions of the dominant and most powerful members of society are analyzed in great detail. As one such treatise describes, "At its simplest, high status can be signaled by an upright posture and its opposite, submissiveness and humility, by a slouch or a generally sagging posture" (Wainwright 2003: 60).

As this quest finds voice in the popular press, men and women who aspire to be upwardly mobile are urged to adopt certain postures, to practice special patterns of eye movement, to dress in certain ways, even to decorate their offices in the suitable style so as to appear to be successful (Korda 1979; Molloy 1975). Those who are truly serious about social advancement can hire "image consultants" and "personal coaches"—the contemporary equivalent of the Renaissance dancing masters. It may well be that the ultimate democratization of modern nations depends upon the uniform acquisition of high-status movement behaviors by all segments of society. "Body politics" may be the means through which the struggle for social equality is at long last resolved—at least, so present-day purveyors of appropriate behavior would have us believe (Henley 1977).

The emphasis on using carefully contrived physical behavior to create favorable social impressions also has a dark side. It is a small step from image management to manipulation. Movements can be misleading. "Politicians and other public figures deliberately use body language to emphasize, persuade, and even deceive their audiences" (Blackman 2008: 43). So do salespersons, ministers, friends, parents, children, lovers, husbands, and wives. "Lying is such a central characteristic of life that better understanding of it is relevant to almost all human affairs" (Ekman 1985: 23). Thus there is a growing branch of movement study dedicated to the detection of deception through nonverbal means.

While we may dislike being deceived in real life, we find it highly entertaining in other contexts. Both theatre and dance use human movement to create a deceptive atmosphere of reality. But actors and dancers are not

Figure 7.8 Unspoken rules govern acceptable physical behavior in public places.
Jan Stanley

liars. By standing agreement, the "audience agrees to be misled, at least for a time" (Ekman 1985: 27). These performing arts provide opportunities to observe human life on display, in carefully constructed simulations of reality.

Theatre

All plays, whether comedic, tragic, realistic, or fantastic, involve the imitation of action. As a sequence of events unfolds, the audience observes the interactions of characters, gaining insight into their desires, values, problems, and conflicts. This dramatic simulation is a group enterprise, involving playwright, director, actors, costume, set, sound, and lighting designers. Movement, however, is the crucial element in theatre, for "man shows in his movements and actions the desire to achieve particular aims and ends" (Laban 1971a: 106). Therefore, the actor must know how to move: "He must know how to mirror life conditions and their fateful outcome in selected bodily attitudes and movement qualities; otherwise the values which he wants to convey remain unrecognisable" (ibid: 107).

Movement study comes into theatre in many ways: in the physical and vocal training of the actor, in developing the actors' powers of observation, in the creation of character, in blocking action on stage, and in establishing a bond with the audience. For example, the actor must learn to exploit the expressive possibilities of the body. Lecoq notes:

> The study of human anatomy enabled me to develop an analytic method of physical preparation, directed towards expressivity and bringing into

play each part of the body: feet, legs, hips, shoulders, neck, head, arms hands, getting a feel for the dramatic potential of each in turn.

(2002: 66)

Vocal expressivity also requires physical training, for "*speech is movement*" (Adrian 2008: 2). Speech, produced as the flow of breath, is shaped by the vocal organs. Breath support is essential for speaking well. Other bodily factors also affect speech.

> The way we stand or sit, for instance, the ways our heads, necks or spines are correctly or incorrectly aligned, the carriage of our shoulders, upper chest and torso, the habitual set of our mouth and jaw—all of these influence the balance and function of our voice.
>
> (Rodenburg 1992: 20)

As Lecoq reiterates, "it would be absurd to claim that voice can be separate from body . . . gesture, breathing and voice join to form a single movement" (2002: 68).

In addition to refining the use of the body and voice, the actor must also become a keen observer of the actions of other people. "The performer must learn to read and exhibit the behavior of the people he meets" (Laban 1971a: 107). Actors must master what Chekhov (1991: 60) called the "Psychological Gesture," the physical action together with the feelings connected with it. As Easty explains:

> There are thousands of motions that the hands, feet, eyes, nose, fingers, shoulders, in short, the whole body go through of which the average individual is totally unaware and in which he is usually not interested. However, with actors it must be different. They must learn from other people what the motivating factors are that produce these seemingly meaningless movements. They must learn that the unspoken word is a powerful one and will be "spoken" even if not with sound.
>
> (1978: 165)

While the individual actor is responsible for devising the actions of his or her character, the director oversees the positioning and movements of cast members on the stage. Staging is dictated in part by the script and set design, but positioning and movement also reveal mood and relationships among characters.

> One of the keys to creating convincing stage behavior is having an instinct about the way proximity (and body language) relates to specific situations . . . Can intimate moments be played between two actors on opposite sides of a room? Probably not. What about moments of encouraging, goading, enticing, or commanding? While there is no correct

physical relationship of a particular action, all good staging justifies the arrangement of actors to effectively express action and relationship.

(M. Bloom 2001: 144)

Finally, movement is essential in establishing the "magnetic current" between stage and audience. "The performance is in reality a mutual creation of actors and audience" (Chekhov 1991: 28). The performers engage the audience empathically, drawing them into the atmosphere and action of the play. At the same time, the audience inspires the actors "by sending them waves of confidence, understanding, and love" (ibid). Even a seemingly solemn and traditional theatrical form like Japanese Noh retains its dramatic vitality by minor adaptations to the particular audience. Based upon audience reactions, the head actor can signal the musicians to indicate that a dance will be repeated or shortened.

> So close and immediate is the relationship between performers and spectators that if the audience is noisy the costumes are changed at the last minute; a kind of homeopathy is tried where brighter costuming is used to calm a too flashy audience.
>
> (Schechner 1985: 143)

Dramatic forms ranging from classical Noh to contemporary musical theatre incorporate music and dance into performance. Dance also stands independently as a popular practice and theatrical spectacle. It is to these secular forms of movement expression that our discussion now turns.

Secular dance

As an ephemeral art that leaves no artifacts, dance in human history is difficult to trace. Its origins in prehistory are speculative at best, and only fragmentary evidence is available for much of recorded time. Nevertheless, dance as a communal form of communication and expression is likely to have preceded theatre, simply because expressive gesture is now considered to be the precursor of spoken language. While dance-like behaviors have been observed in other species, human dancing is unique.

> Community dancing occurs only among humans, if by that phrase we mean a form of group behavior whereby an indefinite number of individuals start to move their muscles rhythmically, establish a regular beat, and continue doing so for long enough to arouse euphoric excitement shared by all participants, and (more faintly) by onlookers as well.
>
> (McNeill 1995: 13)

As McNeill suggests, dance probably started primarily as a participatory practice, rather than a spectacle for onlookers. Its social value came from the muscular bonding and euphoric feeling it generated among the dancers. As more occasions were found for dancing, this form of communal expression wove itself into the social fabric.

> There are birth dances of family and tribal congratulation, initiation dances which instruct new tribal members into cult secrets and sexual information, marriage dances of sexual selection and property endowment, war dances and dances of welcome to strangers, or testimony of good fellowship . . . Food, fish, or game are desired. Or rain is needed. Or floods must be dried up. Then dance for it. A warrior is sick. Dance the demons out of him. A man dies. Dance to lay his ghost and protect his survivors from possible threats of his wandering shade.
>
> (Kirstein 1969: 2)

A wide variety of dances continue to be practiced in social groups around the world. In Western Europe and the United States, however, there has been a bifurcation in the practice of dance, leading to two forms of contemporary expression: professional theatrical dance and popular social dance. Theatrical dance actually evolved from social dance, notably from the court dances of Renaissance Europe. As mentioned earlier, dancing was a means of socializing the individual and "formed an important part of the education of a gentleman" (Au 1988: 13). Dances performed in the European courts were social occasions that incorporated pageantry and spectacle. Parts in these performances were generally danced by aristocratic amateurs, but this changed over time. "Parts were assigned on the basis of ability rather than rank, and noble and commoners mingled in the dances without regard for precedence" (ibid: 17). In 1641, Cardinal Richelieu of France commissioned a ballet in honor of King Louis XIV, which was performed on a proscenium stage—an event with far-reaching effects in the development of professional theatrical dance. The proscenium stage framed the action and "served as a distancing device between the performer and the audience, which was now called upon to admire rather than participate" (ibid: 18). In the ensuing centuries, theatrical dance has developed into a virtuoso display of movement prowess that takes many forms and styles. The professionalization of dance has deepened the division between performer and spectator.

As a staged spectacle performed by professionals for an audience, dance has much in common with contemporary theatre. However, the movements used in dramatic acting and miming must bear a close resemblance to everyday behavior, so that the characters and actions on stage are realistic and believable. "This would not occur in a dance where the movements of the dancer show, on the whole, such dreamlike transformations of everyday actions and behavior that their symbolic character cannot be mistaken" (Laban 1971a: 95). Perhaps this is why dance does not enjoy the same degree of popularity as the other theatrical arts. Indeed, in order to generate a broad television audience for dance, it has been necessary to introduce a competitive element, resulting in programs like "Dancing with the Stars," and "America's Best Dance Crew."

At the participatory level, popular social dance in the industrialized West has gradually shifted from communal folk dances, expressing a variety of sentiments, to couple dances that serve primarily as occasions for courting the opposite sex.

> Within the emotional spectrum aroused by dance, sexual exhibition and excitement are always latent and often become explicit. Since the Renaissance, this aspect of dancing has tended to displace others in European society, first in courtly circles and later in middle-class ball-rooms, until in our own time mass culture has made song and dance almost synonymous with sex throughout the world. This constitutes a specialized, historically exceptional meaning, and has helped to blind us to the other roles that dancing played in other times and places.
>
> (McNeill 1995: 65)

Among all the many occasions in human life that call for dancing, two major categories suggest themselves, "those dances which originate in social aims, and those which have a magic or religious purpose" (Kirstein 1969: 2). Social aims dominate in Western European dancing today for "the European has lost the habit and capacity to pray with movement" (Laban 1971a: 5). As Osterley reminds us,

> The whole idea and object of dancing, among civilized peoples, has now become so purely a matter of pastime and enjoyment that it is, at first, difficult to realize its very serious aspect among men in past ages ... It may be true enough that dancing has always been a means of exercise and pleasure; but from the earliest historical times ... this purpose has always been subordinated to religious uses primarily.
>
> (1923: 19)

In the next section, we contrast contemporary Judeo-Christian worship services with primal movement rituals. We examine the transcendent function of dance, trace the suppression of these functions in the West, and survey contemporary manifestations of a once-sacred function, namely, healing through movement.

Humankind at worship

Contemporary Judeo-Christian worship services tend to be solemn and decorous. Muscular participation is reduced to a few conventional gestures and simple actions such as rising, sitting, or kneeling. Singing and chanting are the major rhythmic activities used to unite the congregation. Some celebrants may enter and exit in a stately processional. Beyond this, there

Figure 7.9
R.W. Moore

is little movement through space. While sects differ in the liveliness of their services and the degree to which the congregation participate physically in expressions of religious fervor, in general "the idea that spirituality can be associated with the body is extremely remote from the Western belief in the dichotomy of mind and body, spirit and flesh" (Highwater 1985: 25).

Worship in the West has not always been so subdued. The Hebrew prophets used song and dance to induce a state of mind conducive to prophesizing (McNeill 1995). In ancient Greece, the cult of Dionysus incorporated music, wine, and violent dancing to drive worshippers into an ecstatic frenzy that was both feared and widely emulated (Kirstein 1969). However, during the later years of the Roman Empire, "the dance of primal ecstasy was sexualized by the Roman mentality and became the first form of intentionally lewd cabaret entertainment" (Highwater 1985: 44). For the early Christians, the bloody spectacle of the gladiatorial games, the risqué theatrical shows, and the sensual pantomimic dances were all evidence of the moral collapse of the Empire. Thus, when Christianity became the official state religion of Rome, the Church fathers "anathematized, without exception, the symptoms, the obvious stench of Roman virulence, among them, dance" (Kirstein 1969: 59). As the ritual of the Christian Mass was developed, full-bodied movement was excluded from the holy ceremony. Moreover, even secular theatrical dancing was banned and disappeared in Europe for nearly a thousand years.

Yet, despite the early ban, dancing continued to crop up in Christian churches and religious practices, and the Church officials had to fight a continuous battle against body movement. "From the fourth to the end of the eighteenth century ecclesiastical and lay authorities issued one prohibition after another against dancing in churches and church porches, in churchyards and for the dead" (Backman 1952: 331). However, because the need to dance is strong, particularly in times of trouble, church prohibitions were never completely successful. Outbursts of popular dancing occurred, as in the medieval "dance manias" provoked by fear of the plague (Sorell 1986). Christian mystics and gnostic cults challenged the orthodoxy of the Church by promising "actual *experience* of God" brought about through somatic practices (Berman 1990: 138). Other Christian groups, such as the Shakers, Anabaptists, and Pentecostals, integrated ecstatic dancing into their worship services. Meanwhile pious Christians continued to participate in mixed-sex social dancing, despite stern warnings from the clergy (Marks 1975).

While the Christian Church has not been totally successful in suppressing dance, it has not been completely unsuccessful, either. Today, to a great extent, movement has been stripped of its sacred functions and relegated to the purely secular domain of human life. "If commentators on the contemporary situation of religion agree about anything, it is that the supernatural has departed from the modern world" (Berger 1970: 1). With progressive secularization, brought about in the West by a variety of historical forces, the "divine fullness began to recede until the point was reached when the empirical sphere became both all encompassing and perfectly closed in upon itself. At that point man was truly alone in reality (ibid: 94).

The modern existential aloneness of human beings, who are condemned to live in a purely material, demysticized world, sharply contrasts the view of primal peoples, who believe in "a world of essences which is embodied in all forces and elements" (Highwater 1985: 23). In this worldview, "nature is never only 'natural' . . . the world is impregnated with sacredness" and power (Eliade 1959: 116). Primal humankind was constantly confronted by manifestations of the power of nature, which simultaneously revealed human limitations. Consequently, "man felt the need to transcend his condition, for his life depended on his ability to establish a lasting bond with the source of power" (Wosien 1974: 8). As Lawrence elaborates,

> The whole life-effort of man was to get his life into direct contact with the elemental life of the cosmos, mountain-life, cloud-life, thunder-life, air-life, earth-life, sun-life. To come into immediate, *felt* contact, and so derive energy, power, and a dark sort of joy. This effort into sheer naked contact, *without an intermediary or mediator,* is the root meaning of religion.
>
> (1976: 36)

Because "life was experienced as constant movement," dance became "man's natural way of attuning himself to the powers of the cosmos" (Wosien 1974: 8). By imitating the movement of animals, trees, streams, clouds, and other natural phenomena, humans attempted to align themselves with the supernatural powers manifest in the natural world. Thus, through dance, primal peoples "touch unknown and unseen elements, which they sense in the world around them" (Highwater 1985: 27). The body becomes "the instrument for the transcendent power; and this power is encountered in the dance directly, instantly and without intermediaries" (Wosien 1974: 9). Accordingly, movement is perceived to be potent and magical, and the body becomes a vehicle for gnostic experience that is both visceral and spiritual. "The dancer saturates his living self, his human body, with forces otherwise perceptible only separately from it and thus when he places his body before us, it appears in a transcended form" (Laban 1975a: 179).

Healing arts

If it is unfashionable today to speak of the "sacred" power of dance, movement nevertheless retains certain magical, transformative properties (Murphy 1992). For example, the physical discipline of dance provides the individual with a means for mastering inner drives and for transcending habitual physical and mental limitations. "Dance has a highly integrative nature" (Halprin 2000: 17). Movement releases the regenerative properties of the body, making dance a healing art. The use of movement and dance to achieve once sacred aims continues, albeit in more secularized and specialized contexts. One such context is therapy. In disciplines such as dance/movement therapy, body psychotherapy, and various somatic practices, movement is utilized to heal the mind, as well as the body, of a person in distress.

(A) DANCE/MOVEMENT THERAPY

Though it no longer carries magical connotations, movement rhythm is experienced even today as transforming. The driving pulse of rock music excites the young, the sing-song cadence of a backwoods evangelist hypnotizes the congregation, and the rhythmic pulse of marching soldiers induces a state of euphoric muscular bonding. The behavioral research of Condon (1982) and Hall (1983) reveals that even in everyday interactions, we are locked into a structured world of dance-like rhythms and, when those rhythms shift, so do our feelings about the interaction. In fact, the profound connection between body and mind, experienced through rhythm, has been reconfirmed by modern study. As Meerloo (1960: 37) observes, "the communion of rhythm and dance enables man also to reach, although temporarily, a plateau of ecstatic living which carries him far beyond his daily troubles and frustrations." The power of movement to affect lives and to transform them has led to the development of two new fields of study and practice—dance/movement therapy and body psychotherapy.

Dance therapy is defined by the American Dance Therapy Association (2010) as "the psychotherapeutic use of movement as a process which furthers the emotional and physical integration of the individual." The field was founded in the United States in the 1950s by a varied group of professionals (e.g., Marian Chace, Trudi Schoop, Mary Whitehouse, Alma Hawkins, Franziska Boas, Lilyan Espenak, etc.) who had in common the belief "that it is possible to reach people's feelings through the exciting, enlivening and calming power of dance"(Bartenieff with Lewis 1980: 143). As Schoop described,

> If psychoanalysis brings about a change in the mental attitude, there should be a corresponding physical change. If dance therapy brings about a change in the body's behavior, there should be a corresponding change in the mind. Both methods aim to change the total human, mind and body.
>
> (quoted in ibid: 141)

In addition to the reciprocal interaction of body and mind, therapeutic practice is based on the assumption that movement reveals both conscious and unconscious aspects of the client's personality. In a dance therapy session, the basic elements of the dance—rhythm, spatial design, coordinated gestures and postural actions—are used to awaken body awareness and evoke spontaneous dancing. The act of creating a movement through improvisation is believed to be inherently therapeutic "since it allows the individual to experiment with novel ways of moving, which generate a new experience of being-in-the-world" (Stanton-Jones 1992: 9). In addition to facilitating self-awareness and emotional expressivity, a key goal is the improvement of the client's ability to form and maintain interpersonal relationships (K. Bloom 2006). This is facilitated by moving with others in a group. As Bartenieff explains, dance as an art of nonverbal behavior serves more than one purpose.

> The "holy" madness of the individual artist and the emphasis on the spectacular aspects of theatrical display constitute merely one side of dance. The other side is composed of the regulatory, interactional forces of the dance that include more than expression of emotion. This second aspect we may call here community dance. It is a central force in the forming and regulating of group and individual relationships, interaction, and definition of role.
>
> (1972/73: 14)

She goes on to note that the dance/movement therapist is an empathic catalyst, one who re-enacts the ancient "role of community healer" (ibid: 10). Chace concurs, adding that "one must subscribe to the belief that rhythm and a shared emotional experience are important to a feeling of well-being" (1975: 171). By drawing on the integrative and regenerative properties of movement, dance/movement therapy aims to lead the distressed individual back to creative functioning within his or her social sphere.

As a distinct branch of the main body of psychotherapy, body psychotherapy "helps people deal with their concerns not only through talking, but also by helping clients become deeply aware of their bodily sensations as well as their emotions, images and behaviors" (United States Association for Body Psychotherapy 2010). Body psychotherapy developed from the work of Wilhelm Reich (1897–1957), who initially studied psychoanalysis under Sigmund Freud. Later, he developed his own theories of healthy psychological functioning and the bodily basis of mental and emotional pathologies. Reich contended that "muscular contraction in various areas of the body," related to emotional attitudes adopted early in life, restricts the healthy flow of energy through the body (Christ and Schwartzman 1999: 405–406). He, and his protégés, Alexander Lowen and John Pierrakos, explored various physical modalities for addressing these muscular blockages, and they are thus viewed as pioneers in treating mental and emotional distress through the body.

Clients seek body therapy for the same reasons they seek verbal therapy (for help with depression, trauma, sexual difficulties, relationship issues, and so on), but may also pursue this approach for treatment of physical problems. Like dance/movement therapy, body psychotherapy assumes a functional unity between body and mind. However, most work is done on an individual basis, with the client lying down, sitting, or standing. Body psychotherapy sessions incorporate many different treatment techniques, including breath work, meditation, sensory awareness exercises, touch, massage, directed physical activity, and mediated verbal interaction and reflection (D. Johnson and Grand 1998). As a growing discipline, "body-oriented psychotherapies aim to give greater freedom and integration to the physical, mental, emotional, and spiritual aspects of human life" (Allison 1999: 381).

(C) SOMATICS

Somatics is an emerging body-based group of disciplines that spans holistic education and complementary medicine. The purpose of somatic movement education and therapy is to "enhance human processes of psychophysical awareness and functioning through movement learning" (International Somatic Movement Education and Therapy Association 2010). The term "somatics" was coined by Hanna, who defined the field as follows:

> Somatics is the field which studies the *soma:* namely the body as perceived from within by first-person perception. When a human being is observed from the outside—i.e., from the third person viewpoint— the phenomenon of a human *body* is perceived. But when this same human being is observed from the first-person viewpoint of his own proprioceptive senses, a categorically different phenomenon is perceived: the human soma.
>
> (1995: 341)

Figure 7.10 Somatic practices aim to enhance sensory awareness and ease of movement.

C.L. Moore

In so positioning somatics, Hanna intended to complement long-standing scientific views that tended to objectify the patient's body and nullify personal agency. The aim was to develop a more balanced and integrative disciplinary approach by acknowledging the intrinsically subjective aspects of bodily experience and the active nature of human movement.

Somatics as a discipline emerged in the early twentieth century, notably in Germany where radical reformers advocated "a new relationship to the body and a return to nature" (Kaes, Jay, and Dimendberg 1994: 673). From the beginning, the somatics movement incorporated a diverse range of approaches and promoted "healthy" lifestyle changes in diet, posture, breathing, exercise, and expressive movement. Founding figures in this field include Joseph Pilates, F. Mathias Alexander, Mabel Ellsworth Todd, and Elsa Gindler, along with subsequent developers such as Moshe Feldenkrais, Ida Rolf, Charlotte Selver, Irmgard Bartenieff, and Milton Trager. Each of these figures has developed his or her unique approach to the treatment of the body/mind, and the somatics field today contains distinct disciplines, each with its own educational and/or therapeutic emphasis, principles, and methods (Allison 1999).

In common with dance/movement therapy and body psychotherapy, the somatic disciplines base practice on a recognition of the unity of mind and body. Alexander emphasized that "human ills and shortcomings cannot be classified as 'mental' or 'physical' and dealt with specifically as such ... all training, whether it be educative or otherwise ... must be based upon the indivisible unity of the human organism" (1955: 2, 3). Somatics, however, focuses primarily on the treatment of the physical manifestations of distress rather than on their emotional or psychological sources.

Consequently, somatic practice draws upon principles of anatomy and motor learning to treat the aches and pains that often result from improper physical functioning. Feldenkrais has noted that "many of our failings, physical and mental, need not therefore be considered as diseases to be cured, nor an unfortunate trait of character for they are neither. They are an acquired result of a learned faulty mode of doing" (1973: 152). Body therapists thus believe that reeducation is the key to improved modes of doing, pointing out that such improvement on the body level is inevitably reflected on other levels of human function as well. As noted by Bartenieff, "There is no such thing as pure 'physical' therapy or pure 'mental' therapy. They are continuously interrelated" (with Lewis 1980: 3).

Regardless of the particularities of each sub-discipline, the rediscovery of the inter-relationship of the physique and the psyche has led to new modalities in the treatment of disease and to a renewed interest in the regenerative powers of movement. Whether dance therapy and body therapy are truly novel disciplines or, rather, a much needed reawakening to the ancient wisdom is perhaps debatable, for as Meerloo has noted,

> the dance of the medicine man, priest or shaman belongs to the oldest form of medicine and psychotherapy in which the common exaltation and release of tensions was [sic] able to change man's physical and mental suffering into a new option on health.
>
> (1960: 24)

Movement experiences that are authentic, that bring about a reintegration of mental and physical functioning for the individual or that draw a person into a stronger relationship with others through a shared movement rhythm certainly carry some vestiges of this ancient sacred knowledge with them. Indeed, moments like these often appear to be quite magical to those who have had such experiences.

In conclusion, we can say that movement retains its capacity to transport the individual beyond the limits of the self. Such transcendental power is seldom tapped in everyday activities anymore, yet some glimmers of the once-sacred functions of movement are revealed in the secular contexts of contemporary therapies. Perhaps we may yet reclaim the use of the body in worship, experiencing again those moments in which "the most potent of expressions, those of awe, surrender and ecstasy, dissolve in turn in the experience of attaining the centre, when the expression through movement is transcended"(Wosien 1974: 105). And by reclaiming this part of our movement heritage, perhaps we may also gain a "new grasp on the universe and a new pact with life" (Meerloo 1960: 25).

Recapitulation

In the opening of this chapter we observed that the human being moves to satisfy a need. The needs that motivate our actions are various. They range from *deficit* needs—those things we must have to sustain our existence, such as sleep, food, water, shelter, safety, love, and esteem—to *being* needs—those things we desire to enhance the quality of existence, such as self-expression, beauty, knowledge, truth, and self-transcendence.

Movement serves a vital function in each of the varied quests for human fulfillment. Movements done in *work* serve a productive function; in *war and contest*, a protective function; in *social display*, a communicative and affiliative function; and in *ritual and worship*, a transcendental and regenerative function.

Tracing the varied functions of movement in work, war, social display, and worship is a bit like entering the lair of a Gorgon. We find ourselves confronting what appears to be a many-headed "movement monster." In each of these areas of human life, the physical activity appears distinct and the kind of body knowledge generated therein looks special. As a consequence, the movements of the worker seem unique, wholly and clearly different from those of the soldier, the athlete, the social climber, the actor, the priest, or the therapist. In the encounter with so much diversity, it is easy to forget that all the visages of movement belong to the same creature.

It is small wonder, then, that the ubiquity of movement in human enterprise is so often overlooked, or that the body knowledge of a given area of activity is thought to be totally specialized and discrete. Yet, despite our tendency to overlook the fact, movement is a common thread running through all human endeavors. The disciplined study of movement has the potential for increasing our appreciation of the essential unity of mind, body, and action. Through such study, we discover that the individual is one with culture, and function with expression, space with energy, dance with work with sport with religion; and human life can never again be seen as a mere collection of isolated endeavors.

8 Movements in context

Introduction

As noted in Chapter 7, movement plays a role in virtually every *human* activity. As a primary extension system, its influence on communication and human relations is enormous. However, this potent influence is mostly subliminal, for the ephemeral nature of motion makes it difficult to grasp, and its very ubiquity inclines us to "tune it out." Nevertheless, all of us have been observing and making sense of human movement in some way or another since birth. Our aim with this text is to refine these powers of observation and provide a means for reflecting on the judgments of others that arise from individual body knowledge and body prejudices.

Diminishing body prejudice and enhancing body knowledge require that we approach movement observation from multiple perspectives, tapping both the objective and subjective skills of the whole being. To begin with, we must find ways to heighten movement awareness and to discern what we perceive with greater accuracy and precision. The videotaped exercises in Chapters 3 and 5 were designed to facilitate development of these objective observational skills. By integrating such procedures into normal perceptual practices, we may become more acute movement observers.

While heightened awareness and refined discrimination are necessary preconditions for becoming a truly knowledgeable observer, these objective skills alone will not suffice. We must, in addition, learn to be more reflective about our subjective reactions. This involves examining not only what we tend to perceive in the movements of others but also how we interpret these perceptions. Chapters 4, 5, and 6 suggested some ways to begin scrutinizing the personal lexicons of movement meaning that we attach to nonverbal behaviors often encountered in everyday life. In these nonverbal encounters, objectivity and subjectivity intermingle, for we exert control over what we *do* and *do not* see. As Myrdal has noted, "we almost never face a random lack of knowledge. Ignorance, like knowledge, is purposefully directed . . . and highly opportunistic" (1969: 29). Becoming a better observer also involves stretching, opening the doors of perception and altering habits of the mind.

Observing and journaling

This chapter is primarily visual. The videotaped materials were chosen to provide further opportunities for exploring your personal powers of observation. The recorded events span a range of functions of movement in human life, including work, sport, social interactions, and creative activities. Specifically, the website portion of Chapter 8 contains four different movement episodes:

1. a martial artist in a park, warming up and practicing maneuvers with a sword;
2. two carpenters in a cabinet-making shop performing similar tasks;
3. a staff meeting at a university, involving discussion between the department chair and his two assistants;
4. a creative dramatics class in a dance studio, including nine children and their instructor.

Unlike the videotaped events in Chapters 3 and 5, which were shown in silence to facilitate concentration on the movement in isolation, the episodes seen in this chapter are accompanied by the words and sounds that occurred in the actual settings. While having a sizeable video crew present undoubtedly had some effect on the behavior of the movers on camera, attempts were made to keep the action as natural as possible. The behaviors had not been staged or rehearsed, and the scenes will appear quite similar to events you might come across in daily routines.

Please watch at least two of these events and record your impressions in a personal observation journal. Focus on recording the nonverbal features that seem most interesting, evocative, and significant to you. You may want to survey quickly all four episodes in order to choose the two most appealing. Jot down any first impressions—taking stock of what immediately stands out serves as a good advance organizer for further study. It is fine to watch each episode more than once, bearing in mind that the journal record is not meant to be a detailed analysis. Rather, the written description should be a snapshot, capturing the high points.

Your entries may be poetic, concrete, impressionistic, or interpretive. The length of each entry is up to you. It should be long enough to properly represent what you saw, recording the features that stood out and were personally meaningful.

Direction for website exercise

The visual portions of Chapter 8 can be accessed on the website. This material includes an introduction and four movement episodes that provide material for journaling.

Recapitulation

This observation and journaling exercise provides an opportunity to learn more about your individual way of describing and making sense of the world of human movement. Please keep the notes you have made on the video-taped movement episodes. These notes will be used again, in conjunction with exercises in Chapters 9 and 11.

9 Basic parameters of movement

> It has often been said that I intend to reform in all the fields of human activities in which I have been working, such as school and home education, industry, the art of the theatre, medicine, and social organisation ... The truth is that I have advocated and experimentally tried to pay more attention to human movement—bodily and mental—which is obviously at the basis of all human activity. Movement research and movement education have been neglected in our time and some failures of our civilisation are surely influenced, if not produced, by this neglect.
>
> Rudolf Laban

In this chapter we will be introducing the basic concepts of one observational framework widely used in movement study, namely, Laban Movement Analysis (LMA). Granted this is by no means the only available framework for facilitation of movement understanding, its comprehensiveness, flexibility, and sound conceptual basis make the Laban system a preferred choice. Likewise, in terms of the number and range of applications, it has been rather peerless.

While the system justly bears the name of its founder, Rudolf Laban (1879–1958), Laban Movement Analysis today is a creative synthesis that has been enriched considerably by concepts developed by Laban's colleagues and later students of human movement, working within the Laban tradition. Nevertheless, the basic tenets of the analytical framework remain unmistakably those of the originator, and no introduction of the system would be complete without first saying a few words about the life, times, and ideas of Rudolf Laban himself.

A man in motion

Laban was born in 1879 in Bratislava, Czechoslovakia, then a part of the powerful Austro-Hungarian Empire. Though groomed for a military career by his father who was a career army officer, Laban wanted to pursue his own interest in art. In 1900 he was permitted to begin studies, first in Munich then later at the *École des Beaux Arts* in Paris (Preston-Dunlop 1998b).

In addition to visual art, Laban showed a special interest in theatre production—stage design, theatre architecture, decor, and costumes—and enjoyed something of a theatrical career as a cabaret performer and organizer of carnival entertainments (Doerr 2008). However, his real vocation did not begin to emerge until 1910, when he founded a communal "dance farm" in southern Switzerland, in which the whole community, after work, produced dances based upon their occupational experiences (Green 1986). Through this experiment Laban is said to have realized that his "dramas, songs and movement-scenes, in spite of the occasional use of the spoken word, did not belong to drama or opera but to the world of dance" (S. Thornton 1971). This insight marked a significant turning point in his career.

From 1910 through 1936, Laban dedicated his energies to developing a modern dance in central Europe. His efforts characteristically took a variety of forms: he choreographed and performed himself; he trained dancers, establishing schools in Basel, Stuttgart, Hamburg, Prague, Budapest, Zagreb, Rome, Vienna, Essen, and Paris, each directed by a former student; he organized a dancers' union; he directed large recreational movement compositions, called "movement choirs," which were danced by non-professionals; and he wrote and published books on dance (Hodgson and Preston-Dunlop 1990).

Prominent among all these accomplishments was his development and publication of a dance notation system in the late 1920s (Laban 1928, 1956). Unlike master works in the performing arts of theatre and music, which can be preserved in written scripts and scores, great works in the history of dance had been completely lost because there was no way to record them in written form. Although there had been attempts to devise a dance notation since Baroque times, these early systems were limited to a depiction of the actions of the legs and the floor pattern travelled. Movements of the torso and arms could not be recorded with exactitude. Laban's notation system solved such problems and made a full recording of the action of all parts of the dancer's body possible for the first time. Additional development of the notation by his students Albrecht Knust (1979) and Ann Hutchinson Guest (1983, 2005) made Laban's system eminently practical, and it is now widely used to document master works of contemporary dance.

Unfortunately, this highly productive period of Laban's career was brought to a close in 1936 when the Nazi Party banned his work throughout Germany, and Laban, then living in Berlin, was banished to Staffelberg, in Bavaria. By 1937, demoralized and in ill health, Laban managed to emigrate to Paris. Then in 1938, through the intervention of colleagues who had found political asylum in England, he was able to cross the Channel (Preston-Dunlop 1998b). This relocation in England seems to mark another significant turning point in Laban's life and career (Hodgson 2001). After 1938, Laban retired from an active role in the dance world and applied his energies instead to the study of industrial work functions (Laban and

Lawrence 1974), the promotion of movement education in British schools (Laban 1975c), the movement guidance for stage actors (Laban 1971a), and the assessment of personality through movement observation and interpretation (Laban 1957). In this final period, Laban crystallized many of his theories about human movement in their most complete form (Moore 2009).

No recounting of Laban's life is complete, of course, without mention of his influence as a teacher. From 1910 until his death in 1958, Laban always worked closely with students, in the theatre, studio, even in the factory. He is remembered as a charismatic educator who possessed the uncanny ability to sense a student's potential and draw it out. Laban also used teaching to help develop ideas, experimenting in the classroom with whatever problem was occupying him at the time. In this way Laban often took the role of a catalyst. He would lay the groundwork of a concept or practice, then consign it out to a student for further development as he himself moved on to the consideration of new problems and ideas.

Laban's own career was characterized more by diversity of endeavor than by the single-minded devotion to a particular discipline (Maletic 1987). Yet he could engage in a variety of efforts without dissipating his energy. This is perhaps due to the fact that his constant interest in movement provided a unifying theme throughout his many activities. For Laban, movement was the essence of life and the mirror of humankind. His discovery that there are core elements and general organizational principles common to all movements unified his own professional endeavors. Moreover, Laban's vision continues to provide a synthesizing perspective for others concerned with the study of movement behavior in a variety of contexts. In the following section we will take a closer look at the general principles that underlie Laban's conception of human movement.

General principles of the Laban system

While Laban Movement Analysis is subject to various interpretations, the following premises may be said to guide its application.

(a) Movement is a process of change

Commonly, movement is defined as a change in place or position. That is, an action begins in one place and ends in another. Through the perception of this change, we know that movement has occurred. But while the difference between the beginning and ending locations of an action may be indicative of motion, movement itself is *not* a position or even a change of positions. Rather, movement is the *process* of the changing.

The difference is subtle but important. If we take a simple action, like moving the arm from point A to point B, and rapidly photograph it, we will be able to see all the intermediate locations through which the arm has passed as it swept from A to B. But as Laban points out, "heaping up the single pictures in a pile can never give the impression of a movement." The "uninterrupted flux" of the motion itself becomes visible only "when we let the pictures unroll" (Laban 1974: 3).

Moreover, human movement involves not merely a change in position, but also a change in the activation and involvement of the body and in the quantity and quality of energy necessary to effect the motion. In other words, human movement is a fluid, dynamic transiency of simultaneous change in spatial positioning, body activation, and energy usage.

(b)   The change is patterned and orderly

Describing movement as a "process of change," an "uninterrupted flux," or an "indivisible streaming" often gives an observer the uneasy feeling that the very process one is trying to see has already ceased to exist just at the moment one glimpses it. Indeed, it takes a while to get used to the "rolling and pitching" spectacle of movement as a process of change (Bergson 1946: 150). But catching a glimpse of change as it is occurring is made easier because, beneath the appearance of unceasing fluctuation, there is a governing pattern and order that prevents movement from being chaotic. Laws of sequencing, the alternating rhythms of stability/mobility and exertion/recuperation, as well as the fact that people develop movement habits that are repeated—all these provide an underlying pattern to change that may be perceived.

For example, at first glance the spatial pathways traced by a body in motion may appear random and disorderly. But closer study reveals that

> a series of natural sequences of movement exists which we follow in our various everyday activities. Such sequences . . . are determined by the anatomical structure of our body. These sequences . . . always link the different zones of the body and its limbs in a logical way.
>
> (Laban 1974: 37)

Another kind of patterning can be found in the rhythmic alteration of stability and mobility. Stability, as Laban defined it,

> does not mean either complete rest or absolute stillness. Stability has the tendency to facilitate temporary and relative quietude which is equilibrium. Mobility on the contrary means a tendency towards vivid, flowing movement, leading to a temporary loss of equilibrium. For instance, in a flying turning leap . . . the whole body is in a mobile state. When the jump is terminated and the feet touch the floor again, there is a tendency towards quietude and equilibrium . . . All our steps and gestures of the arms are rhythmical changes between stability and mobility.
>
> (ibid: 94)

Moreover, the use of energy is governed by an alternating rhythm of exertion and recuperation. Just as phases of work and rest are paired in the involuntary action of heart and lungs, the alternations of activity with recovery are paired in the voluntary actions of the whole body. For instance, in rowing, recovery occurs in the movement,

> which, after completion of a stroke, brings the body and the oar into position for the next stroke. In fencing or sparring the act of regaining the position of guard after making an attack is called recovery . . . Effort used in actions and that used in recovery serve and help each other in alternating . . . in a definite rhythm; they are rhythmical opposites within acts of vital function.
>
> (Laban 1971b: 45)

(c) Human movement is intentional

The human being moves to satisfy a need. Actions are guided and purposeful, and the intentions of the mover are made clear by the way in which the person moves. While the uses of space and of the body reveal the mover's purposes, Laban believed that the uses of energy, or the dynamics of an action, were particularly evocative of intentions. Thus, he used the term, "effort," to delineate the dynamic energies exerted in movement and noted

> the distinction of two contrasting inner attitudes with which the effort invariably preceding any movement can be activated. The inner attitude of fighting against something contrasts with the inner attitude of yielding to something . . . There exists no effortless action or movement— physical or mental—and the effort used with a non-fighting indulgence does not always involve a low degree of exertion.
>
> (ibid: 44)

A study of the manner in which a person applies energy, to fight against or indulge in an experience, allows an observer to penetrate the "inner world in which impulses continually surge and seek an outlet in doing, acting, and dancing" (Laban 1971a: 17). While individuals do show habitual predilections for certain effort configurations, human beings also possess the capacity to comprehend the nature of effort qualities and their patterning in dynamic sequences. Moreover, we may intentionally seek to alter our movement habits through conscious training. Laban used the term "humane effort" to characterize such developmental attempts and noted that "with his humane effort man is able to control negative habits and to develop qualities and inclinations creditable to man, despite adverse influences" (ibid: 15). Humane effort is rarely taken into consideration when speaking of movement study and training. But, as Laban emphasized, "it is a most important manifestation and perhaps the very source of the possibility of movement education, which is of paramount importance . . . to every individual's self-development" (ibid).

It is this intentional capacity, to vary widely and at will the kind of energies employed in an action, that distinguishes human movement from the automatic, instinctual actions of animals and the mechanical motions of inanimate objects.

(d) The basic elements of human motion may be articulated and studied

Through his scrutiny of human movements in a variety of contexts, Laban discovered basic elements of physical actions that are common to all human motion. "Whether the purpose of movement is work or art does not matter," Laban explained, "for the elements are invariably the same" (1971a: 103). These basic elements make up the "alphabet of the language of movement: and it is possible to observe and analyse movement in terms of this language" (ibid: 115). In fact, knowledge of these elements of movement and their combinations and sequences makes possible a "new approach to the understanding of the mystery of doing and dancing" (Laban 1984: 12). In the following section of this chapter, key elements of the system of Laban Movement Analysis are articulated in greater detail. [Note: visual examples of these elements can be accessed in Chapter 9 on the website.]

(e) Movement must be approached at multiple levels if it is to be properly understood

As noted above, movement is a dynamic, fluid process involving simultaneous changes in spatial positioning, body activation, and energy usage. Any attempt to capture this process must therefore include description of each of these aspects. Moreover, how basic space, body, and effort elements are combined and sequenced must be taken into account. Movement study, as Laban envisioned it, should incorporate multiple levels of analysis. The observer should consider not only *what the movement is made of*, but also *how it is put together*. That is, analysis at the molecular levels of a given movement event (the basic elements that comprise the action) needs to be integrated with observation at the molar levels (the laws of sequencing and rhythmic patterns), if the movement is to be understood.

Another point, mentioned briefly in Chapter 5, is Laban's idea that an individual may approach movement observation from various perspectives. For example, movement may be explored and appreciated from a bodily perspective, through physical immersion in the on-going stream. Or, movement may be studied objectively, with an eye to improving its function. Finally, movement may be approached intellectually, with the aim of interpreting its significance in more abstract terms. According to Laban, we waver between these perspectives and "sometimes we compress them in a synthesized act of perception and function" (1974: 7).

Each of the principles—(a) movement is a process of change; (b) the change is patterned and orderly; (c) human movement is intentional; (d) the basic elements of human movement may be articulated and studied; and (e) movement must be approached at multiple levels if it is to be properly understood—may be used to guide us towards that "synthesised act of perception and function" described by Laban. In addition, these principles may be seen to shape the entire framework, known as Laban Movement Analysis (LMA).

Introduction to Laban Movement Analysis

The basic elements common to all movements may be categorized under three broad headings: (1) the use of the *body*; (2) the use of *space*; and (3) the use of *dynamic energy*. We shall take up these one by one to provide an initiation to Laban Movement Analysis. While the discussion cannot be exhaustive, we will touch upon the key concepts of the descriptive-analytical system.

Use of the body

When we move, different parts of the body are brought in and out of play just like instruments in an orchestra. Sometimes a single body part will solo, as when we tap a foot or raise an arm. At other times the simultaneous motions of two or more body parts may provide a kind of visual counter-point, as when we nod the head while leaning forward in a chair. Finally, just as there are moments when all the instruments in an orchestra are brought into simultaneous play, so too all body parts may unite in a single action, as in a well-coordinated spin or a startled jump.

Among all the many possible patterns of bodily coordination, two major categories may be delineated—those actions that are *gestures* and those that are *postures*. A *gesture* is an "action confined to a part or parts of the body" (Lamb 1965: 16). Nodding the head, swinging the lower leg, clenching a hand, or shrugging the shoulders are all examples of gestures that are limited to a single body part. It is also possible to do two or more gestures simultaneously. For instance, the ballerina may extend one leg while lifting and opening both arms. Or a businessman may impatiently tap his fingers while glancing at his watch. The ability to isolate an action to one part of the body with precise differentiation and articulation and to coordinate two or more gestural actions simultaneously makes possible a great range of functional tasks and expressive actions.

On the other hand, a *posture* is a position assumed by the whole body or an action in which the whole body participates uniformly. Examples of

Figure 9.1 A postural action involves all parts of the body.
Jan Stanley

postural actions may be found in everyday life. During a conversation, the stiffly erect posture of one person may relax into a sprawled but attentive position as the other party leans forward chattering, the whole body straining with excitement. A child in a classroom raises her hand to attract the teacher's attention. When this gesture is ignored, the child begins to wave her whole arm urgently and soon she is almost jumping out of her seat in her postural attempts to be recognized. Sports also provide many examples of postural actions. A diver balances on the edge of the high board, the whole body in taut alignment to spring and somersault into the pool. The baseball player throws his body forward in a postural slide toward a base. Each of these full-body actions involves "a continuous adjustment of every part of the body with consistency in the process of variation" (Lamb 1965: 16).

Throughout all activities, gestures and postures alternate. Gestures may expand into postures. For instance, imagine that someone starts to pick up a box. The first attempt is gestural—the arms are extended, the box is grasped, and the arms contract to lift it. But if the box is heavier than anticipated, this gestural approach will not succeed. Instead the whole body will be brought into play, as the lifter squats, grasps the box firmly, and presses the weight upward using the legs, torso, and arms in a concerted move.

Postures may also be turned into gestures. Imagine, for example, that the boss tells an employee he has been promoted. At first the employee may leap to his feet shouting "Hooray!" Then, glancing at the shocked boss, the employee recovers himself, and contains his postural elation in a gestural handshake, accompanied by a polite, "Thank you, Ms. Smith."

Almost any action may be performed as a gesture or a posture. However, when a movement requires full concentration (e.g., a high dive), or when the mover participates wholeheartedly in the activity (e.g., an excited spectator cheering the home team), postural movement is more likely to occur. When minimal involvement suffices in a task (e.g., brushing crumbs off a table), or when the mover feels constrained or artificial (e.g., going through a formal reception line), gestural movement is more likely to occur. The differentiation of posture and gesture is a powerful tool for studying both the functional and expressive aspects of movement.

Another differentiation that is useful in studying the body use deals with the body part(s) with which a movement sequence is started. This concept is called *initiation*. While discriminating postures from gestures is analogous to noting whether a single instrument or the whole orchestra is playing, observations of initiation focus on the sequence in which body parts are brought into play; that is, on what might be called the "melody" of bodily coordination.

Four broad distinctions may be drawn about initiation: movement may begin *distally*, with the head, arms, or legs leading the action; movement may begin *centrally*, with the chest or pelvis initiating the motion; movement may begin *in the lower body*, distally in the legs or centrally in the pelvis; or movement may begin *in the upper body*, distally in the arms and head or centrally in the chest.

Many common actions may be initiated either distally or centrally. In rising from a chair one may begin distally, by uncrossing the legs and planting the feet on the floor, then shifting the center of weight forward to stand. Or one may initiate the action centrally, by first shifting the pelvis forward in the chair until the body is positioned over the legs to rise. In both these instances, the lower body is the primary initiator of action.

It is also possible to rise from a chair by initiating the action from the upper body. This is sometimes the way we rise when tired. We begin the movement by tilting the upper body forward towards the feet, sometimes even assisting the rising by using our arms to push against the chair. Little motion is required in the lower body to stand up in this way.

In addition to functional facilitation of movement tasks, a given type of initiation may characterize expressive movement, such as a dance style. For

Table 9.1 Basic elements of body part usage

Gesture	An action confined to a part of the body
Posture	A position of the whole body, or an action in which the whole body participates consistently
Initiation	Where any movement originates in the body
	• *Distal initiation*: Movement begins in the arms, legs, or head
	• *Central initiation*: Movement begins in the torso
	• *Upper body initiation*: Body parts above the waistline (arms, head, chest) begin an action
	• *Lower body initiation*: Body parts below the waistline (i.e., leg or pelvis) *start a movement*
Sequencing	The overall organization of body part activation in a given moment

instance, the modern dance form created by Martha Graham emphasizes central initiation almost exclusively. In Graham's dances the lower spine is used like a spring. All movements are driven through the coiled contraction and springy release of the lower back; the arms and legs are meant to move only in response to impulses emanating in the center of the body. On the other hand, classical ballet emphasizes the distal initiation of motion. The ballet dancer's arms and legs inscribe spacious arcs and lines around a still and held torso. The motive force of the movement comes from the periphery of the body, not its center. Thus, the discrimination of different types of initiation is another powerful tool for studying both the functional and expressive aspects of movement.

To summarize, basic parameters of body part usage include elements shown in Table 9.1. Visual examples can be accessed on the website.

Use of space

We are used to thinking of space as an emptiness. But Laban has pointed out that space is much more than something that is not there. Space is "a locality" in which movement changes take place. In addition, "Space is a hidden feature of movement and movement is a visible aspect of space" (Laban 1974: 4).

As we begin to analyze physical action more closely, we find we need both these ways of thinking about space if we are indeed to capture and describe movement accurately. First, we must be able to picture the locale in which the movement occurs—is it small, large, cramped, crowded? Can one circulate through the space freely or is one compelled to stay in one spot? Secondly, we must be able to articulate the spatial design that is in the movement itself; that is, to describe where motions go in the changing process of flowing from place to place.

Let us begin this discussion of the basic elements of space with the view of *space as a locale*. Space as a locale in which movement occurs may be categorized in three ways: first there is the *general space* in a given environment; next, the *interpersonal space* or distances between people moving in a given environment; and finally, the *personal space* or the sphere of territory defined by the areas we can reach while standing on one spot (Laban 1974).

We gain access to general space through locomotion. We may travel in straight lines or curved paths through an environment. We may crawl, leap, stroll, skip, slither, tiptoe, or glide. We may concentrate on what is above us, at our feet, or at waist level. We may feel cramped, uplifted, intimidated, or oppressed by the size of the environment, be it architectural or natural, and by what we sense to be the potential for movement within the locale. All of these kinesthetic aspects have to do with movement through general space.

Interpersonal space touches upon the changing distances and orientations that appear among several people moving in the same locale. Are people bunched together or spread out, moving towards one another or away? Are they side by side or back to back? Interpersonal space is fraught with drama. Is someone standing too far, or breathing down your neck? Do you prefer to face someone or sit alongside when conversing? Do you talk down to a child or kneel to be on the same level? All of these many movement variables have to do with the changing relationships created in interpersonal space.

Finally, whether the body moves through space or stays in one spot, it occupies space and is surrounded by it. This occupied area comprises personal space or what is called the "kinesphere." Personal space may be defined as "the sphere around the body whose periphery can be reached by easily extended limbs without stepping away from that place which is the point of support when standing on one foot" (ibid: 10). One can get a sense of the farthest reaches of the kinesphere by standing on one leg and swinging the free leg, as well as the arms, in widely extended paths all around the body, allowing the torso to tilt and twist for balance. The middle reach area of the kinesphere may be experienced with similar motions performed with slightly bent limbs. And finally, actions held close to the stationary body indicate the nearest reach area of the kinesphere.

Beyond the kinesphere lies the rest of general space, which can only be reached by stepping away from the stationary stance. However, even in locomotion, the kinesphere goes along for the ride, for, as Laban noted, "we never . . . leave our movement sphere but carry it always with us, like an aura" (ibid).

As a consequence, a great deal of movement occurs within the kinesphere itself. As we seek to describe where bodily actions flow within the kinesphere, we experience space as a "hidden feature" of movement and movement as a "visible aspect" of space. Let us imagine for a moment that there are jet engines in the joints of our limbs that leave vapor trails as we move. The contrails make visible the *spatial design* of kinespheric movements. And three patterns may be discerned: movement that leaves *straight lines* as vapor trails; actions that result in *curved* and arc-like trails; and motions that leave behind complex *three-dimensional loops*, twists and spirals. Laban called these invisible shapes in space "trace-forms" (1974: 5). Let us take a closer look at the properties of each of these trace-forms.

Straight lines provide the simplest orientation to space. These trace-forms support unswerving motions towards a fixed goal (e.g., reaching for a glass on a shelf) and simple repetitive sequences involving linear reversals (e.g., erasing a smudge or poking a hole in cardboard with an ice pick). On the body level, linear trace-forms may be accomplished simply with flexion and extension of the various joints.

Curved trace-forms allow a more varied approach to space and, while they still support motion towards a fixed goal (e.g., swinging a heavy box to heave it into the garbage bin), curved paths lend themselves to more cyclical movement sequences (e.g., polishing a silver plate or performing cartwheels). On the body level, curved trace-forms require abduction/adduction and sometimes rotation in addition.

Twisted and spiraling trace-forms allow the most flexible and complex approach to space. Three-dimensional pathways create volume and support actions with multiple goals, as in slashing weeds or tying a knot. These trace-forms tend to be less common than linear and curved pathways, possibly because the bodily coordination required is more complicated, often involving flexion/extension, abduction/adduction, and rotation. Three dimensional trace-forms are found, however, in certain virtuosic movement events, such as a reverse somersault, twist-tuck high dive; axel jumps in figure skating; or martial arts defense patterns in which multiple attackers are fended off simultaneously.

In addition to the shape inscribed by a trace-form, the overall pathway itself shows a directional orientation. As Laban has articulated:

> The basic elements of orientation in space are the three dimensions: length, breadth and depth. Each "dimension" has two directions. With reference to the human body, length, or height, has two directions up and down; breadth has two directions left and right; depth has two directions forward and backward.
>
> (ibid: 11)

As we consider each of these dimensional orientations more closely, we see that the *vertical* dimension emphasizes the process of rising and sinking or falling. Reaching for a container on a high shelf, kneeling to dust a baseboard, stamping the floor in indignation, or lifting an eyebrow quizzically—

Figure 9.2 Both tennis players reach backward, emphasizing the sagittal dimension
        of depth.

Juergen Kuehn

all are actions that stress the vertical dimension. Trace-forms that rise and fall may be linear, curved, or twisted and voluminous.

The *horizontal* dimension (which Laban referred to as "breadth") emphasizes the process of widening and narrowing. Ironing a shirt, scattering crumbs for birds, opening one's arms to embrace, clasping someone in a hug, sprawling in a chair, or huddling in the cold are actions that primarily utilize the horizontal dimension. Of course, trace-forms that widen and narrow may be linear, curved, or twisted and voluminous.

The *sagittal* dimension (which Laban referred to as "depth") stresses the process of advancing and retreating. Throwing darts, recoiling from a stomach punch, springing forward at the start of a race, hanging back in hesitation, reaching out to shake someone's hand, or relaxing in the bathtub are all actions that emphasize advancing and retreating. Again, trace-forms that advance and retreat may be linear, curved, or twisted and voluminous.

As with the analysis of body usage, the differentiation of locale, trace-form shape, and dimensional orientation provide valuable tools for elucidating both the functional and expressive aspects of movement.

To summarize, basic parameters of the use of space include the elements shown in Table 9.2. Visual examples can be accessed on the website.

Table 9.2 Basic elements of the use of space

Spatial locale
- *General space*: The environment or area in which action occurs
- *Interpersonal space*: The changing distances and orientations among movers in a locale
- *Personal space (kinesphere)*: The area of space reachable without taking a step

Trace-forms
The invisible "vapor trails," inscribed by the moving body in the kinesphere
- *Linear*: Straight kinespheric pathways
- *Planes*: Curved kinespheric pathways
- *Volumes*: Three-dimensioal twisted, looped, or spiraling kinespheric pathways

Dimensions
The basic spatial scaffolding used to orient movement
- *Vertical*: Includes the directions of up/down and stresses rising/falling processes
- *Horizontal*: Includes the directions of left/right and stresses widening/narrowing processes
- *Sagittal*: Includes the directions of forwards/backwards and stresses advancing/retreating processes

Sequencing
- The overall organization of a spatial design and orientation in a given movement phrase

---

Dynamics

In addition to articulating bodily activation and spatial design, a thorough description of movement must also incorporate *how* the action is performed. Was the movement abrupt or hesitant? Was the rhythm jerky or smooth? Was too much energy applied or not enough? All these questions touch upon the many rich and differentiated dynamic qualities with which movement may be performed.

Laban called the dynamic aspect of movement "effort," and discerned four motion factors that may be varied in any given action (Laban and Lawrence 1974). We can change the focus, the degree of pressure, the timing, and the degree of control or kind of flow with which a motion is done. Laban believed that the dynamics of effort are derived from the inner attitudes of the mover towards each of these four motion factors (*Focus*, *Pressure*, *Time*, and *Flow*). As North paraphrased, "The attitude of the moving person towards each motion factor is a discernible and classifiable fact. Either the factor is 'indulged in,' 'yielded to' or it is 'fought against,' 'resisted.'" (1975: 232). Thus, two contrasting qualities may be identified for each motion factor, as shown in Table 9.3. Visual examples can be accessed on the website.

Table 9.3 Basic effort elements

Motion factor	Attitude		
	"Indulging in"	⟷	*"Fighting against"*
Varying *focus*	Indirecting	⟷	Directing
Varying *pressure*	Decreasing	⟷	Increasing
Varying *time*	Decelerating	⟷	Accelerating
Varying *flow*	Freeing	⟷	Binding

At first the idea that effort qualities represent inner attitudes may appear to be rather peculiar. After all, attitudes are not usually things we believe we can see. Yet if we notice someone walking rapidly down the street, we easily deduce the person to be in a hurry. If this same person always moves swiftly (i.e., accelerating action whenever possible), we come to sense that the individual is *always* rushed. Through observation of the quality of the person's motions, we conclude that he or she has the attitude that there is never enough time. In fact, we might even say that the person is fighting against time, constantly accelerating actions in order to squeeze more into a given period. When we think about it, therefore, there is much in the premise that "*Effort* is the common denominator for the various stirrings of the body and mind which become observable in . . . activity" (Laban 1975c: 18).

However, the observation of effort presents some challenges because of the extremely ephemeral nature of each dynamic quality. It is not stretching the point too far to say that, properly understood, the dynamic aspect of movement is the most variable and fleeting of all movement changes. That is, a given effort quality cannot be maintained for a long period of time without our ceasing to perceive it as dynamic. For example, when riding in an airplane we perceive the process of speeding up as the plane takes off, but once airborne, when maximum speed has been reached and is maintained, we lose the sense of travelling rapidly. It is only if the plane slows down a little in flight and then speeds up again, that we perceive its deceleration and/or acceleration. Similarly in human movement, it is variation, not maintenance, of kinetic quality that we perceive as dynamic. Within the rapid walk of our hurried person-on-the-street, there will be fluctuations in speed, moments of decelerating and accelerating, that contribute to the urgency of the walk. Inner attitudes are manifested in moments of fluctuation in focus, pressure, timing, and control. In other words, effort is made visible only as it changes.

Let us consider more closely the effort element of *focus*. To begin with, focus involves varying ways of physically attending to the environment and

Figure 9.3 The effort quality of *directing* facilitates precision of focus.
Jan Stanley

orienting one's motions in space.* There are two contrasting ways to apply
focusing energy—one may physically home in on a single point of interest
by directing, or one may scan multiple points of interest by indirecting.
Laban noted that, "In bodily actions of great directness all active muscle
groups co-operate in producing, as a rule, a well-traced pattern having no
plasticity" (1975c: 71). Directing would be used in the effort, for example,
to place a key in a lock, cut out a pattern with scissors, or thread a needle.
Directing movements often appear channelled in attentiveness, specific,
pinpointing, straight, aimed, and unswerving.

* The motion factor called "focus" in this book is often referred to in other sources as the "space"
factor, because it involves the effort to orient oneself. The term "focus" is used here to prevent
any confusion with the "use of space" category discussed in the preceding section.

On the other hand, a movement can be considered indirect when "the effort of multilateral muscular function prevails in it. This effort brings about continuous changes of the direction of the movement" (Laban 1975c: 68). Indirecting efforts would play a role in, for instance, feeling around for a light switch in the dark, waving a scarf to keep away mosquitoes, or peering around to find a familiar face at a crowded cocktail party. Indirecting movements often appear multifaceted in attentiveness, circuitous, round-about, meandering, and flexible.

The effort factor of *pressure* involves varying attitudes towards physically exerting force and using one's weight* to have an intentional impact on the environment. There are two contrasting ways to apply force in movement —one may utilize body weight and muscle power resolutely by increasing pressure, or one may achieve delicate yet persistent impact by decreasing pressure. In movements of increasing pressure, the power of muscular resistance is used to produce a powerful exertion. Here, as Laban describes, "the prevailing effort is of muscular tension" (ibid: 60). Increasing pressure would be used in, for instance, forcing open a tightly closed container, throwing a heavy object, or wringing out a thick towel. Actions of increasing pressure appear firm, powerful, solid, strong, and forceful.

On the other hand, in movements of decreasing pressure "a feeling of intensive lightness and relaxed buoyancy is experienced" and "muscular relaxation prevails" (ibid: 62). Decreasing pressure would be used to, for instance, maneuver delicate objects, smooth tissue paper, or gently guide an elderly person to a chair. Movements of decreasing pressure often appear light, delicate, airy, gentle, and buoyantly resilient.

The effort factor of *time* involves varying attitudes towards the urgency of an action. There are two contrasting approaches—an effort may be made to speed up the pace of an action decisively by accelerating, or to delay the culmination of the motion by decelerating. A movement may be considered to accelerate when

> the effort of an abrupt or sudden muscular function prevails in it . . . Physically, this abrupt character of a sudden motion is to be found in explosions or in the released jerk of a spring. Bodily actions of quickness cannot be prolonged without losing their character . . . but will themselves always have a short duration.
>
> (ibid: 64–65)

Accelerating would be seen in, e.g., a startled response to an unexpected sound, the lunge to catch a falling glass before it smashes to the floor, or the snap when pitching a baseball. Accelerating motions appear sudden, quick, instantaneous, fleeting, and abrupt.

---

* The motion factor called "pressure" in this book is sometimes referred to in other Laban Movement Analysis sources as the "weight" factor.

On the other hand, decelerating actions resemble "the hovering of smoke" rather than the "abruptness of a spark." The duration of the movement is prolonged and "the effort of continuous muscular function prevails in it" (Laban 1975c: 66). Decelerating would be found in such instances as a dawdling walk, the motions made to soothe an over-excited person, or pressing a seal in hot wax. Decelerating motions appear gradual, leisurely, drawn out, unhurried, and languid.

The effort factor of *flow* involves varying attitudes towards the precision and control with which a motion is performed. There are two contrasting attitudes towards controlling the flow of a motion—an effort may be made to keep the action contained at all times through binding flow or to let the inherent inertia of the movement take over by freeing flow. Binding flow is seen in a movement "when the prevailing effort is the readiness to stop" (ibid: 75). Moreover, "the bodily means of performing bound movements is the participation of antagonistic muscles which help in the steady control of an action" (ibid). Efforts to bind the flow of motion would be found in, for example, carrying a cup brimming with hot coffee, maneuvering carefully through a narrow aisle in a china shop, or shaking hands stiffly with a polite host. Actions done with bound flow appear controlled, restrained, careful, taut, and precise.

On the other hand, in freely flowing movements, "the muscles antagonistic to the fluent character of the action remain passive, without readiness to function." As a result, in a movement showing free flow, "the effort of stopping is almost absent" (ibid: 73). The inertia of the movement is allowed to take over. Free flow would be found in such movements as the helter-skelter running of a child on the beach, shaking out a duster, or throwing up the hands in exasperation. Motions performed with free flow appear abandoned, fluent, easygoing, loose, and unrestricted.

As might be imagined, multiple effort qualities are often manifested simultaneously in actions. For example, typing on a computer keyboard is often done with dabbing movements that combine directing, decreasing pressure, and accelerating. In a moment of extreme anger an individual may flail about vehemently with free flow, increasing pressure, and accelerating. Passengers on a subway train are often seen staring vacantly into space with bound flow and direct focus, while the person walking down a deserted street at night maintains alertness by quick, indirecting movements. Combining differing effort qualities with each other facilitates the performance of a vast range of functional tasks as well as the expression of a gamut of movement moods (Laban 1971a; North 1975; Maletic 2005).

However, as Laban has pointed out, moods do not accumulate only in effort combinations. "Following one another in movement sequences, the consecutive efforts will build up a kind of melody or sentence-like structure, the collective mood of which is an important part of movement experience" (Laban 1975c: 46). For example, a movement sequence may begin quietly with indulging effort qualities and build up to a crashing impact. Or a dynamic phrase may explode with fighting effort qualities and wane in a decrescendo of indulgent dynamic energies. The intensity of an action may build and fall, build and fall, creating a repetitive swinging rhythm. Or in a given movement one may observe an evenness of dynamic quality throughout. Other types of phrases can also be identified (Maletic 2005).

In describing these rhythmic patterns of effort sequences we only touch upon the complicated, manifold, and changing dynamic energies that are observable in human movement. Laban has sometimes used the metaphor of an inner landscape to depict this world of effort combinations and sequences, noting that, "We cannot easily describe in words the roads and landscapes of this realm . . . This does not mean that the vistas and delights of this world are altogether indescribable, but we have to use special words and special connotations" (1971c: 40–41).

The language of effort, body, and space provide us with a rudimentary vocabulary for describing the ever-changing landscapes of human movement. While we may discuss these basic elements of movement in writing, it is most useful to see actual demonstrations of these motion factors. The visual portions of this chapter, which can be accessed on the website, illustrate each of the basic elements of Laban Movement Analysis that we have been describing.

Direction to website

Please proceed now to view the video portions of Chapter 9 on the website.

Recapitulation

The system known today as Laban Movement Analysis, notwithstanding the considerable enrichment by later contributors, still bears the unmistakable stamp of its originator, Rudolf Laban. He initially pursued an interest in the visual arts and design before turning to the study of human movement. However, once crystallized, Laban's interest in movement was wide-ranging, encompassing the fields of professional and lay dance, industrial work study, education, theatre, and therapy. Among his many accomplishments, Laban is best remembered for his development of a movement notation system, as well as for elucidation of the core elements and organizational principles common to all movements.

The following premises may be said to have guided Laban's inquiry into human movement: (a) movement is a process of change; (b) the change is patterned and orderly; (c) human movement is intentional; (d) the basic elements of movement may be articulated and studied; and (e) movement must nevertheless be approached at multiple levels if it is to be properly understood. These principles provide the conceptual foundation upon which the framework of Laban Movement Analysis is built.

The basic elements common to all movements, as elucidated by Laban Movement Analysis, may be categorized under three broad headings: (1) the use of the body; (2) the use of space; and (3) the use of dynamic energy. The differentiation of gestures, postures, and types of initiation provide analytical tools for studying body usage. Attention to the locale or area of space in which the movement occurs, the shape of the trace-form, and the dimensional orientation of the action help us to decipher the use of space. Finally, the perception of the qualitative variations in focus, pressure, time, and flow provide insight into the changing dynamics of human effort.

A thorough description of movement must take each of these factors into account—the use of body, space, and dynamics, as well as the rhythmic sequences in which variations occur over time. Movement is indeed a complex, multifaceted phenomenon whose description and analysis challenge the observer. By offering a terminology for movement description and a framework for movement study, Laban Movement Analysis provides a powerful tool for deciphering the ever-changing and indivisible streaming that is human movement.

Now that you have been introduced to the framework of Laban Movement Analysis, look over your original observation journal entries, based on the movement events viewed in Chapter 8. You can gain insight into your personal observation style by reflecting on the following questions:

1. To what extent do I observe the elements of body usage, space, or effort? Are there any movement parameters that I tend to overlook? What are they?
2. Do I tend to describe actions sequentially, in the order in which they occurred? Or do I capture high points and significant actions, but not in sequence?
3. Is it important to me to describe the setting and context of action? Or do I focus on the movement behavior alone?
4. Do I tend to stick to a concrete description of movement actions? Or do I operate at higher levels of abstraction, capturing the mover's feelings or thoughts, discussing social roles, or describing what occurred poetically or metaphorically?

These reflections pave the way for developing your personal observation skills. The next chapter provides further practical guidance.

10 Observation in practice
Process and structure

I was once given advice by an old man. "You must learn to look at the world twice" he told me as I sat on the floor of his immaculately swept adobe room. "First you must bring your eyes together in front so you can see each droplet of rain on the grass, so you can see the smoke rising from an anthill in the sunshine. *Nothing* should escape your notice. But you must learn to look again, with your eyes at the very edge of what is visible. Now you must see dimly if you wish to see things that are dim—visions, mist, and cloud-people . . . animals which hurry past you in the dark. You must learn to look at the world twice if you wish to see all that there is to see."

Jamake Highwater

In the preceding chapter the framework of Laban Movement Analysis was introduced. This comprehensive analytical system makes it possible to examine body part usage, spatial design, and movement dynamics in fine detail. Indeed, *nothing* will escape the notice of a well-trained movement analyst, as will be demonstrated in Chapter 11, "As Experts See It."

On the other hand, pinpointing its parts is not the only way to look at a movement event. As the old man advised in the story above, there is a second way of looking at things, a less sharply focused and more global mode of perception. Indeed, if one wants to see not only all the different parts of an action, but also the elusive motion as a whole, one must learn to look at the world twice.

Michael Polanyi, a physical chemist and also a social scientist, has dealt with this double vision of the world in his concept of subsidiary vs. focal awareness. He points out that both modes of perceiving are involved in, for instance, using any tool. If we are driving a nail with a hammer, we pay attention to both the nail and the hammer, but in a different manner.

We *watch* the effect of our strokes on the nail and try to wield the hammer so as to hit the nail most effectively. When we bring down the hammer we do not feel that its handle has struck our palm but that its head has struck the nail. Yet, in a sense we are certainly alert to the feelings in our palm and the fingers that hold the hammer. They guide us in handling it effectively, and the degree of attention that we give to the nail is given to the same extent but in a different way to these feelings . . . They are not watched in themselves; we watch something else while keeping intensely aware of them. I have a *subsidiary awareness* of the feeling in the palm of my hand which is merged into my *focal awareness* of my driving the nail.

(Polanyi 1962: 55)

In the skillful performance of any task, our focal awareness operates "with a clear view to the comprehensive activity in which we are primarily inter-ested," while we remain subsidiarily aware of the details of the performance; consequently, "subsidiary awareness and focal awareness are mutually exclusive" (ibid: 56). Switching our focal attention to details of which we had previously been only subsidiarily aware nearly always leads to confusion. For example, in competitive sports the phenomenon of "choking" under pressure may be caused by a shift in awareness. With highly practiced skills, focusing on movement rather than the goal of the action as a whole appears to impair performance (Yarrow, Brown and Krakauer 2009).

An altered relationship of focal and subsidiary awareness can negatively affect not only our performance but also our ability to see meaningful wholes. For example, if we listen too keenly to the individual notes and chords of a musical composition, we may fail to hear its melody. The notes of a tune, the colors and shapes of a painting, and the body, space, and dynamic elements of a movement event must be perceived as subsidiary to the whole if they are to make sense. As Polanyi opines, "all particulars become meaningless if one loses sight of the pattern which they jointly constitute" (1962: 57).

This twofold vision of focal and subsidiary awareness has an impact on our observation skills and our ability to use movement analysis meaning-fully. There is a technique to observing and one can learn *how to* do it better. Yet this craft must be subsidiary to a larger purpose, to *why* one is looking carefully at a given event. Similarly, while various elements of motion can be delineated through analysis, these parts must remain subsidiary to the whole movement event if the analysis is to prove meaningful. "Thus an alternation of analysis and integration leads progressively to an ever deeper understanding of a comprehensive entity" (Polanyi 1969: 125).

In this chapter we will look twice at the act of observing movement. First we will consider four *process* principles that can be applied to enhance observational skill. Then we will consider how to *structure* an observation so that one obtains meaningful results. In both instances we will bear in mind the roles of subsidiary and focal awareness in helping us explore the world beyond words.

Observation as process

The act of movement observation and analysis can be seen as a process consisting of four phases: (1) relaxation; (2) attunement; (3) point of concentration; and (4) recuperation. First the observer must get in a relaxed and receptive mood, then tune up his or her kinesthetic sensibilities for the concentrated effort of analysis that follows. Finally, recuperations are necessary to keep the observer fresh and alert. Each of these phases provides a vital link in the process of observation. While there are many ways to go about each phase, omitting any one tends to make the act of watching movement more difficult and tiring. Let us see how each part of the process facilitates movement perception.

Relaxation

The initial preparatory stage involves *relaxation* as the observer strives to "get in the mood" for whatever will come. This takes the form of letting go in order to achieve a state of mind analagous to the "unfocused focus" of the naturalist. As Wilson describes,

> The naturalist is a civilized hunter. He goes alone into a field or woodland and closes his mind to everything but that time and place, so that life around him presses in on all the senses and small details grow in significance. He begins the scanning search . . . His mind becomes unfocused . . . no longer directed toward any ordinary task or social pleasantry.
>
> (1986: 103)

This unfocused state of receptiveness is also conducive to the observation of movement.

All too often, unfortunately, we see the opposite approach in observers (especially over-eager beginners) who prepare to look at movement by getting "all keyed up." These viewers poise in their chairs tensely, heads jutting forward, eyes bulging out in excited alertness. Body and mind assume an attitude of taut eagerness. Not the smallest twitch shall escape their notice! And then the movement event begins to unfold and, horrors, they find they cannot see anything! This state of tense over-readiness actually interrupts the process of observing.

A more fruitful preparation induces relaxation. There are some simple things an observer can do to get ready to observe. To begin with, one should make oneself as physically comfortable as possible by assuming a calm yet alert position with an unobstructed view. Try not to sit in such a way that you have to huddle, strain, or twist to see. While making yourself physically comfortable, allow yourself to unwind mentally as well. Set aside current concerns or preoccupations. If possible, let your mind go blank for a few moments, worrying about neither the observation task ahead nor the everyday duties that await you. If this process is difficult, you can try doing a structured exercise to relax. *Seeing without Words (Exercise 4)* from the Chapter 3 videotape is one such exercise designed to facilitate relaxation. Any number of other approaches are also helpful, such as yawning and stretching, taking some deep breaths, tensing and relaxing various parts of the body, closing your eyes and listening to sounds in the environment, or visualizing a pleasant scene in the mind's eye.

The key to achieving and maintaining a state of relaxed attentiveness while observing may be summarized in two words: moderation and monitoring. Relaxation is not an end in itself. Some people have developed such elaborate relaxation rituals that they put themselves in a trance and, by overdoing it, never get around actually to observing movement! Relaxation is a preparatory state only. Do whatever is necessary to make yourself physically comfortable and to clear your mind, and then proceed to the subsequent phases. Relaxation in moderation is the key to a functional observation process.

Second, remember that it is possible to become tense at any point during an observation process. If you are becoming physically uncomfortable or terribly sleepy, if you have trouble concentrating, or if you begin to feel panicky because the observation is not going smoothly, take a moment to breathe. Movement occurs in recurrent patterns and it is most likely that whatever you feel you are dozing through, missing, or overlooking will be repeated. The key is to get yourself into a receptive organismic state and to stay there. Monitoring how you are feeling throughout the observation process is essential to keep the windows of movement perception open and clear.

Attunement

A second phase in the observation process is *attunement*. Attuning is analogous to focusing an old-fashioned manual camera. When one looks at a scene through the lens, one sees the general configuration, but the picture is often blurred. As the photographer adjusts the camera, the scene comes into sharper focus, objects becoming clearer, and one is able to make choices about what is the most interesting angle and meaningful composition for the shot. Attunement serves much the same function in movement observation. One senses the general configuration of the movement and is able to bring the elements into focus, prior to making decisions about which features are most important. Attunement provides a transition from relaxed attentiveness to the honed analytical phase of intense concentration to come.

As discussed in Module A, movement perception involves multiple senses, drawing mostly upon vision, hearing, and kinesthesis. Each of these sense modalities is available to us as a means of attuning with movement. Many different attunement exercises were demonstrated on the videotape of Chapter 3. For example, *Mirroring (Exercise 1)*, or imitating the movement as it occurs, enhances the viewer's kinesthetic awareness and identification with the changing movement process. Simply saying *Watch, Watch* (*Exercise 2*) whenever a movement occurs helps the observer to pick up the rhythmic structure of the movement event. Attempting to *Echo* (*Exercise 3*) the dynamics of an action through one's tone of voice allows the viewer to identify with the dynamic qualities inherent in a given movement sequence. *Doodling* (*Exercise 5*) what one sees also provides a means of attuning with the changing shapes, rhythms, and energies of the actions under observation.

Attunement is to detailed movement analysis what a rough draft is to a finished chapter. Attuning allows one to sense the movement process in a sketchy and general way without feeling pressured to describe these perceptions in detail. We have all been observing movement since we were born. Nevertheless, when we are *asked* to observe, the process often strikes us as novel and difficult. Attuning allows us to use our senses of sight, hearing, and kinesthesis to establish contact with what we perceive, thus warming us up for more demanding tasks to come.

Point of concentration

In a previous chapter we noted that movement is comprised of multiple, on-going changes in the use of body, space, and dynamics. When we try to pin down what we see, as we do when analyzing movement with the Laban system, the multifaceted nature of the movement can prove to be mind-boggling. For this reason, it is often very useful to choose a single *point of concentration* and to study that element of movement only. Such concentration sorts the complex movement experience into simpler and more familiar units and keeps the observer from being overwhelmed. For this reason, it is one of the most useful techniques available to us as observers.

The majority of the exercises on the videotape for Chapter 5 utilized the point of concentration technique. *Silly Walks* (*Exercise 3*) asked the observer to focus on how each of the three performers used different parts of their bodies. *Moving Sculpture* (*Exercise 4*) used spatial orientations as the point of focus, while *Dynamics* (*Exercise 5*) emphasized the use of effort qualities. Points of concentration serve to clarify and sharpen the observer's impression of a movement event by revealing more details and subtle inter-relationships of elements. By shifting one's point of focus from body usage to, for instance, spatial design, then onto effort dynamics, a complex and multifaceted picture of a movement event may be gradually built up. This was the technique demonstrated in the exercise called *Instant Replay* (*Exercise 7*) in Chapter 5.

While point of concentration has the aim of focusing attention on a single aspect of movement behavior, it also has the paradoxical effect of allowing attention to wander. This relates back to Polanyi's concept of subsidiary awareness. While the observer is concentrating on delineating, say, body part usage, other aspects of the movement event are glimpsed subsidiarily. One sees not only that the hand initiates the action, but also that it traces an arc-like vertical spatial pattern. Sometimes, in fact, these subsidiary perceptions become so outstanding that the observer forgets to attend to the original point of focus and concentrates on another aspect of movement altogether. While one may seem to be straying from the point, this is not actually a problem, since the element of concentration is still working in the way it was intended—it is helping the observer to take apart and make sense of the mind-boggling complexity of movement behavior.

The aim of this third phase in the observation process is to penetrate the movement event, teasing out the separate elements that comprise it, bringing details into sharp relief, and, in general, elucidating the action through analysis. Two additional techniques, each demonstrated on the videotape for Chapter 5, are also of use in this process. The first involves "embodiment." One can *Learn a Phrase* (*Exercise 1*) so thoroughly as to be able to teach it to somebody else. Accurate imitation requires detailed observation and penetrating analysis of all aspects of the movement event in question. Moreover, the experience of embodying what one sees provides information about the movement "from the inside." Watching the movement sequences and comparing them, as in the *Two Entrances* (*Exercise 2*) of Chapter 5, also facilitates close study of a given movement, and serves to elucidate elements of each action through comparative description.

Recuperation

As might be expected, the intense concentration needed for the third phase of the observation process can be quite draining. As a consequence, the observer must build phases of *recuperation* in, if he or she wishes to keep the powers of perception fresh and acute. Recuperation is used here to signify an active and positive recharging of energy. This recharging can be brought about by simply changing what one is doing or how one is doing it. For example, it is possible to stare so fixedly while observing that you virtually hypnotize yourself. One way to prevent this from occurring is to make a practice of periodically looking away from the scene you are observing.

Glance down at your notes, look around the room, peer out the window. Even a momentary variation in focal length refreshes the eyes and restores the observer. Monitoring one's state of tension and making ongoing adjustments to remain relaxed will also serve the function of recuperation. More obvious changes in the nature of the activity will be found to be refreshing as well. For instance, taking time to jot down your impressions and to discuss your observations with others can serve as a recovery from the concentrated solo effort of analyzing movement.

Returning to earlier phases of the observation process can also be recuperative. We have already noted that the constant monitoring and prevention of tension is restorative. In addition, many techniques of attunement can be used to relax and refresh the movement analyst. Let us say, for example,

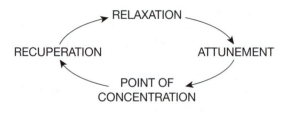

Figure 10.1 Phases of the observation process.

that one is struggling to discriminate postures from gestures. After a period of sustained concentration, one begins to doubt his or her judgment. And the harder one tries, the more the postures and gestures begin to look alike. Phasing back to an attunement exercise, such as *Watch, Watch* (*Exercise 2*, Chapter 3), can relieve the observer from feeling pressured to identify every little movement accurately, an impossible task in any case. After taking a breather by attuning, the person typically finds that postures and gestures, or whatever else one wants to sort out, have become distinct again. When recuperation serves its purpose, it reinvigorates the observer to continue the study of human movement with renewed energy.

Structuring observation for results

At the heart of any observation process is the question, "Why?" Why are we observing? What do we wish to learn? What is our purpose in studying a given movement event? Obviously, there are many possible answers to the question of "Why?" We might be observing someone's movement just because we are idly curious about the person. Perhaps we are watching the person move for more diagnostic reasons, for instance, to help a friend improve his or her tennis serve. Or we may be auditioning someone for a part in a play, or selecting someone for a job. If the movement event is a basketball game or a dance concert, we may be observing just for fun. Then again, we might be harnessing movement observation in a research project, for example, studying student–teacher interactions in the classroom, comparing American and South African styles of hip-hop dance, or observing plaintiff behavior in family court.

Having a clear purpose is the first step toward attaining meaningful results. We must know why we are looking in order to get started at all. However, there are five other elements that also play a role in structuring an observation: (1) the role of the observer; (2) the duration of the observation; (3) the selection of movement parameters for observation; (4) the mode of recording impressions; and (5) the process of making sense and drawing conclusions. In the sections that follow we will discuss each of these elements and how it affects observation.

The role of the observer

The changing nature of our roles as onlookers affects the observation process. In viewing movement, as perhaps in all life, we alternate between two roles—we are either spectators, observing the action from the sidelines without being directly involved, or participants who are called upon to observe while acting and interacting. Obviously, the qualitative nature of observation is very different when we are active participants rather than sideline spectators.

Generally speaking, when we think about being observers, we typically think of ourselves in the role of spectator rather than in that of participant. Given the fact that movement occurs in virtually all human activities, however, the participant observer role is quite common. Nevertheless, there are many occasions when we are merely spectators. Watching television, going to a movie, attending a sporting event, seeing a performance, even observing strangers in public places—all these are primarily non-intervening observation situations. Watching the online videotapes that accompany this text also emphasizes spectator-like observing.

From a process point of view, there are advantages to being a non-intervening observer. Here, one is at leisure to concentrate exclusively on the movement and to reflect upon the composition and meaning of a given event, progressing through the relaxation, attunement, concentration, and recuperation phases in an unhurried fashion. Movement can be viewed with some degree of detachment and objectivity. The spectator may indeed see deeply into a physical activity, yielding an impression that is elaborate and detailed. Consequently, it is very useful to practice movement observation and analysis in situations where one is free to be a spectator, especially in the beginning stages of learning to analyze movement.

On the other hand, in participatory observation situations, such as teaching, coaching, counseling, supervising, or simply conversing, movement awareness must compete for our attention with a dazzling onslaught of other situational stimuli. Self-presentation, other people's reactions, what to say next, how much time is passing, and myriad other concerns distract our attention from a single-minded concentration on the nonverbal dimensions of the experience. As a consequence, observations of movement behavior made by the actual participants in the event itself may be less elaborate and detailed than the leisurely impressions cultivated by a spectator. Participant observers tend to see only as much as they need to see in order to be able to act or react. On the other hand, participant observing is multisensory. By entraining with others in the ongoing stream of interaction, the observer can get a "feel" for what is transpiring nonverbally. Through personal involvement, the subjective dimension is richer for the participant observer than for the spectator.

Participatory observation presents a challenge from a process point of view. Here, the participant must perceive movement behavior, interpret it, and properly intervene in the on-going movement event, which is in flux. Obviously, the process and content of observation must be kept relatively simple if the flow of activity is to proceed at a natural pace. Needless to say, the same observation principles apply—one must remain relaxed and perceptive; one must kinesthetically attune to the movers with whom one is interacting; one must, from time to time, apply concentrated attention to detail to clarify nonverbal impressions; and one must somehow establish a recuperative rhythm to keep going. When a person is a participant observer, maintaining focal awareness of movement is more difficult to manage. However, the rewards are worth the effort. When one can observe movement deeply *while being absorbed in everyday activities*, reality "affirms itself dynamically" (Bergson 1946: 157). Interactions become richer, revealing another dimension of aliveness.

Duration of observation

The length of time spent in observing also has an influence on the kind of results one will obtain. As you recall, in Chapter 2 we discussed the two metaphors for time, noting that it may be thought of as a line with a discrete beginning and end, or as a circle that is continuous. When time is thought to be linear, sequences of events are seen to have clear beginnings and endings and to be historically unique. Linear time keeps moving on; it never doubles back on itself. In contrast, when time is thought of as a circle, sequences of events are seen to be cyclical, for time turns back on itself, repeating endlessly.

Movement, like time, can be thought of as linear progression of unique acts or as a cyclical pattern of repeated actions. In fact, human movement behavior reveals *both* these attributes, and the duration of the span of observation that influences that attribute will be revealed, as shown in Table 10.1. For example, a very brief observation of several minutes' duration usually leaves the observer with an impression of a unique linear sequence of individual acts. However, if one observes an activity for a more extended period of time, several hours for instance, movements will be seen to repeat themselves in a cyclical fashion. If one can observe an activity over a much longer time span, sampling the behavior over a number of years, one may see a progression of changing and developing movement patterns. At this durational level, movement begins to reveal a linear aspect again, although the action units are conglomerate patterns rather than single acts. Hypothetically, if one could survey movement events over decades or centuries, a historical cycle of patterns might be discerned.

The point is this: the characteristics of movement behavior that are revealed are a function of the duration of the observation. Observing briefly (Level 1) allows one to capture a unique sequence of acts in a given context. First impressions and snap judgments are usually based on what is perceived in the blink of an eye. Such judgments can be accurate, especially

Table 10.1 Duration of observational span and revealed attributes

Duration of span of observation		Revealed attributes of movement behavior
Level 1:	*Brief* Say, several minutes	A unique linear progression of individual acts
Level 2:	*Extended* E.g., several hours and days	A cyclical pattern of repeated actions
Level 3:	*Longitudinal* Sampling over several years	A unique linear progression of changing action-patterns
Level 4:	*Historical* Survey of decades/centuries	Presumably, a recurring cycle of repeated patterns

in the case of experienced observers (Gladwell 2005). At an audition, for example, dancers learn and perform a movement sequence that is only a minute or two long. Yet the choreographer can cast the piece on the basis of this brief duration.

To capture a characteristic pattern of behavior, however, a brief observation is not sufficient. It is only when movement is observed for a more extended period of time that a cyclical pattern of repeated actions becomes apparent. Consequently, observations of the second durational span (Level 2) are employed when the purpose of the observation is to establish characteristic features of movement style, as this applies to an individual, a dance form, or even culturally inscribed behaviors (M. Davis 1975).

Longitudinal sampling (Level 3) suggests itself as being the appropriate observational duration if one is interested in how movement patterns and traits change and develop over time. For example, sequential changes in movement patterns are evident as babies mature. While a general developmental sequence has been discerned, each child modifies this sequence to some extent, based upon his or her own movement characteristics (Hartley 1995; Amighi et al. 1999). Observational sampling over several years is necessary to discern the unique linear progression of changing action patterns.

Lengthy temporal spans (Level 4) are appropriate for historical study of movement patterns and styles. Admittedly, there is a dearth of material available for direct observation, since, prior to the twentieth century, movement artifacts are fragmentary at best. However, twentieth-century chronicles do reflect cyclical patterns of change, such as the cycle described in McDonaugh's *The Rise and Fall and Rise of Modern Dance* (1970).

It is clear that as we move from Level 1 to Level 4 in the duration of the span of observation, there is a corresponding shift from specific and unique behaviors to the more general and enduring patterns. In structuring an observation, therefore, it is important to exercise control over the length of time spent observing if one is to answer appropriately the question chosen. If, for instance, we want to improve a friend's tennis service, a brief observation of a few moments' length may suffice. If, on the other hand, we wish to delineate his or her style of play, we may need to watch several matches, observing over hours. If we wish to track the development of a tennis champion throughout his or her career, we will need to do longitudinal sampling. Finally, if we are interested in the historical evolution of tennis, we will need to survey decades or centuries, working from artifactual-archival materials as well as observable movement events.

Selection of movement parameters

Another aspect of structuring an observation has to do with selecting the movement parameters that will be studied. Any movement event involves activation and interplay of body parts, use of dynamic energies, and change in spatial placement. Additional factors addressing how the body shapes itself in space, as well as the types of relationships among movers may also be delineated, as shown in the expanded taxonomy of human movement (Table 10.2). Individual and group movements can be quite complicated, and analytical systems based upon Laban's work reflect this complexity.

While a thorough analysis of a movement event would give equal weighting to body, space, effort, and other elements, in reality not every parameter will be equally salient in solving a given problem. Researchers who have utilized movement observation and analysis have tended to concentrate on certain movement elements that seemed focal to their areas of inquiry, while excluding others as being only of subsidiary relevance. Examples can be found among the Laban-based studies described in Chapter 7. For instance, the Movement Pattern Analysis profile used to identify managerial decision-making styles focuses on dynamic and spatial components of movement rather than detailed analysis of body part usage (Moore 2005). In contrast, the Choreometric analysis of dance style concentrated on the use of the body and space, while a detailed description of dynamics proved to be less salient for detecting cross-cultural variations in dance style (Bartenieff with Lewis 1980). Clearly, it is not necessary to analyze every element of a movement event to derive meaningful interpretations.

In a seminal examination, M. Davis reviewed diverse social science studies of nonverbal behavior and found "consistent relationships between the character of movement patterns and what they were associated with" (1975: 96). Using the prism of Laban Movement Analysis, she noted that body and effort parameters were highlighted in psychological studies of intra-psychic processes, while space and relationship parameters were the focus of sociological and anthropological studies of interpersonal processes. There were areas of overlap in research foci and the movement parameters chosen for analysis. As Davis noted at the time, her study should be considered a

Table 10.2 Expanded taxonomy of human movement

I   *Body*

   A   Body attitude
   B   Body actions (locomotion, turning, jumping, gesturing, pausing, etc.)
   C   Use of center of weight
   D   Body part actions (flexion, extension, rotation, tilting, shifting, etc.)
   E   Body part relationships (posture, gesture, posture–gesture merger, etc.)
   F   Relationships of limbs (support, gesture, bilateral, unilateral, upper, lower, etc.)
   G   Body shapes (ball, pin, wall, screw)
   H   Use of trunk (one unit, differentiated, etc.)
   I   Body usage (most active parts, isolations, part leading, included, held, etc.)
   J   Body part phrasing (simultaneous, successive, blending, etc.)

II   *Effort*

   A   Tension flow attributes (even, fluctuating, high intensity, abrupt, gradual, etc.)
   B   Pre-efforts (gentle, vehement, flexible, etc.)
   C   Effort elements (flow, weight space, time)
   D   Effort qualities (bound, free, etc.)
   E   Effort combinations (states, drives, full efforts)
   F   Effort phrasing types (explosive, emphatic, even, etc.)
   G   Rhythm (metric, non-metric, breath, etc.)
   H   Tempo (slow, moderate, etc.)

III   *Space*

   A   Level (low, high, etc.)
   B   Direction (dimensions, diameters, diagonals, peripherals, transversals, etc.)
   C   Spatial path (straight, curved, angular, spiral, etc.)
   D   Reach space (near, middle, far)
   E   Approach to kinesphere (central, peripheral, transverse)
   F   Dimensionality (one, two, three dimensions)
   G   Specific forms (octahedral, cubic, icosahedral, etc.)
   H   Use of general space (in place, small, large, varied levels, etc.)
   I   Orientation (above, below, in front, to side, etc.)

IV   *Shape*

   A   Symmetry/asymmetry
   B   Monolinear, polylinear, chordic
   C   Modes of shape change (shape flow, directional movement, carving, etc.)
   D   Shape qualities (spreading, enclosing, rising, etc.)
   E   Shape flow design

V   *Relationship*

   A   Groupings (single file, line, circle, etc.)
   B   Contact (touching, grasping, supporting, etc.)
   C   Relationship play (with, sharing, against)
   D   Facing (eye contact, relating to, etc.)
   E   Orientation (vis-à-vis, alongside, above, etc.)
   F   Kinespheric relation (near to, far apart, etc.)
   G   Leading/following/contrasting
   H   Mirroring
   I   Echoing
   J   Synchrony/asynchrony

---

work-in-progress and the associations viewed as tentative. Consequently, "one could make an argument for a very open-ended approach to movement research" when selecting movement parameters for study (M. Davis: 107).

Three decades later, the systematic use of movement analysis as a tool for studying individual and group behavior continues to be refined (Tortora 2006; Van Zile 2006). Nevertheless, identification of relevant parameters remains challenging. Since it is difficult to predict what will be salient for a particular problem, the following course of action suggests itself. Begin with some open-ended observing, allowing oneself to respond to the event metaphorically or poetically. Then, in a more analytical frame, try out various points of concentration, focusing in turn on body, space, and dynamic parameters. Some of these parameters will seem to leap out while others will remain elusive and hard to see. Reflect on what leaps out. If these elements seem to support your initial metaphoric or poetic impression, then you are on your way to selecting parameters to observe. As you continue to study the movement event using these selected parameters as points of concentration, some will hold up as being relevant to your central purpose in observing, while other elements that initially seemed meaningful will not prove to be so on closer scrutiny. In short, selecting parameters to concentrate on is a trial-and-error matter, and it is only as one progresses through the next two aspects of structure that the overall effectiveness of this selection process can be assessed. As Beveridge summarizes,

> Accurate observation of complex situations is extremely difficult ... Effective observation involves noticing something and giving it significance by relating it to something else noticed or already known; thus it contains both an element of sense-perception and a mental element. It is impossible to observe everything, and so the observer has to give most of his attention to a selected field, but he should at the same time try to watch out for other things, especially anything odd.
>
> (1950: 140–141)

Mode of recording impressions

As the observer progresses through the phases of the observation process, impressions and insights arise that should be recorded. There are a variety of ways to document movements, ranging from verbal notes to pictographic stick figures, from coding sheets to elaborate symbolic notations.

Keeping running notes of one's impressions is an immediately feasible means of documentation, since most of us already possess the necessary language skills for this sort of record keeping. The drawback to this method is that the complexity of movement is troublesome to capture concisely with words. One picture is often worth a thousand words, and moving pictures can be worth a million. Consequently, verbal descriptions of movements may become quite cumbersome.

An alternative to running written notes is the use of some sort of schematized verbal coding sheet, which serves a dual purpose of structuring the movement elements to be observed and of streamlining the amount of required note taking. Such coding sheets may be quite simple and general, as in Example A, or more elaborate, as in Example B. Coding sheets can also be designed to record the occurrence of particular elements, by using check marks or ticks instead of words. Example C illustrates this approach to documentation. [These examples and all following ones can be found at the end of this chapter.]

There are also a variety of means for graphically recording one's movement perceptions. These range from simple iconic representations, like stick figures, to complex symbolic notation systems. In some cases, combinations of verbal phrases, stick-figure drawings, and symbols work admirably well as recording devices, especially if the record is meant to serve mainly as a mnemonic device for the observer (see Example D). There are also simplified versions of symbolic notation systems, such as motif writing in the Laban system (Example E). Simplified notations allow the viewer to capture the most salient aspects of a movement sequence. As with stick-figure notes, simple motif notations will not allow a movement to be recorded in sufficient detail to be exactly reproduced when read back. However, if one only wishes to document a limited number of movement parameters, simplified symbolic notation like motif writing can prove to be quite sufficient.

If, on the other hand, the recording of a movement event needs to be detailed enough to allow it to be exactly reproduced when read back, full notation, using one of the existing symbolic systems, is the logical choice. Labanotation is shown in Example F. In addition to this Laban-based system, the Benesh notation system and the Eshkol-Wachman system have been used widely for movement documentation (Benesh and Benesh 1969; Eshkol and Wachman 1958).

Of course, the drawback to any of these symbolic systems is that the observer must be trained to write and read them. Because the symbology must be elaborate to match the complexity of movement, learning a notation system of this sort can be quite time-consuming. Currently, therefore, documentation via symbolic notation lies mostly in the province of specially-trained observers.

In general, the choice of a recording method depends on the observer's intent. For example, if the observer wishes to convey the results of his or her studies to the general public, verbal description, whether as an initial recording method or a later translation, is the obvious choice. If, on the other hand, one wishes to preserve a great dance work or a vanishing folk dance tradition, symbolic notation would be the best means for documentation, albeit with limited accessibility for anyone but select movement professionals. Coding sheets have been used extensively in movement research and are the best choice when the observer needs to quantify the data for certain analytical purposes. Motif writing and other simplified symbolic systems also show promise for their applicability in studies where the observer only wishes to record a small number of motion variables. Finally, a personalized short-hand of verbal phrases and pictograms works best when one needs to make a quick record for immediate personal use.

Making sense

Either as a spectator or a participant, an observer will have watched a movement event for the length of time judged appropriate for the type of question he or she is trying to answer. In this process, the observer has teased out salient movement parameters and found a suitable way to record them. But the observation process is still incomplete until she or he has made certain interpretations of the movement data in relation to the original question and drawn some kind of conclusion. This final link is necessary if the whole effort is to prove meaningful.

In some cases, making sense may be as simple, for better or worse, as relating what you have seen to your store of body knowledge/body preju-dice. This is probably what we do when we have been watching someone or some event out of idle curiosity or during a casual interaction. That is to say, we simply find the most readily available explanation for what we have witnessed and then go on about our business, having made an informal judgment. On the other hand, we may need to contrast what we have actually seen with what we want to see in order to draw our conclusions. This may be the case when we are using movement observation diagnostic-ally, as in correcting a friend's tennis serve. In our mind's eye we may see a smooth arcing motion as the racket connects powerfully with the ball. But in reality we notice that our friend's arc has a slight wobble at the end because she pulls back slightly at the critical moment of contact. And so our conclusion is that she is losing power in her serve by ever-so-slightly drawing back at the moment when she should be smashing the ball.

In these first examples, it is possible for the process of sense-making to be rather informal and for the interpretive framework used therein to remain implicit. However, in other applications of movement observation, such as job selection, performance evaluation, personality assessment, or social science research, the interpretive framework will need to be made more explicit and the drawing of conclusions more formal. For example, the Movement Pattern Analysis assessment correlates dynamic and spatial elements of an individual's movement style with a three-stage model of decision making in order to draw conclusions about how the person will handle a particular job (Moore 2005). The Kestenberg Movement Profile is another Laban-based movement assessment in which the correlation of action with psychological interpretation is specified clearly (Amighi et al. 1999). In instances like these, the interpretive frameworks are quite explicit and the drawing of conclusions highly formalized.

These various examples suggest the following model of sense-making. At the center of this model, as shown in Figure 10.2, is the set of movement data collected through observation. Now, these data are linked with (1) one's implicit body knowledge/body prejudice; (2) a vision of desired behavior; or (3) an explicit interpretive framework, via the operations of, say, comparing, contrasting, or correlating. The first approach, based upon one's body knowledge/body prejudice, is most likely to be followed when making informal judgments as a spectator or participant observer. The second, which involves contrasting observed behavior with performance criteria of some sort, is most likely to be used when one is teaching, coaching, or critiquing a movement event. Finally, the third approach, wherein a more systematic framework of interpretation is utilized, is most likely to be resorted to when arriving at formal assessments and judgments, or conducting research inquiries.

With this final, sense-making link, we can now complete our design for structuring the observation, as illustrated in Figure 10.3. At the heart of this model is the question, "Why?" or the purpose for observing. Around this center are five other structural elements: (a) the role of the observer; (b) the duration of the observation; (c) the selection of movement parameters; (d) the mode of recording impressions; and (e) the process of making sense. Some elements, such as observer role or duration of the observation, may be dictated by the nature and context of the movement event itself. To the extent possible, however, structural elements should be carefully chosen in relation to the purpose of the observation. Each element influences the process of making

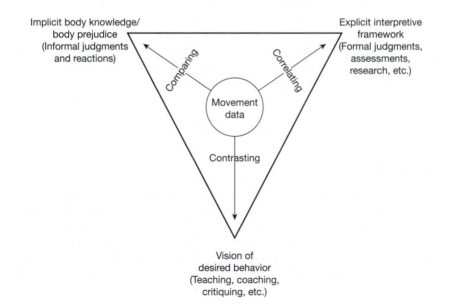

Figure 10.2

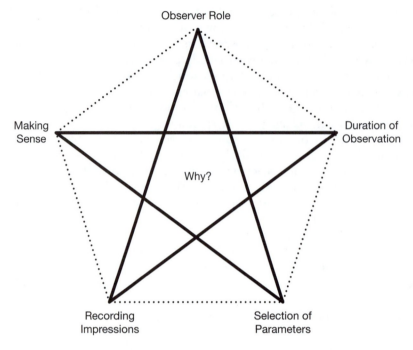

Figure 10.3

sense and elements influence one another. For example, being a spectator or participant observer influences how many movement parameters can be considered and how these parameters can be recorded. The duration of the observation affects what can be perceived about the movement event and the types of inferences that can be drawn. How the movement data are recorded can facilitate interpretation or confound the process of making sense of what has been seen. Decisions made at each point of the star will influence other parts of the structure, the overall effectiveness of the observation process, and the likelihood of obtaining meaningful results.

Recapitulation

Movement observation and analysis may be thought of as a *process* consisting of four phases. The observer prepares by inducing a state of attentive *relaxation*. This is followed by a period of *attunement* in which the observer uses various sense modalities to tune into the rhythms, shapes, and patterns of the movement event. Various *points of concentration* are then brought into play to help the observer discern the body, space, and effort elements of the event in a detailed and analytical way. Finally, periods of *recuperation* must be interspersed throughout the observation process if the movement analyst is to remain fresh and attentive.

It goes without saying that the experience of observation must be understood in relation to the *purpose* of movement study. We analyze movement so that we may better understand the actions of others and of ourselves, and hopefully, behave more humanely to each other as a result of this understanding. Towards these ends, we need to exercise some control over the *structure* of the observation effort if we wish to obtain meaningful results. Five structural elements occupy important positions in relationship to the central purpose that guides the observation. These elements are (a) the role of the observer; (b) the duration of the observation; (c) the selection of movement parameters for observation; (d) the mode of recording impressions; and (e) the process of making sense.

Observers can be detached spectators or lively participants in the movement event being studied. Spectators are obliged to be more objective, but also have the leisure to concentrate on the movement behavior without competition from other concerns. More things compete for the attention of participant observers, but since they are plunged in the ongoing stream of movement behaviors themselves, they can also draw on their subjective bodily impressions. Both roles impact the nature of what can be perceived.

The duration of the observation influences the characteristics of the movement event that can be perceived. An observation of only several minutes is likely to reveal a unique linear progression of individual acts. A more extended observational duration of several hours or days will show a cyclical pattern of repeated actions, whereas a longitudinal sampling over years tends to disclose how movement patterns themselves change and develop over time. Finally, a historical survey of decades and centuries is likely to reveal a cyclical pattern of repeated patterns, although direct observational data have been difficult to obtain at this level.

While thorough analysis of a movement event would focus equally on body, space, effort, and additional parameters, in reality some elements usually prove to be more salient than others. Generally, through trial and error, the movement parameters most relevant for a particular question or line of inquiry may be identified.

How to record one's movement perceptions also becomes a concern. Various means of documenting movement observations are available. Verbal notes and coding sheets, stick figures and do-it-yourself notations, motif writing, and full symbolic notations are among the methods from which the observer may choose, according to the purpose of movement analysis. Examples of these modes of recording follow this recapitulation.

Finally, the work of the observer is not completed until meaningful interpretations are made of the movement data and appropriate conclusions are drawn in relation to the original question. Generally speaking, body knowledge/body prejudice, a vision of the desired behavior, or a formal interpretive framework will be called into play to complete this vital last step—making sense of movement.

Example A **Simple coding sheet**

Movement coding sheet   Date _____

Person under observation   _____

Observer   _____

Place of observation   _____

Most active body parts

Use of energy

E.g. forceful, delicate, quick, leisurely, direct, meandering, easy-going, controlled

Use of space

Direction of gestures (e.g. forward, sideward, upward, etc.)

Reach space (e.g. gesture near to, mid-reach, or far from body core)

Relation to others in group (e.g. near to, facing, side by side, etc.)

Example B Elaborate coding sheet

Dance style analysis

I   **First impression** (make notes after first viewing)

_____

_____

_____

II   **General description**

Number of performers _____

Costumes/props _____

Performance space _____

Accompaniment _____

Dance genre _____

III   **Relationship and group form**

Group form (line, circle, cluster, facing, front to back, side to side, etc.)

_____

_____

_____

Example B Elaborate coding sheet—continued

Use of symmetry and asymmetry in group forms

_____

_____

_____

Use of synchrony in group movement

_____

_____

_____

IV   Use of the body

Types of action (locomotion, jump, turn, level change, gesture, stillness, etc.)

_____

_____

_____

Body part orchestration (most active body parts, parts that are not emphasized, posture, gesture, body attitude, etc.)

_____

_____

_____

Phrasing of bodily action (simultaneous, sequential, etc.)

_____

_____

_____

Use of body contact (touching, grasping, supporting, etc.)

_____

_____

_____

Example B Elaborate coding sheet—continued

Other forms of relating (eye contact, near to, surrounding, etc.)

_____

_____

_____

V   Use of space

Type of path through general space (straight, circular, in place, etc.)

_____

_____

_____

Use of level (low, middle, high, etc.)

_____

_____

_____

Use of kinesphere (near, middle, far reach; zones of kinesphere—in front, behind, to sides, below waist, above waist, etc.)

_____

_____

_____

Approach to kinesphere (central, peripheral, transverse)

_____

_____

_____

Predominant spatial form (octahedral, planar, cubic, etc.)

_____

_____

_____

Example B Elaborate coding sheet—continued

Modes of shape change (shape flow, directional movement, carving, etc.)

_____

_____

_____

VI   Use of effort

Effort mood (predominant effort elements or states that are stressed)

_____

_____

_____

Effort intensity (use of drives)

_____

_____

_____

Phrasing (even, increasing intensity, decreasing intensity, accented, etc.)

_____

_____

_____

VII   Summary: how do movement elements come together to create a coherent "style?"

_____

_____

_____

_____

_____

_____

_____

_____

Example C Numerical coding sheet

Observation Form

Subject: _____   Date: _____   Observer: _____

directing ⌐	indirecting ⌐	increasing pressure ⌐	decreasing pressure ⌐	accelerating ∕	decelerating ∕	2 efforts	3 efforts

| | | | | | | effort flow ∕ | |

enclosing ∕⌐	spreading ⌐	descending ⌐	rising ⌐	retreating ∕∕	advancing ∕∕	2 shapes	3 shapes

| | | | | | | shape flow ∕∕ | |

Observation Form

Subject: ___Jane Person___   Date: ___Summer 2010___   Observer: ___CLM___

directing ⌐	indirecting ⌐	increasing pressure ⌐	decreasing pressure ⌐	accelerating ∕	decelerating ∕	2 efforts	3 efforts
卌卌 卌卌 ⲗ卌 卌卌 卌卌 ‖((28)	卌卌 卌卌 卌卌 ‖) (18)	卌卌 ‖‖ (9)	卌卌 卌卌丅 ((((13)	卌卌 卌卌 卌卌 卌卌 ⲗ卌丅 卌卌 ‖‖ (32)	卌卌 ‖‖ (2)	卌卌 卌卌 ⲗ卌丅 ‖ (16) effort flow ∕ 卌卌 卌卌 ‖ (12)	‖‖‖ (3)

enclosing ∕⌐	spreading ⌐	descending ⌐	rising ⌐	retreating ∕∕	advancing ∕∕	2 shapes	3 shapes
‖)) (4)	‖( ) (3)	卌卌 ‖‖ (7)	∕ (1)	‖‖ (2)	卌卌 卌卌 卌卌 ⲗ卌丅 ‖) (22)	‖‖‖ (3) shape flow ∕∕ 卌卌 ‖ (6)	

Example D Do-it-yourself notation/mnemonic device

Class Warm-up

— heel rock

— ⚬┼⚲   ⚬┼⚲   thigh lift, toe tap into
                    hip extension

— 🧍   condensing ◁ ▷ / leading w/ upper /
     leading w/ lower to ⌐⌐

— leg swing rising ⌐⌐ ⌐⌐ ⌐⌐ 🧍 🧍
  (sink back to
       floor)

— 🧍 sitting arm circles /
     🧍 hip walk ⬛ ⬛ /

     🧍 🧍 🧍 🧍 🧍
     propulsion sequence

Example E Simplified notation—"motif writing"

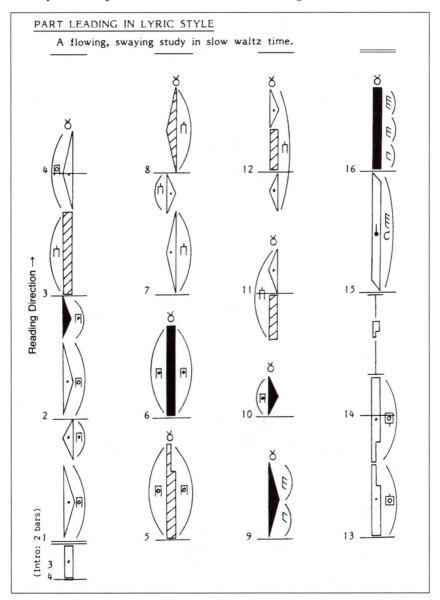

PART LEADING IN LYRIC STYLE

A flowing, swaying study in slow waltz time.

Example F Full Labanotation

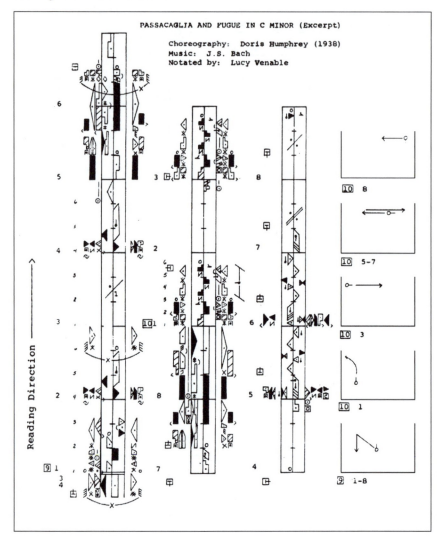

Reprinted by permission of the Dance Notation Bureau

11 Observation in practice

As experts see it

God is in the details.

Ludwig Mies van der Rohe

In Chapter 9, we introduced the basic parameters of human movement, that is, *body*, *space*, and *dynamics*, as delineated by the system of Laban Movement Analysis. In Chapter 10, we discussed practical aspects of movement observation, taking a closer look at the process and structure involved in arriving at meaningful results. In this chapter we will continue to pursue the theme of observation in practice, demonstrating how experts use Laban Movement Analysis to elucidate human movement.

Each of the sections that follow was written by a different movement analyst. Each analyst was asked to study one of the movement episodes you too saw on the video portion of Chapter 8, "Movements in Context." The individuals chosen are all experts in Laban Movement Analysis, who are familiar with the setting and type of movements they were asked to observe. Peggy Berger, who herself practices and teaches Aikido, was chosen to analyze the episode with the martial artist. Warren Lamb, a management consultant, who collaborated with Rudolf Laban himself in the 1940s in the analysis of industrial work movement, was solicited to study the workers in the cabinet-making shop. Pam Schick, a university instructor and choreographer, who has created dances based on the analysis of conversational movement, was asked to examine the university staff meeting. Finally, Sharon True, an experienced teacher of creative dance and movement for children, was selected to study the children's dramatics class.

Following her or his agreement to participate in this project, each analyst was given the same basic instructions: observations were to demonstrate the use of the Laban system for movement description, to show how movement analysis can be used to draw inferences about behavior, and to reflect how such knowledge might be integrated and generalized to enhance understanding of behavior occurring in contexts similar to the ones shown on the Chapter 8 videotape.

Aside from these instructions, each person was free to go about the task of observation according to his or her personal judgment and preferred way of working. Their reports indeed show that a variety of methods of inquiry may be chosen while utilizing the common descriptive language of the Laban system. [Authors' commentary preceding the individual analyses highlights how each observer structured the observation.]

Consequently, this chapter can be used syntactically as well as substantively to improve observation practice. Syntactically, you will be able to see how each of the experts created a structure for observing: how they chose a central question and subsequently managed the observer role, duration of observation, selection of movement parameters, and choice of the mode of impression recording to make sense of their movement data. Substantively, on the other hand, you will be able to study their use of the Laban Movement Analysis terminology and concepts.

As you recall, you were asked to save the notes of your own impressions of each episode on the Chapter 8 videotape. You might like to compare your observations with those of the expert. In this manner, the expert's analysis can be used to establish a standard of practice. By studying and analyzing the tape again by yourself to determine if you can see what the expert saw in each of these movement episodes, you can gain valuable practice in observing and analyzing, using the Laban system.

Now, let us see what the experts have to say . . .

EPISODE 1: MARTIAL ARTS DEMONSTRATION OF AIKIDO

Authors' commentary

The movement episode described here consisted of two parts. First, the Aikidoist performed a series of motions to warm up. This was followed by a number of maneuvers using a wooden sword. Peggy Berger chose to comment on these two aspects of the episode separately, dividing her observations into several sections. She begins with opening remarks on the episode as a whole, followed by an explanation of the purpose and style of Aikido warm-ups. She then describes the martial artist's performance in detail, commenting on each warm-up exercise in the order in which it appears on the tape, following up with remarks on the sword maneuvers. Ms. Berger concludes with an analysis of this particular practitioner's style, noting some areas in which improvement could be made.

The central question ("Why?") that seems to interest Ms. Berger is determining how effective the Aikidoist would be in an actual martial engagement. Because she is working with videotaped material, she is cast mostly in the role of a bystander and, accordingly, her detailed descriptions reveal an elaboration often characteristic of spectator observation. Meanwhile, since Ms. Berger practices Aikido herself, she has a kinesthetic feel for the material she is watching. Being familiar with the functional demands of this martial art, as well as with its underlying philosophy, helps her to put her immediate response into some sort of meaningful context.

The duration of the observation is necessarily brief, only a few moments in length, and reveals a unique linear progression of individual acts. While Ms. Berger offers a summary of the Aikidoist's movement patterns, she does so tentatively. Additional remarks indicate that she feels further study would be necessary to pinpoint his style.

In terms of movement parameters, Ms. Berger is quite thorough in her analysis. Although she does point out that body, space, and dynamics (effort) are not always equally important, she includes the following elements in her analysis:

- *Body*: gesture, posture, initiation, and sequencing;
- *Space*: traceforms and dimensions;
- *Dynamics (effort)*: single qualities, combinations of factors, and sequences of qualities.

Since the results of her observations were to be published in this book, they have been recorded in words. In terms of making sense of her data, Ms. Berger adopts a coaching attitude, comparing the Aikidoist's actual performance with her vision of desired behavior. Here her concern is that his practice of the forms of the martial art be of use in an actual fighting engagement. Her conclusions are that more variation in the dynamic factors of pressure and focus, along with better postural integration of the upper and lower body would make him a more effective defender.

Because of the detailed nature of Ms. Berger's analysis, photos have been placed throughout the section to help the reader identify the exercise to which she is referring. Moreover, we strongly recommend that the reader replays the Aikidoist episode (the first of the Chapter 8 episodes on the website) in conjunction with reading this expert's observations.

Expert's observations

1. Opening remarks

(a) Warm-ups in Aikido are done for many different purposes:

- – to prepare the body for action;
- – to ready or focus the mind;
- – to open up or initiate flow of the energy ("ki").

It would be interesting to know which of these reasons motivated this practitioner.

(b) It would also be interesting to see the difference between his warm-ups and his actual practice, which is most often done with a partner rather than alone.

(c) It would have been helpful if the video had shown the whole body the entire time, since Aikido consists of postural movements, mainly weight shifts, which are used to transfer power.

All of this is to say that the context of performance, as well as that of observation, may (and probably will) change the understanding of the movement being viewed.

2. Aikido warm-ups—purpose and style

The following is a general analysis of the movement parameters in Aikido warm-ups, with some implications about why the movement is done as it is.

Effort

This is mostly dependent on the practitioner. However,

(a) Frequent variations in pressure and flow help the Aikidoist sense his or her body weight and keep "centered."

(b) Often, combinations of two different effort qualities (e.g., variations of time and flow factors) are used as a preparation for an "action drive" exertion, i.e., threefold combinations of pressure, time, and focus factors.

Body

(a) Generally centrally initiated movement.

(b) Generally postural movement.

(c) Weight shifting in the lower body often occurs while arms are gesturing and torso remains vertical. So there is an overlapping of postural movement in the lower with gestural movement in the upper. This gives the impression of much mobility (weight shifting) while maintaining a stable feeling (through the verticality of the torso).

(d) Maintenance of vertically held torso gives a constant central support for the body.

Space

(a) Vertical torso while arms are often moving in other dimensions or planes.

(b) Mostly planar and linear movement in the arms, especially emphasizing the sagittal dimension. In fact, arms are usually in front of the torso. This allows the defender to maintain stability and balance.

(c) Generally the knees are bent, with the feet placed in a wide stance, one foot slightly in front of the other or side by side. Both positions are very stable. The feet leave contact with the ground only for locomotion.

(d) Most movement is in mid-reach space in the kinesphere. Again, this allows practitioners to maintain their verticality and balance so they do not overextend themselves and lose their stability (or the fine balance between stability and mobility).

(e) Though it often seems as though the arms are moving a lot, it is usually the torso that does most of the movement. Arms stay in front of the center of weight (in the pelvic region) while the practitioner steps, pivots, and changes level.

Implications

(a) *Center*: The prevalence of weight shifts and pivoting during which the Aikidoist maintains her or his vertical dimensionality is the physical form of maintaining center (centrally supported, centrally initiated, and centrally aligned). "Center" is the spiritual or philosophical stance of the Aikidoist.

(b) *Mobility and stability*: There is a balance between stability and mobility. The erect torso is important for balance. However, sometimes the upper body tilts off the vertical while the lower body maintains a grounded stability. At other times, while locomoting for instance, the torso is held in the vertical dimension to maintain stability over the fluid mobility of the moving legs. Dynamics also play a role in the balancing of stability and mobility. For example, fluid variations in timing alternate with focused changes in pressure to contrast a flowing mobile state with a weighty stable state. Many other examples of this precarious relationship between mobility and stability are found in Aikido.

3. Analysis of Aikido warm-ups

[I am choosing to observe and note only what stands out as the most important—either when watching Aikido or when understanding this particular Aikidoist. Effort, space, and body use are not always equally important.]

3.1 Arm circles

Space and body

(a) These start out as centrally initiated, gestural movements of the arms in the vertical plane. The lower body is quiet.

(b) When he adds the bending of the knees, the movement becomes a fully postural movement. The knees cause the body to rise and sink in the vertical dimension while the arms continue to inscribe a vertical plane.

Effort

(a) During the gestural movement, the effort phrase begins with a controlled deceleration, changing to a free acceleration with passive heaviness.

(b) When the bending of the knees is added the effort phrase changes:

- the weight factor of passive heaviness changes to a diminished increasing pressure;
- there is less fluctuation between freeing and binding flow;
- deceleration is accentuated.

Figure 11.1 Arm circles.

(c) There seems to be an internal focus with little if any attention paid to external space.

3.2 *Shake*

Effort

Movement is rapidly performed with firm control. Again there is little attention to external space, but the internalized focus is maintained. This gives the impression that the mover is preoccupied with sensing his body weight or that he is in a dream-like state. Perhaps this is what this Aikidoist uses to warm up his internal parts?

Body

Gestural beginning turning into a full postural movement.

3.3 *Rowing exercise*

[There is a difference between the movement when the right foot is forward and when the left foot is forward. Though only the upper body is viewed, the movement from the hips down can be inferred from what is visible and from later exercises.]

(a) Left T-stance
   There is a disconnection between the upper body and the lower body here. Ideally, the weight should be shifted clearly forwards and backwards, while the arms swing congruently in the sagittal plane. In fact, however, the hips seem to be swaying slightly from side to side. This diminishes the strength and power that would occur with a more integrated movement. Because this exercise is about the transfer of power by using the lower body to pull and push, it seems that it is of utmost importance that the upper and lower body be unified.

(b) Right T-stance
   The lower body is more involved, thus making this movement more clearly postural than the above one. The pelvis is more synchronous with the arms. As the pelvis moves forwards and backwards, the arms swing in the sagittal plane. This congruity between the upper body and the lower body allows more power and strength to come through.

3.4 *Rowing exercise with arms in forward triangle*

(a) The same difference between right and left T-stances as in Exercise 3.3.

Figure 11.2 Rowing.

(b) Central initiation both posturally (right T-stance) and gesturally (left T-stance).

(c) Effort:
   – generally a dream-like combination of heaviness and free flow;
   – less attention paid to timing than in Exercise 3.3;
   – little effort made to orient the movement in space; very inwardly focused.

3.5 Rowing exercise in two directions

(a) Basically a sagittal movement with the pivot in the horizontal plane.

(b) Everything else is the same as the prior exercise. The lack of synchrony between upper and lower is more apparent as there is more movement involved. Note how the hands flop passively backwards towards the pelvis at a different moment than the backward weight shift of the pelvis itself. These two motions should occur at the same time.

3.6 Rowing exercise with eight direction changes

The prior three exercises lead up to this exercise. As noted before, these exercises are primarily about transfer of power through a pull/push type of movement with the thrust of the power centered in the pelvis—the weight shifting forward and backward in the sagittal dimension.

In this last exercise in the series, this Aikidoist has lost his sagittal orientation because of the lack of effort to focus while making multiple spatial changes (8 pivots). It seems that the more spatial changes he has added, the more he relies only on flow to carry him from place to place, and the less his upper body and lower body are spatially and dynamically consistent and clear.

Effort

While his hands flop heavily back to his body and past it, they should stop when the movement is done. It would be more effective to start and stop the movement by controlling the flow and focusing the action clearly in space (there might be an attacker there!).

Figure 11.3 Rowing with eight direction changes.

Body

His arms and lower body are not congruent. The arms are not in front of his body, i.e., he does not face his arms. Usually in Aikido, the arms are more or less in front of the center of the body, and in any type of rowing exercise this is necessary in order to transfer power. In this case, the arms are doing more movement than the lower body and going different places in space.

Space

Often at the end of a throw in Aikido, a peripheral counter-tension is used to keep the attacker at a distance. This Aikidoist pays no attention to space, and this affects the efficiency of the movement. There needs to be a counter-tension between the pelvis and the hands as the arms swing forwards and upwards. If this movement were done as a response to an attack, the defender would need to be more attentive to space, to get rid of the passive heaviness in hands, and to create a clear peripheral countertension to keep the attacker at a distance. [Clearly, the context of the movement is important. Simply as an exercise teaching one to move by pivoting to eight different directions, perhaps flowing and revolving around the vertical axis would be enough. However, for effective martial use (or partner practice), clarity of the sagittal pathways, activation of increasing pressure, the coordination of the upper and lower body, and a direct focus to aim the movements are crucial.]

3.7 Two step (with turn)

Space

While stepping and turning, the arms trace a horizontal arc, emphasizing widening and narrowing.

Body

Slight gesture into a full postural movement.

Effort

Decreasing pressure.

3.8 *Sword block*

Body and Space

(a) A gesture of the arms into the horizontal dimension is followed by a postural step and turn to sink along a diameter of the vertical plane.

(b) Widening is what is common to both parts of this action.

Figure 11.4 Sword block.

3.9 *Block*

Body and Space

(a) A postural advancing movement prepares for the next action.

(b) The mover steps back, posturally retreating while the arms trace a volume, ending in front of the body to block a blow.

Effort

As in previous exercises, the effort combination used at the end of the phrase results in a momentum that allows the arms to flow at the sides rather than be held in space. This effort would never work as a block against a forceful punch, for example.

3.10 Tenkan (turning move)

Space

Emphasis on the sagittal dimension, with a step forward, a pivot, and a step backwards.

Body

The most interesting thing to note is that alternating hands create a held focal point in front of the body, as the mover performs postural half turns around the extended arm.

Effort

What is interesting is the absence of variations in timing, the occasional presence of indirecting and, most importantly, the emphasis on flow fluctuations. What results is an impression of the mover's remoteness, in spite of the seeming spatial focal point established through the use of the body.

4. Sword maneuvers

General comments

(a) There is more use of the efforts of directing/indirecting and fully crystal-lized increasing pressure than in any of the warm-up exercises.

(b) There is much more binding of flow at the end of phrases, stopping the sword and controlling its weight and momentum.

(c) Spatial patterning and orientation is clearer when mover uses the sword.

(d) Aikidoist shows a tendency toward sinking and narrowing at the end of phrases.

Further observations

The last sequence in which the Aikidoist turns to face different directions is reminiscent of the prior 8-direction rowing exercise. It is interesting to note, though, how different the effort configurations and use of space and body are between the two exercises. With the sword in his hand, this Aikidoist is much clearer in his spatial orientations. The sword cuts arcs in the sagittal plane, thrusts forward, or outlines a three-dimensional trace-form with definite attentiveness to external space. Moreover, his arms are more congruent with his lower body, thus making these clearly powerful postural movements.

Figure 11.5 Sword maneuvers.

The efforts crystallize into dynamic, two- and three-element combinations. At the end of the phrases, bound flow is used to control precisely where the sword stroke ends. The mover activates his own weight to lift and control the weight of the wooden sword. Therefore, active increasing pressure replaces passive heaviness. And because aim is important in the effective use of a weapon, there is more attention to focusing his motions, with the effort of directing often being used to pinpoint the sword's destination. Preparation for slashes and thrusts with the sword are accomplished through mobile combinations of variations in flow and time. The slash itself is a punching action comprised of increasing pressure, directing, and accelerating. The linear forward thrust is a pressing action comprised of increasing pressure, directing and decelerating.

It is quite interesting to note how differently the Aikidoist moves simply because a weapon has been added. We can safely assume, then, that the context of an action, and the props that are used, often affect performance profoundly.

5. Summary of movement patterns

Body

(a) Keeps relatively vertical with a tendency towards sinking and narrowing or immobilizing the chest.

(b) Tendency towards disconnection between upper and lower in body use, creating "floppy" hands and lack of spatial clarity. This might create a weak base of support for any power moves in an actual martial encounter or partner practice.

Effort

(a) Tendency towards free flow and heaviness, especially in arms and hands. This continues in all the free hand warm-up exercises, with a noted absence of fully crystallized combinations of pressure, focus, and timing variations.

(b) Very little attention paid to external space, with little effort to direct or indirect his focus. This gives the feel of a very internalized awareness, of sensing how the inside of the body is working. In defensive situations, this attitude would make the martial moves ineffective.

(c) When the sword is introduced, the efforts crystallize into full action-oriented configurations, combining pressure, focus, and timing variations. Bound flow is also brought into play to control the weight and momentum of the sword. This sword work makes me think that this practitioner is relatively advanced because there is a clarity of effort, space, and body that makes the movements crisp, powerful, and credible.

Space

(a) Clearer use of space in right T-stance than left T-stance warm-up rowing exercise.

(b) Clearer use of space in sword practice.

(c) Much of the spatial use emphasizes the sagittal dimension.

6. Recommendations

In working with this practitioner of Aikido, I would encourage a more active use of pressure variations and a more congruent mobilization and integrated usage of the upper and lower body. I would also suggest that he become more attentive to external space, utilizing the directing and indirecting of focus to make the martial maneuvers more effective and full of "ki" (energy).

EPISODE 2: TWO WORKERS IN A CABINET-MAKING SHOP

Authors' commentary

The movement episode described here consisted of two parts. First, one worker sprays adhesive onto some plastic trim, then fixes the trim to the edge of a counter-top, and finally cuts away the excess trim with a power tool. In the second part of the episode, a different worker performs these same three operations. Warren Lamb concentrated his observations of this episode in four parts: a general description of each worker's movements, a comparison of their gestures and postures, an assessment of each worker's skill relative to the task, and finally a brief discussion of the implications of their individual movement patterns.

In the opening of his description of the two workers, Mr. Lamb outlines three possible approaches to studying this event and makes it clear what his approach will be. The central question he pursues deals with job selection: what movement qualities are needed for this job and which worker seems to possess these qualities and to be the better suited for the task?

Under the particular circumstances, Mr. Lamb was a spectator observer, able to play and replay the videotape at leisure, and his findings are quite detailed. Although the duration of the event is brief, representing a unique linear progression of individual acts, Mr. Lamb uses his observational data to generalize, positing overall behavioral tendencies of each worker.

Mr. Lamb is relatively selective in the number of movement parameters he analyzes, emphasizing single effort factors, spatial dimensions, and the relationship of posture and gesture. Again, for the purposes of this book, he has recorded his observations verbally.

Finally, at the sense-making stage, Mr. Lamb adopts a more formally diagnostic stance, correlating his movement data with an interpretive framework for decision-making. In the Movement Pattern Analysis scheme, which Mr. Lamb himself developed, the dynamic factors (of focus, pressure, and time) and the spatial shaping (in the horizontal, vertical, and sagittal planes) represent problem-solving motivations that affect how a job is done. The basic interpretive framework is shown in Table 11–1.

Although the sample of movement behavior for these workers is too brief for a thorough assessment, Mr. Lamb is able, by analyzing where movement variation is present in posture, to delineate behavioral tendencies

Table 11.1 Movement Pattern Analysis: basic interpretive framework

Element of movement	Variation in movement	Preponderant orientation of action
Effort		
Focus	Indirecting ⟷ Directing	Precise investigation of problem/task
Pressure	Decreasing ⟷ Increasing	Persistence in problem solving
Time	Decelerating ⟷ Accelerating	Adjusting action moment by moment
Flow	Freeing ⟷ Binding	Adjusting the degree of control
Space		
Horizontal plane	Enclosing ⟷ Spreading	Exploring alternative approaches
Vertical plane	Descending ⟷ Rising	Clarifying a problem
Sagittal plane	Retreating ⟷ Advancing	Systematically implementing action

for each and to suggest relative strengths and weaknesses of their individual approaches to the job.

As with the previous description of the Aikidoist, photos have been placed throughout this section to help clarify the detailed analysis. However, the description will be most meaningful when the Chapter 8 videotape of the episode has been reviewed.

Expert's observations

1. Introduction

Worker *A* is wearing the yellow sweatshirt and appears first on the Chapter 8 tape, Worker *B* is wearing the blue jacket and appears second on the tape. An approach to the study of these two workers' movement needs selection among three alternatives.

(a) Attempt to record all the movement that happens. While this attempt can be made, it is almost impossible as video obscures some of the movement and, in any case, the human eye has its limitations.

(b) Concentrating on those movements directly relevant to the task from the point of view of effectiveness (standards of performance having been previously defined).

(c) Concentrating on those features of movement that indicate a different characteristic way of moving to fulfill the task.

The only choice for this study is (c), but some reference will be made to (b) on a speculative basis. The results of observations from (c) will be reviewed as to the implications for selection and training.

2. General impression

Worker *A* is more gentle and careful in the spraying operation, using decelerating and decreasing pressure, and placing the spray gun deliberately, using directness and deceleration. He faces the bench and moves with an advancing sagittal inclination. *A* also emphasizes bound flow; this can be observed in movements of the hand and arm.

Worker *A* appears to fix the backing from the trim in a recess, an operation which Worker *B* does not do, but in which he (*A*) continues with his directing and decelerating qualities.

Laying out the trim, *A* introduces increasing pressure alternating with decreasing pressure, and free flow alternating with bound flow. *A*'s hand in relation to his wrist moves in a widening horizontal path, but hand and arm in relation to the body reveal an advancing sagittal stress.

In using the trimming tool, *A* handles it with deceleration and directness, similarly to the spraying tool earlier, and orients himself with advancing movement, emphasizing bound flow.

The overall impression is that *A* uses predominantly decelerating and directing movement qualities, together with bound flow to give an impression of care, concentration, and meticulousness. He shapes his movement so that he can easily advance towards the bench.

On the other hand, Worker *B* is more casual and speedier when using the spray gun, emphasizing acceleration and an alternation of directing and indirecting focus.

Worker *B*'s movement in laying out the trim is somewhat obscured. We see him fixing the trim at the end of the board with increasing pressure, especially obvious in the wrist. In this operation, *B*'s hand and wrist in relation to the body retain a predominant widening horizontal orientation.

In using the trimming tool, *B* emphasizes increasing pressure with acceleration, together with a predominant narrowing horizontal stress in space. He also introduces some falling and rising vertical movements and alternates between freeing and binding flow.

The overall impression is that Worker *B* uses accelerating together with alternating free and bound flow to give an impression of speed with ease and casualness. His widening shape emphasizes the casual impression. This impression changes, however, at the end of the operation (use of the trimming tool), when narrowing is seen together with vertical plane falling and in conjunction with increasing and decreasing pressure.

Figure 11.6 Worker *A* laying out trim.

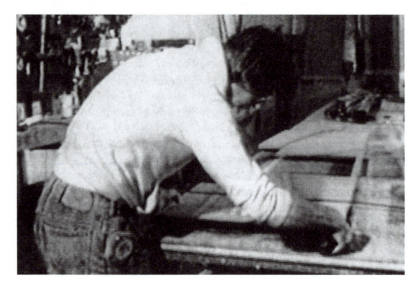

Figure 11.7 Worker *A* using trimming tool.

Figure 11.8 Worker *B* laying out trim.

Figure 11.9 Worker *B* using trimming tool.

3. Hand and arm gestures in relation to the body postures

(a) Worker *A*'s predominantly decelerating hand "gestures" alternate with relative acceleration as he moves the spraying tool to and fro, but it is impossible to see this reflected in whole bodily movement ("posture"). There is little *time* variation to be seen in posture and in this respect *A* is more or less *timeless*, neither accelerating nor decelerating.

Worker *B* shows many examples of acceleration changing to momentary deceleration and this is reflected in posture movement. He performs a range of *time* effort variation, i.e., accelerating and decelerating, while *A* (in posture) makes little such variation.

While *B* is obviously quicker in terms of time duration (a stop watch would show that), the impression that *A* is more careful needs questioning. Does *B*'s postural command of *time* effort give him a more positive control of the job?

(b) In spraying and, more particularly, handling the trim, *A* emphasizes directing. In the spraying his body supports this, and there is a posture range of variation of indirect/direct, with emphasis on direct. In handling the trim this directing comes close to rigidity, i.e., becoming a fixed stare.

Worker *B*'s indirecting is observable in posture, and a range of indirect/direct, with emphasis on indirect, can be seen throughout. Note when he lifts the trim, roves around with the spray gun, places the gun, adjusts the protruding end of trim.

(c) In Worker *A*, however, there is bodily variation in respect to advancing/retreating to a small degree constantly, but obviously so, for example, towards the end of the spraying operation. Such variation cannot be seen anywhere in *B*'s movement.

(d) Worker *B*'s widening is seen repeatedly to be backed up by posture movement, and there is a momentary narrowing which precedes each new widening. *A*'s widening hand movement is seen in conjunction with his predominant advancing/retreating posture. Also *B* introduces falling/rising (see the trimming operation), which appears nowhere in the case of *A*.

(e) Worker *A*'s increasing pressure is confined to his hands. With *B* there is more decreasing pressure seen in postural effort combined with gestural increasing pressure—see positioning of the trim and use of hand tool.

(f) Similarly, with *flow*. *B* shows more flow variation in his body compared to *A*—note *A* in the spraying operation particularly.

Analysis of where movement variation is mainly present in the posture is summarized in Table 11.2.

Table 11.2 Movement variations in the posture

Element of movement	Variation in movement	Worker A	Worker B
Postural effort			
Focus	Indirecting ⟷ Directing	Moderate	Moderate
Pressure	Decreasing ⟷ Increasing	Low	High
Time	Decelerating ⟷ Accelerating	Low	High
Flow	Freeing ⟷ Binding	Moderate	High
Postural space			
Horizontal plane	Enclosing ⟷ Spreading	Moderate	High
Vertical plane	Descending ⟷ Rising	Low	Moderate
Sagittal plane	Retreating ⟷ Advancing	High	Low

4. Movement analysis as an aid in skills training

Without detailed "on the job" study it is difficult to say what the skills of the job are, but they might include:

(a) Hand–eye coordination in spraying the trim to get even spreading, correct thickness of adhesive: directing and widening.
(b) Accuracy in fixing trim: directing, increasing pressure, and narrowing.
(c) Accuracy and consistency in using trimming tool: directing, decelerating, and narrowing.
(d) Overall speed without prejudice to accuracy: accelerating/decelerating in addition to above.

In terms of hand and arm movements, Worker *A*'s directing suggests that he could meet (a) and (c). The need for more increasing pressure and narrowing could probably be taught by means of hand/arm exercises. The need for improvement in overall speed would depend upon job specifications and behaviors valued in the shop (see the following section).

Worker *B* has the overall speed, and his increasing pressure plus variation in widening/narrowing suggest that he has the required skills to a greater extent than *A*. Recognizing these tendencies would be a good basis for working with him to improve his directing.

Worker *B*'s greater flow variation makes him more suited to learning the skills while on the job. Worker *A* would benefit from classroom training.

However, the learning of skills should be linked to understanding of individual behavior. If the movement required for work is confined to hand and arms and perhaps eye focus only, without integration into whole body movement (posture), there will be a danger of stress, fatigue, unpredictability, and lack of motivation for the work.

5. Behavioral tendencies indicated

The categorization of posture movement shown in (3) (e) above (under *Hand and arm gestures in relation to the body postures*), when matched against a decision-making model, suggests the following:

- Worker *A* has an operational approach (his high *sagittal* movement) and is more motivated than *B* for a job that is highly systematized and where the programming is done for him (low *time*).

- Worker *B* is more suited to a job where he can apply his high *pressure* and *time* and where he takes the initiative to sort out problems and adjust the programming. His high *horizontal* shaping puts him more in touch with alternative ways of doing the job and he is likely to show higher resourcefulness than *A*.

Such behavioral interpretation, from the movement analysis, can be a guide for selection. If a worker is required who will do the job exactly as instructed and accuracy is more important than speed, *A* should be preferred. If output is more important, and the job requires adjustment to different quality materials, variety of sizes, new embellishments, etc., then *B* should be preferred.

The findings go part way to answering the questions raised in (3) above (under *Hand and arm gestures*). Although *A* seems more careful and meticulous, and *B* more casual and indifferent, in fact *B* could prove both a more skilled worker, and more highly motivated, relative to the job and the job situation.

EPISODE 3: THE UNIVERSITY STAFF MEETING

Authors' commentary

The movement episode described here consists of a short segment of a longer staff meeting in which three people are present. Pam Schick began her study of this episode by watching the tape *without sound* to highlight the nonverbal behavior. She recorded her first impressions and used subsequent study of the videotape *with sound* to reflect upon questions that arose from her first silent viewing. In her analysis she describes each person's movement behavior individually. She follows this with a comparison of similarities among the three people and concludes with various inferences based on these observations.

Ms. Schick lists five questions that arose after her preliminary viewing of the videotape without sound. Each of these questions probes some aspect of either the feelings and motivations of the individuals or their relationships with each other. Were we to capture the gist of these initial relationships with, and feelings for, one another?

As with the previous episodes, Ms. Schick is cast in the role of the spectator observer. Although the material viewed is quite brief in duration, her observations reveal a subtlety and detail characteristic of such bystander observation, especially when the replay option of videotape is available.

Ms. Schick is relatively selective in the number of movement parameters she considers, emphasizing dynamic factors, spatial dimensions, and posture in relationship to gesture. Her mode of recording here, as with the other experts, is verbal.

In terms of making sense of her observations, Ms. Schick appears to go down the route of informal judgment, comparing her movement data with a more implicit interpretive scheme, possibly metaphoric in nature. As a consequence, the linking of data with conclusions must be followed intuitively, as is often the case when one makes informal judgments of people and situations.

Again, a close viewing and reviewing of Episode 3 on the Chapter 8 videotape will enhance the reading of the expert's analysis.

Expert's observations

A: The blond woman on the left in the red sweater;
B: The man in the center;
C: The brunette woman on the right in the pink sweater.

1. First impression: without sound

The man is in charge or giving information. The woman on the left (*A*) is attentive initially. Then she begins to cast glances at the other woman (*C*). The woman on the right (*C*) is impatient and holds back. She pays attention to *A* visually and to *B* vocally. The man (*B*) and *A* exchange some words about her paper. *A* looks a little surprised by the information, or questioning. She is ready to write while *C* has her hands in her lap or on her paper with no intention of writing. *C* is impatient, mocks *B*'s drone by side-to-side movements of her upper body, holds back, and then talks only to *B*. After some discussion with *B*, *C* seems content or in understanding with him, smiling congruently. It's as if they accomplished their task (she came to his rescue?). *A* has watched *C* during this transaction, but appears less involved until she nods understanding once near the end. Woman *A* seems left out of the harmony between *B* and *C*, although she is being informed of something that will affect her. *C*'s rhythmical efforts directed at *B* seem to have enlivened the interaction. Communication was greatest when *B* addressed *A* in directness and got a direct response and when *C*'s acceleration and combination of direct/bound acceleration, direct/firm acceleration, and firm acceleration reached *B* and he responded similarly with rhythmic variations of time and pressure or a direct/firm acceleration. Although *B* was in charge of the meeting, you get the feeling that *C* runs the show.

Figure 11.10 Woman A (left), Man B (center), Woman C (right).

Questions that arise:

(a) Is the woman (C) mocking the man during his presentation?
(b) Are the two women in cahoots originally? Their eyes imply they are (i.e., "he goes on and on, but what does it mean to *us*?").
(c) Does he *care* about this matter?
(d) Is C manipulating him or just trying to get information?
(e) Is the man being "tactful" to A or just informing her?

2. Analysis and description of A: actions and interactions

A sits in a concave posture with neutral flow and narrow limbs. She uses her left side as a buffer between her and B initially but drops her left arm once they get started. She directs her focus and body to B, seemingly available for communication in her upper body. She looks down at her paper when he focuses on her (subordinate behavior). She uses free flow when writing. Although it is difficult to "see" on the video, I get the impression that her flow fluctuates little, tending towards a maintained bound quality in her torso while listening. Her concave sagittal posture barely changes throughout the episode. When B says, "We've got to modify our check sheets," she focuses directly upon him and they share head nods, hers within a slight sagittal forward emphasis.

Woman A's movements are primarily gestural. She uses decreasing pressure and bound flow in self-touch and head-holding gestures, with directness and flow fluctuation in her eye movements when she glances at *B* or *C*. *A*'s eyebrows gesture up and down once in response to *C*. Woman *A*'s active movements are in nodding, looking down or up, or drawing on her paper with a direct, free flowing delicacy. When man *B* touches her paper, she draws her left hand backwards and upwards slightly with a delicate control. Postural movements are rare.

A shares the quality of directing with *B*, and looks directly at *C* as well, though not in synchrony with *C*'s meaningful glances. Both *A* and *B* give an impression of stability—*A* with her directly focused delicacy and *B* with his precise firmness. However, *A* shares only once in the rhythmic congruity that connects *B* and *C*, with the light, quick eyebrow gesture described above.

A appears subordinate, willing to follow directions but not sure of herself (eyes down, no postural weight assertion, rounded, concave posture). She is willing to follow the implications of a new policy by listening to woman *C* who teases out what it means in terms of action. *A* asks only one question about time, moves eyes, hands, and head gesturally. She never uses pressure in a postural shift. She initiates movements distally in a sequence *after B* or *C*. The indication she has heard or understood is an in-breathing with a postural flow near the end, with an "I get it" slight head nod. I have the feeling *A* will wait to hear how woman *C* thinks this new information will affect them and what its real impact will be.

3. Analysis and description of B: actions and interactions

B sits between *A* and *C* with a broad vertical stance and speaks in a slow, deliberate tone of voice. Looking down, he flips through the pages leisurely as if what he needs to say is in the text and gradually it will occur to him. He directs his gaze from side to side and turns the pages in a gliding or floating manner that seems to annoy woman *C*, while *A* just waits or writes patiently. *B* is decelerating (stalling?) in time and focusing intently or delicately, without getting to the point. He does move quickly on the word "modify." He is concerned that *A* change the check sheet. His gestures often flow downwards and across his body, with recuperative upward rebounding. Even when gestures of the hands emphasize points with direct quick jabs, *B*'s body remains stably rooted, so that gesture and posture are incongruent. He seems to be uncomfortable implementing change, even though it is his job to inform his staff of the need for action ("We intend, to begin, to implement, . . . immediately.")

Although he maintains a sagittal "fourth position" in his legs (knees turned out, one foot in front of the other), he seldom moves sagittally except for retracting and then sliding forward his left leg. Ironically or intentionally, this movement "kicked" woman *C* into action. Most of *B*'s gestures descend and rise vertically or open and close horizontally with directing and indirecting of focus. His hands move with the pen between them in delicate variations of freeing and binding. In fact, *B* has an extensive effort range in his distal hand gestures, but he seldom activates movement posturally or initiates movement centrally.

I get the impression of a man who is the authority here, although he is less than excited by these new changes and possibly grateful for *C*'s anticipatory explication of what it will mean in practical terms to the staff.

4. Analysis and description of C: actions and interactions

When the segment begins, woman *C* is sitting with her right leg crossed over her left, facing 45 degrees away from *B* and smiling. This orientation gives the impression that she might be communicating with woman *A*, but that she is not paying attention to man *B*. *C* taps her foot with quick fluctuations of bound and free flow and tilts her head in the vertical plane in rhythm with the man's words, as if she's heard it all before. She darts quick/direct glances at *A* and *B*, thrusts her arm forward swiftly and then drops it in passive weight on the table, lowering her eyes. She maintains a concave posture, curls backward in her chair as if her impatience requires a little distance to give the man time to say his "spiel."

Then *C* readjusts her position, facing slightly more towards *B*. Pressure variations become more apparent in the rhythmic gestures of her foot. At one point, she advances posturally, taking a deep breath and centrally initiating a lurch forward as if she is going to interrupt *B* and *A*. Then she releases her breath, binds her flow, and does not interrupt. As if on cue, when the man slides his foot towards her, she begins to speak firmly and quickly, punctuating her words with quick/direct glances and hand gestures to clarify what actions to take as a result of this new policy. Her acceleration seems infectious and the man picks up his tempo. They jab little quick/direct/firm/bound gestures across, down and forward, dancing more in effort synchrony with one another now. Woman *C* tilts her head and smiles seeming to signify her understanding and implied agreement as to what they should *do* about this new policy. I have the impression she has seen a lot of directives come and go and even this new policy can be seen in terms of channels of action that she can now control or implement. The indirectness of the head tilt and smile at the end seem flirtatious and feminine, as if she has charmed the man somewhat by figuring out what to do and who to send where to get the new policy in action.

5. Summation of similarities in movement styles during the meeting

A uses space effort in her eye focus a great deal, but avoids direct eye contact except when asking a question. Usually she relates to paper and pen more than to the other people. Woman *A* has head-nodding and the use of controlled lightness in hand gestures in common with the man. She shares a preference for directness with woman C and often echoes her gestures— woman A nods after C nods and lifts her eyebrows after C does so. Man B shares a preference for indulging effort qualities and direct focus with woman A, while with woman C he uses more fighting effort qualities to establish rapport. Woman C quickens the man's stable state into action and alertness.

A has a small kinesphere, while B a large one that extends to encompass fleetingly woman A's paper and woman C's leg space. C's centrally initiated linear movements are more controlled when speaking to B. She seems to make her kinesphere smaller to relate to him.

A emphasizes upper body gestures with a maintained concave shape in the torso. Man B caters in his gestural style to the preferences of each woman, but never deviates posturally from his position of stable power and authority. C expresses her lack of cooperation initially by not sharing her focus or orientation with the others. She later reorientates herself towards B, controlling her own impatient need to speed things up and moderating her gestures in pressure and size.

6. Inferences

The man, B, is not inspired by this new change. The women defer to him but are not terribly respectful or concerned. They seem to be familiar with his style and somewhat impatient with it on the one hand. A would not rock the boat but looks to C for how this is going to impact them. She seems ready enough to follow the orders she writes down but does not anticipate or have strong personal intentions in relation to them. She just nods. The man is delicate but firm with her about change. C defers to him as an authority, but not without showing her irritation at his slowness. Her ability to defer to him due to protocol (sex, rank) does not hide her impatient, nervous leg bounces, her jerky, jabby gestures as she expresses nonverbally a need to clarify what this new policy really will mean in terms of decisions and anticipated actions. She looks down or smiles coyly in agreement but one wonders what she will do later.

B's presence is felt through his accelerating and decelerating pressure as well as his wall-like stance. C's presence is felt through quick jabs, darts, and glances as she gets into the conversation and withdraws from it. A's presence is less dramatic, as she maintains a small kinesphere, moving little and interacting with the others mostly through nods of agreement.

7. Teamwork: inferences and suggestions

In terms of teamwork, B needs to be aware of his own impact or lack thereof. He needs to know his personal purpose in his work so he can either enthuse or motivate his staff with the need for change and their contribution to it —or—he needs to "lighten up" in his communication about how important this new directive is in the larger scheme of things. In any case, greater familiarity with the implications of the new policy for his staff would aid communication.

A needs encouragement to come forth with her contribution or explicit instructions regarding what she is to do. She is not good at drawing implications and needs more detailed guidance.

C is using fairly stereotypical subordinate and "female" behavior (gender cues) to interact with a male superior. Her persona is something of a "front" and only partially hides her impulsive intention to take charge and do it. She has disdain for the man's style of authority and could benefit from having either more personal responsibility and scope for initiating action or more appreciation for the leadership styles of others.

EPISODE 4: THE CREATIVE DRAMATICS CLASS

Authors' commentary

The movement episode described here is taken from a class in creative dramatics for children. Initially the teacher and the class of nine students are seated on the floor while the teacher explains the exercise they are to do next. Following this, the students rise and enact the exercise, while the teacher directs the activity from the side.

Sharon True chose to watch the videotape initially *with sound*, jotting down first impressions and questions. Then, reversing the process described by Ms. Schick in the previous episode, Ms. True viewed the tape *without sound* to complete her more detailed analysis.

As with all the other experts, Ms. True is cast in the role of a spectator observer, watching a brief movement event and recording her observations verbally. In the well-integrated description that follows here, she articulates very clearly her central questions, her choice of movement parameters, and her process of making sense of the movement data. Lest this commentary prove redundant, we shall simply let Ms. True speak for herself. As with all the other episodes, reviewing the segment on the Chapter 8 videotape is recommended.

Expert's observations

My process in observing the videotape of the creative dramatics class was, first, to watch it a couple of times to see what struck me, what questions came to mind; then, to turn off the sound and analyze the movement and determine what parameters and which moments seemed particularly significant; and finally to see if this movement information could suggest some answers to my questions, and some directions for further development of the exercise and the individuals involved.

The first viewings of the tape produced the following notes and questions: "The girl at the teacher's right side is 'in her own world.' Is teacher contributing to her detachment in some way? Children seem relaxed and uninhibited in front of cameras and are fully committed in their participation in the exercise. There is confusion about holding the statue shape, though. What does that mean? How could this exercise be developed?"

My initial notes seem to revolve around three issues: the problem of presenting an activity in such a way that students' interest and involvement is engaged; the problem of confusion about holding the statue shape, and the question of "Where could we go from here?" The subsequent movement analysis suggested some answers to my questions, and also changed my initial interpretations and perspective in some instances.

For example, I used the term "in her own world" to describe the movement of the girl to the teacher's right. It initially appeared to me that she was largely oblivious to what was being said. This impression was based on my observation of her fidgetiness, face-making and lack of eye contact with the teacher. A closer analysis revealed that she was more attentive than I suspected, and the fact that she seemed to know what to do once the exercise started confirmed this idea. The key to recognizing her attentiveness was seeing her use of indirecting focus, in conjunction with flow changes. Her all-encompassing attentiveness to her surroundings and to the teacher did not involve direct eye contact. Rather, her attentiveness was revealed in the way she "echoed" a couple of the teacher's movement phrases and acted out some of the teacher's verbal phrases.

At the beginning of the discussion, she shifts herself forward to align her body in the vertical dimension a moment after the teacher has shifted herself backward to vertical uprightness. The girl echoes, almost imperceptibly, two advancing postural movements the teacher makes. The clearest "echo" occurs when the teacher makes a large, upward and slightly backward gesture of the arm and torso, which the girl echoes in a movement of the arm and head a moment later. (The teacher is saying, "Some of them are going to be standing . . .") The girl's face-making behavior looked quite odd and inappropriate until I turned the sound back on and realized she was responding to the teacher's words, "funny," "ugly," and "yelling." It became clear that, contrary to my first impression, this girl *was* paying attention, although she did not behave in a stereotypically attentive manner. (Compare her with the light blond in the lavender blouse, or the curly-haired girl who sat across from teacher.)

However, the girl to the teacher's right *did* become somewhat cut off from the rest of the group, a situation exacerbated by the teacher's predominant use of advancing and retreating movements in the sagittal plane, which limited her access to children seated to her right and left. In the beginning of her presentation of the exercise, the teacher performs a series of sagittal movements (sliding forward on the knees, rising back and up as she looks at her watch, falling forward and down to emphasize "two kinds of statues"), balancing these with horizontally-inclined movements of head and torso to glance at the children at her sides. However, as the teacher begins to field

Figure 11.11 Teacher interacts with girl on right.

questions, her movements become almost exclusively sagittal. (Observe her planal, cyclic arm and hand gestures as she answers the question of the girl in white top.) A very significant moment occurs toward the end of the discussion, when the teacher realizes she has lost contact with the children to her right and left, and she makes a break from the sagittal plane with a quick, direct, linear arm gesture in the horizontal dimension to touch the head of the girl on her right, and a twist to the left to glance at the boy on her left. The girl's response to the touch was swift and positive—she moved in closer to the group, and focused her gaze on the other children.

The teacher's emphasis on movement in the sagittal plane did not prevent her from engaging her students in other ways. She used different aspects of her repertoire, such as a variety of dynamic qualities and changes in the size of her kinesphere. An attention-getting effort phrase she repeated several times began with a light, free upbeat, accelerated in time to become increasingly direct and bound, and ended with a "pregnant pause." For instance, this happened as she said, "First we're going to start with walking around in a circle [free/light]. Now I want you to think about two kinds of statues [accelerating, becoming bound/direct], a funny statue [pause] and an ugly statue." Through variations in effort qualities, particularly punctuated with accelerations, the teacher holds the students' attention through this long series of explanations.

The teacher moved primarily within the middle reach space of her kinesphere, but when she suddenly expanded her kinesphere with a far reach gesture of her arm and torso along the vertical dimension to indicate high level, shrunk it to indicate low level, and returned to middle reach to show

Figure 11.12 Teacher gestures sagittally.

middle level, she captured the children's attention. I wondered if the clarity with which the children later demonstrated their understanding of the idea that changing levels was an option available to them had something to do with that relatively dramatic sequence of changes in the size of the teacher's kinesphere.

I noted in my first impression of the class that the children seemed relaxed and uninhibited by the camera. In subsequent viewings my attention shifted to the teacher, who in contrast to the children, appeared ill at ease. She verbally indicated a concern with lack of time, which could explain her frequent use of the accelerating quality of time and its affinity for the sagittal dimension. Perhaps the intensity of her bound flow and directness, her occasional self-touch gestures (push-up sleeves, hand to mouth, rubbing hands downward on legs), and the postural retreating movement into the background once the exercise began could be attributed to her attempt to cope with her discomfort with being videotaped.

In the second part of the taped episode, when the children actually do the exercise, the teacher had to remind them repeatedly to make a statue and hold it still before moving it. I have two theories about why the children had trouble making and holding a shape, particularly in response to the "funny" cue. The first that came to mind is that, due to lack of time, the teacher tried to incorporate too many ideas at once. For example, with more time she might have had students practice making ugly and funny statues in place first, then with walking in between, and finally with travelling in character. Another theory emerged as I analyzed the children's movement more closely: perhaps the word "funny" is more strongly associated with a

Figure 11.13 Children make statues as teacher watches.

movement impulse than the word "ugly" is. Therefore "funny" would be more difficult to conceive of as a non-moving statue. Further, the effort qualities the children most often used with "funny"—quickness and free flow—tend to be more "infectious" than the slower, stronger qualities the children often chose for "ugly" characters (see the funny-happy and funny-waving goodbye segments). It would also be interesting to see if the children had as much difficulty making a "funny" statue if they were spread out into a much larger circle, with less proximity to one another.

Inasmuch as acting requires the ability to control sensitively inner move-ment impulses, so that they may be released at the appropriate moment, it would be valuable for the children to begin to learn to recognize and control their impulsive urge to move. But the question arises whether this is a realistic expectation for children, especially those whose ebullience is at the core of their being. For very young children, it is probably not realistic to expect that they could control their impulse to bounce around in response to the cue, "make a funny statue," but I feel that children of the age shown on the tape are ready to learn how to manage their impulses.

Further practice with containing and letting out an urge to move is one direction I could see this exercise taking. Another option would be exploring movement opposites of what many of the children did spontaneously; for example, making a tall, narrow, ugly character that moves quickly or freely, or a low, wide, slow-moving funny character. I was struck by the variety of stepping rhythms and placement of body weight that the children spontaneously exhibited. It would be interesting to see how the children would respond if asked to create their own character on top of so-and-so's "legs" (way of travelling). I also observed that some children repeated certain movement elements again and again, a tendency that, if left unchallenged, could limit their expressive range. For example, the brown-haired girl in the pink sweatshirt repeatedly used a wide, concave wall-like shape and a right body-half/left body-half unilateral mode of travelling. She could be encouraged to use the sagittal dimension more and to explore contralateral patterns of locomotion. The blond girl in plaid pants repeatedly used inward-turning movements (perhaps she and the "wide" girl could team up). The tall girl with the long blue top rarely varied the width of her stance, or used her lower body expressively. She could benefit by working with the girl in front of her, whose lower body movement showed greater variety.

In sum, the Laban framework of movement analysis helped me to correct a stereotypic view of attentive behavior; suggested some reasons for the teacher's degree of effectiveness from one moment to the next as she sought to engage her students' attention and clearly communicate what was expected of them; gave rise to the question of impulse control for this age group; and provided a means for quickly grasping similarities and differences in children's movement responses, contrasts that could be used as a basis for expanding each child's awareness of the movement choices available for developing unique characters.

Recapitulation

"Observation in Practice" has been the theme of this and the preceding chapters. In Chapter 10, with an emphasis on the "Process and Structure," we attempted to specify as closely as possible the various factors that contribute to skillful movement observation and meaningful analysis. In this chapter, "As Experts See It," we have been able to witness the embodiment of expert observational skills in the descriptions of each of the episodes from the Chapter 8 videotape.

These episodes present a range of observational challenges with variations in the size of the group of participants, the type of event, and the level of skill of the movers. It requires one approach to study the actions of a highly skilled solo performer, as in the Aikido demonstration, and quite another to watch a whole class of wiggly children, as in the creative dramatics episode. Likewise, the comparison of two different individuals performing the same physical task, as in the cabinet-making episode, demands a different strategy than the study of several people engaged in "intellectual" teamwork, as in the staff meeting.

It is interesting to note that each expert observer meets these various challenges through careful strategic planning and decisions at the outset. While using the same basic concepts of body, effort, and space, each observer anchors her or his study to some question or concern that is personally relevant.

For instance, Peggy Berger is interested in how the skill of the Aikidoist might be improved in relation to his potential martial engagements. She uses her own body knowledge of Aikido in tandem with her analytical probings to explore this concern. Warren Lamb pays attention to the practical applications of movement study in selecting and training workers, and these interests shape the nature of his analysis of the cabinet-making episode. Pam Schick is absorbed in the human relationships among the conferees in the staff meeting, and her study reveals a constantly changing drama of alliance, flirtation, detachment, ambition, and control. Sharon True's interest is engaged by the behaviors of the teacher and children, as well as by how the class content might be improved or expanded. This focus enables her to pinpoint salient actions amid the myriad movements in the scene.

The manner in which these experts relate their analyses to a central question or concern and also how they vary what they look at, from a close-up on the basic elements of body, effort, and space, to a wide shot of larger patterns of behavior, calls to mind again Polanyi's concept of subsidiary versus focal awareness. For each expert, the process of observing is properly subsidiary to the purpose of the observation. Similarly, while the application of movement analysis reveals many details of each movement event, the elaboration of these details draws its meaning from the way these parts enter into the whole behavior in its human context. Thus, by maintaining the sensitive relationship of subsidiary and focal awareness, the experts anchor their movement observations "in context" and connect their perceptions to a unifying question and purpose.

It is at the point of making these connections that we pass from skills that are specifiable to ones that are not. In making sense of what they see, each expert brings his or her personal knowledge to bear on the problem. For each, the movement episode evoked some question (or questions) that subsequently gave form and direction to the whole observational task. Yet none of the experts has described exactly *how* these guiding questions arose or were chosen from many other possibilities that might have suggested themselves. Seemingly, this crucial aspect of structuring an observation for results is handled by processes that are typically unspecified and largely unspecifiable.

Observation in practice, particularly as demonstrated by the experts in this chapter, consists of both specifiable and unspecifiable skills, and embodies the kind of double vision described in Chapter 10. If we wish to understand the world beyond words, nothing must escape our keen analytical attentiveness. And yet, when we wish to make sense of what we see, we must look again at the very edge of what is visible. For it is probably there that the greatest discoveries are waiting to be made.

12 Challenges and horizons

All of Rudolf Laban's life—whether as dancer/choreographer, teacher/
theoretician, or philosopher/humanist—was an intensive, constant involvement with all facets of movement. It was an unending process of defining
the inner and outer manifestations of movement phenomena in increasingly
subtle shades and complex interrelationships.

Irmgard Bartenieff

The investigation of movement is still in its infancy.

Rudolf Laban

Reports of the experts in Chapter 11 demonstrate how much can be
discovered about movement through conscious people watching. Their
detailed accounts also show how the system of Laban Movement Analysis
can be applied to tease out meaningful aspects of very diverse types of
movement events. Movement is ubiquitous in human life, and happily, there
is increasing interest in understanding this vital phenomenon. A wide variety
of disciplines—from philosophy to neuroscience, anthropology to dance
history, physical education to robotics design and computer animation—
are involved in movement study today. New tools exist to capture motion.
There is a growing body of recorded material available for study, and new
methods that can be brought to bear in these inquiries. Consequently, we
stand on the threshold of an explosion of knowledge, one that has the
potential to radically alter our understanding of body and mind, function
and expression.

In this chapter, we examine the expanding horizons of movement study.
We survey how far we have come, where we are now, and what possibilities
lie ahead. With every possibility, there are also obstacles to be overcome.
Discussion of a perennial challenge—how to make sense of movement in all
its complexity and contextual variety—closes our excursion into the world
beyond words.

Laying a foundation for the study of human movement

Dance provides a useful example in surveying progress in the field of movement study. In the early twentieth century, when Rudolf Laban began his

investigation of human movement, dance was the "poor relation" among all the arts. There had been means of documenting and preserving great works of literature, theatre, and music for centuries, but there was still no good way to record a dance. The dancers' movements disappeared as the dance progressed, leaving behind nothing more than a memory trace in the mind of the performer and the observer. Thus the survival of folk or theatrical dances depended on the recollections of the performers, and their knowledge had to be transmitted directly person to person, through physical demonstration and oral elaboration. Unlike the visual arts, in which complete works survive for centuries, dance and movement left only fragmentary material artifacts—usually drawings with some notes, photographs, programs, and possibly reviews or other types of verbal accounts. Reconstructing a dance from such fragments was quite difficult. Consequently, the art of dance was ahistorical—valued for the moment in which it existed and then lost in the annals of time.

In other art forms, scripts, scores, and visual artifacts provided a rich mine of historical materials that could be studied, copied, reconstructed, even performed again. Education in the arts depended heavily on such historical examples—and still does today. Theatre students perform Greek tragedies and Shakespearian dramas; musicians develop their skills by playing Bach, Beethoven, and the Beatles; and visual artists-to-be can be seen in museums, copying the masterworks of earlier painters and sculptors. Moreover, these historical materials can be analyzed to develop theories of dramatic construction, to discern laws of musical harmony, and to articulate visual principles of design and composition.

In dance, the relative dearth of historical materials for study not only impacted dance education but also affected the development of dance and movement theory. How can one identify elements of movement and theorize compositional principles of an art that is constantly disappearing? Of course, attempts were made to articulate physical techniques for performance, to capture movement in written notation, to spell out its component parts, and to establish guidelines for choreographic practice. But compared to the other arts, the scope of theoretical materials addressing dance and movement was quite limited.

Two developments in the early twentieth century laid a foundation for the study of dance and, by extension, human movement—cinematography and dance notation. Cinematography was preceded by the development of instantaneous photography. Photographs by Muybridge, Marey, and Eaton captured sequential images of movement that the human eye could not see, providing some of the first useful records for analysis (Chapter 7, and Moore 2005). The subsequent development of cinematography enhanced the quality of movement recording. Film and notation made it possible to record dance and other types of movement events, thereby creating a visual archive and written movement literature that provides material for study and research. Film captures a particular artistic performance. However, "a film cannot reproduce a dance step by step, since the lens shoots from but one angle and there is a general confusion of blurred impressions which even constant re-showing can never eliminate" (Balanchine 1970: xii). In contrast, dance notation "records the structure of the dance, revealing with perfect clarity each of the specific movements of each performer" (ibid).

Finding a way to notate the specific movements of each performer took a long time. Prior to the twentieth century, many attempts met with only partial success because "dance exists in space as well as time and because the body itself is capable of so many simultaneous modes of action" (Guest 2005: 1). Moreover, dance styles change. Methods suited to recording one style were seldom flexible enough to accommodate the "continual changes as dance developed" (ibid).

In other words, to be widely practicable, dance notation also had to function as a generalizable system of movement analysis, identifying the "motor elements, which can be freely combined to reveal something about the inner state of the moving person" (Laban 1975b: 5). Through a sound identification of body, space, and effort motor elements, Labanotation and its European cousin, Kinetography Laban, finally proved flexible enough to "be applied to all forms of movement" (Guest 2005: 3). As a consequence, notation has proved to be important, not only to the development of dance history, scholarship, and theory, but also "in non-dance fields such as movement therapy, sport, psychology and anatomy" (Jordan 2005: xiv). Laban Movement Analysis was chosen as the analytic terminology for this textual and visual introduction to the study of movement because it is broadly applicable.

While centuries of dance and movement history have disappeared into oblivion, cinematography and practicable movement notation and analysis systems have now been in place for the better part of the twentieth century. There are reasonably complete records and materials available for study, and this development creates many possibilities for dance and physical education, movement scholarship, and the development of movement theory. As Mlakar points out,

> In the field of theatrical dance, concepts and inherent laws exist which have a scientific character beyond the ephemeral experience of dance. In the course of notating whole works of dance the structures become apparent, and they remain patient and immovable ready for analysis and study.
>
> (1979: xx)

With these possibilities comes a challenge. Mastering any symbolic movement notation system and its associated analytic terminology is analogous to learning to read music or speak, read, and write in a foreign language.

Becoming literate in the language of movement is difficult, particularly because so many movement skills have always been and continue to be taught enactively; that is, through imitation of a more skilled mover. Whether in the studio, gym, or on the playing field, there has been little recourse to analytic discussion or symbolic representation among movement teachers and students. The tradition of embodied movement study runs counter to developing movement literacy and theory, and this is one of the challenges facing the field.

Contemporary developments

Documentation of movement events has also been enhanced by the invention of video recording. Videotaping reduced the cost of recording considerably, making it possible to capture a dance or other movement event from more than one angle, thereby providing multiple views and more complete information. Video cameras have become smaller, more portable, and easier to use. Their inclusion in cell phones makes ad hoc filming possible. Internet websites allow movement recordings of all kinds to be posted for wide viewing. If one wants to watch people in motion, there is material of all sorts available for study today. Moreover, computer technologies such as motion capture, gesture recognition, and animation programs offer new ways to record movement and provide new methods for reconstructing and analyzing movement data. These types of studies feed into creative applications such as video games and film-making, as well as into scientific applications such as biomechanical research and robotic engineering.

Additionally, medical devices, such as functional magnetic resonance imaging, are allowing neuroscientists to see into the human brain in altogether new ways. As a consequence, there has been a knowledge explosion regarding brain and sensorimotor functioning. For example, the discovery of neuroplasticity suggests that the central and peripheral nervous systems possess more extensive powers of regeneration than previously thought. Greater understanding of neuroplasticity opens the way for new healing interventions to treat both mental and physical disabilities (Schwartz and Begley 2002; Doidge 2007). In addition to research on physical injuries, brain imaging is being used to study exceptional physical achievements, such as musical virtuosity (Levitin 2007). Rare accomplishments, once attributed solely to talent or genius, may now be related also to biological structures, neural processes, and behavioral practices. More "evidence for human transformative capacity" is coming to light (Murphy 1992: 7). Discovering how to tap these capacities is an emerging horizon that will inevitably be linked to movement study because movement plays such a critical role in the acquisition of skill.

Increasingly sophisticated technological devices allow movement to be captured in many new ways. These devices only do part of the work, however.

It takes real human beings to make sense of mechanically recorded data, to employ new technologies meaningfully in artistic expression, and to apply discoveries appropriately for the improvement of human conditions. Movement studies being conducted in many different fields have the potential to reshape our understanding of the most fundamental human capacities, elucidating how we think, feel, sense, act, learn, and heal. To achieve this potential, however, certain challenges must be accepted.

Emerging challenges in the study of human movement

Movement is a psychophysical phenomenon, a "common denominator of the mind/body functioning which also takes in the expression of emotions and the spirit" (Lamb 1986: 12). One of the most marvelous and distinctive aspects of skilled movement is its integrative character. Motoric elements combine spontaneously, function melds with expression, and volition is translated into a meaningful action that flows seamlessly through space and time. Exactly how this occurs is a mystery. Nevertheless, significant action is coherent and holistic. As M. Johnson explains,

> In order to have human meaning, you need a human brain, operating in a living body, continually interacting with a human environment that is at once physical, social, and cultural. Take away any one of these three dimensions, and you lose the possibility of meaning.
>
> (2007: 155)

Laban agrees:

> To separate bodily actions (meaning anatomical and physiological functions) from the spatial activity (meaning that which creates the shapes and lines in space) is in reality as impossible as to separate the mental and emotional parts of movements from the space-time forms in which they become visible.
>
> (1974: 49)

Yet this is exactly what has been happening. Anatomical and physiological functions have been studied in isolation from the mental and emotional aspects of movement behavior. The space–time forms of movement have been dealt with as ornamental motoric elements devoid of mental, emotional, and social significance. While many disciplines study movement, each discipline has its jealously guarded territory, and the holistic phenomenon of body–mind functioning is broken up along disciplinary lines. Understanding gleaned in one field often does not cross these territorial boundaries, and the comprehensive entity of human movement is reduced to particularistic bits of information.

Of course, even partial knowledge can shed some light on the complex phenomenon under examination. Problems occur, nevertheless, when one wishes to generalize the inkling too broadly and prematurely. For instance, cognitive neuroscience has been "probing the neural underpinnings of social behavior" to produce tons of information "that are both tantalizing and deeply puzzling" (Adolphs 2003: 165). For one thing, most studies have been laboratory experiments with typical research participants of certain age range. "While abstract stimuli can be precisely defined and controlled, it is unclear how one might come to understand the complex interactions between real-world behaviors and sensorimotor processes with stimuli that do not correspond to behaviorally relevant entities found outside the laboratory" (Shiffrar 2010: Conclusion).

For another,

> The data that are available at present raise as many questions as they provide answers. How can the diverse findings that we accumulate be situated under a single functional framework? ... What are the relative contributions of innate and acquired factors, culture and individual differences to social cognition? To what extent do these factors contribute to psychopathology? Can large-scale social behaviour ... be understood by studying social cognition in individual subjects? Finally, what power will insights from cognitive neuroscience give us to influence our social behaviour, and hence society? And to what extent would such pursuit be morally defensible?
>
> (Adolphs 2003: 176)

To date, most movement researchers have been content to study the elements of movement, not its human meaning. Meaning is comprehensive. Indeed, movement meaning would seem to depend upon the interrelationships of several variables. To begin with, the quality and structure of the movement event contribute to its meaning. Even if one does not subscribe wholeheartedly to the physiognomic theory of expression discussed in Chapter 6, it is nevertheless true that the dynamics and form of an action support certain interpretations while failing to suggest others. For example, passive, weak, curvilinear movements that droop slowly towards the earth will seldom suggest ebullient elation to an observer. Similarly, explosively forceful linear thrusts seldom convey a feeling of calm contemplation. Movement meaning is due, partially at least, to the manner in which the mover uses body, space, and effort. As Arnheim notes, there is a "structural kinship between the stimulus pattern and the expression it conveys"(1974: 450).

Of course, the expression conveyed by a stimulus pattern is affected by the context of the event. "Explosively forceful linear thrusts" would convey different impressions if directed against another person, oneself, a heavy box, or empty space. As noted in Chapter 6, a given action may convey, at one and the same time, multiple meanings, some that are pan-human, others that are culture-specific, and still others that are singularly individualistic. Thus, context too defines, to a considerable degree, the significance we attribute to an action.

Meaning is also in the eye of the beholder. What one notices about a particular movement (indeed, whether one notices it at all) is highly individualistic in nature. As discussed in Chapter 4, meaningful interpretation of movement depends to a large extent on the observer's past experiences and the inductive generalizations (body knowledge/body prejudice) associated with the behavior. Personal background, biases, even taste greatly influence the interpretation of movement, although these variables are often hidden in the construction of meaning.

Despite the inevitable divergence between the meaning attached by the mover and the significance perceived by the observer, the movement event itself remains a point of concrete contact amenable to open inquiry. Laban observed that investigation of the emotional and volitional content of movement promises to yield new insights into human behavior. "In trying to reach this very remote goal," he cautioned, "we must content ourselves for the time being with the clarification of our conceptions of space, time and energy" (1984: 12–13).

There is a danger in following this advice, because "operations of a higher level," such as insight into human behavior, "can never be derived from the laws governing its isolated particulars" (Polanyi 1966: 37). Polanyi goes on to explain:

> Every time we concentrate our attention on the particulars of a comprehensive entity, our sense of its coherent existence is temporarily weakened; and every time we move in the opposite direction towards a fuller awareness of the whole, the particulars tend to become submerged in the whole.
>
> (1969: 125)

Gordon Allport concurs;

> Niels Bohr's principle of complementarity contains a lesson for us. He showed that if we study the position of a particle, we do not at the same time study its momentum. Applied to our work, the principle tells us that if we focus on reaction, we do not simultaneously study proaction; if we measure one trait, we do not fix our attention on pattern; if we tackle a subsystem, we lose the whole; if we pursue the whole, we overlook the part-functioning. For the single investigator, there seems to be no escape from this limitation. Our only hope is to overcome it by a complementarity of investigators and theorists.
>
> (1960: 52)

Making sense of movement

In advocating a complementarity of investigators and theorists, Allport reiterates a principle discussed in Chapter 9, namely, *movement must be approached at multiple levels if it is to be properly understood.* More tools exist for the study of movement today than ever before. More disciplines find movement study relevant to their concerns. Cross-fertilization of ideas is beginning to occur. If these trends continue, then the potential contributions of movement study to comprehension and improvement of human life may yet be realized.

For the lay observer there are many ways to approach learning more about movement. Participating in movement yields insight, as does practicing movement analysis. Paying attention to one's first impressions and identifying their nonverbal bases provides an opportunity to reflect on one's personal lexicon of movement meaning. Shifting between these modes of perception facilitates a holistic appreciation of this vital dimension of human life. As Laban affirms, "movement is a synthesis, i.e., a unifying process, culminating in the understanding of personality caught up in the ever-changing flow of life" (1971a: 107). Consequently, life is never dull for the conscious people watcher. Human movement is ever-present and always revealing.

As Freud asserted, "he that has eyes to see and ears to hear may convince himself that no mortal can keep a secret. If his lips are silent, he chatters with his fingertips" (quoted in K. Bloom 2006: 3). This excursion through the world beyond words can draw to a close now, because you, dear reader, have eyes to see. In every bodily movement "both infinity and eternity are hidden. Sometimes the veil seems to be lifted for an instant. Inspiration, clairvoyance, and a heightened awareness can thrive from this fissure in the part of the world which we see as eternity" (Laban 1974: 54).

Body movement is the first seat of knowledge for the human child. So too it was the first source of knowledge for the species. It would therefore seem that we *should* know a great deal about human movement. But what we do *not* yet know is greater still. Perhaps as we continue to explore the world beyond words, we may lift the veil of ignorance a little more and, by so doing, illuminate not only where we have been but also where we are going.

Figure 12.1 Movement reveals where we have been and where we are going.
Juergen Kuehn

References

Adolphs, R. (2003) "Cognitive Neuroscience of Human Social Behavior," *Nature Reviews Neuroscience*, 4: 165–178.

Adrian, B. (2008) *Actor Training the Laban Way*, New York: Allworth Press.

Adshead, J. (Ed.) (1982) *Dance Analysis: Theory and Practice*, London: Dance Books.

Alexander, F.M. (1955) *The Use of the Self*, Weybridge, Surrey, UK: Re-Educational Publications.

Allison, N. (1999) "Body-oriented Psychotherapies," in N. Allison (Ed.) *The Illustrated Encyclopedia of Body–Mind Disciplines*: 378–381. New York: Rosen Publishing Group.

Allport, G.W. (1958) *The Nature of Prejudice*, Garden City, NY: Doubleday Anchor.

—— (1960) *Personality and Social Encounter*, Boston, MA: Beacon Press.

American Dance Therapy Association (2010) "What is Dance/Movement Therapy?" Columbia, MD: Author. Online. Available www.adta.org (accessed December 30, 2010).

Amighi, J.K., Loman, S., Lewis, P., and Sossin, M.K. (Eds.) (1999) *The Meaning of Movement*, New York: Routledge.

Armstrong, D.F., Stokoe, W.C., and Wilcox, S.E. (1995) *Gesture and the Nature of Language*, Cambridge: Cambridge University Press.

Arnheim, R. (1969) *Visual Thinking*, Berkeley, CA: University of California Press.

—— (1974) *Art and Visual Perception*, Berkeley, CA: University of California Press.

Au, S. (1988) *Ballet and Modern Dance*, New York: Thames & Hudson.

Axtell, R.E. (1991) *Gestures: The Do's and Taboos of Body Language around the World*, New York: Crown.

Backman, E.L. (1952) *Religious Dances in the Christian Church and in Popular Medicine*, London: George Allen & Unwin.

Balanchine, G. (1970) "Preface," in A. Hutchinson, *Labanotation*, 2nd ed.: xi–xii. New York: Theatre Arts Books.

Banes, S. (2007) *Before, Between and Beyond: Three Decades of Dance Writing*, Madison, WI: University of Wisconsin Press.

Bartenieff, I. (1972/73) "Dance Therapy: A New Profession or a Rediscovery of an Ancient Role of Dance?" *Dance Scope*, Fall/Winter: 6–18.

Bartenieff, I. with Lewis, D. (1980) *Body Movement: Coping with the Environment*, New York: Gordon & Breach.

Bartenieff, I. and Paulay, F. (1970) "Dance as Cultural Expression," in M. Haberman and T. Meisel (Eds.) *Dance: An Art in Academe*: 23–31. New York: Teachers College Press.

Battcock, G. (1966) *The New Art: A Critical Anthology*, New York: E.P. Dutton.

Belth, M. (1977) *The Process of Thinking*, New York: David McKay.

Benesh, R. and Benesh, J. (1969) *An Introduction to Benesh Notation*, New York: Dance Horizons.

Berger, P.L. (1970) *A Rumor of Angels*, Garden City, NY: Anchor Books/Doubleday.

Bergson, H. (1946) *The Creative Mind*, trans. M.L. Andison, New York: Citadel Press.

Berman, M. (1990) *Coming to Our Senses*, New York: Bantam Books.

Berthoz, A. (2000) *The Brain's Sense of Movement*, trans. G. Weiss, Cambridge, MA: Harvard University Press.

Beveridge, W.I.B. (1950) *The Art of Scientific Investigation*, New York: Vintage Books.

Birdwhistell, R.L. (1970) *Kinesics and Context: Essays on Body Motion Communication*, Philadelphia, PA: University of Pennsylvania Press.

Blackman, L. (2008) *The Body*, Oxford: Berg.

Blakeslee, S. and Blakeslee, M. (2007) *The Body Has a Mind of its Own*, New York: Random House.

Block, R. (1990) "Models of Psychological Time," in Block, R. (Ed.) *Cognitive Models of Psychological Time*: 1–36. Hillsdale, NJ: Lawrence Erlbaum.

Bloom, K. (2006) *The Embodied Self: Movement and Psychoanalysis*, London: Karnac Books.

Bloom, M. (2001) *Thinking Like a Director*, New York: Faber & Faber.

Bronowski, J. (1977) *A Sense of the Future*, Cambridge, MA: The MIT Press.

—— (1981) *The Ascent of Man*, London: Futura MacDonald.

Brown, S. and Parsons, L.M. (2008) "The Neuroscience of Dance," *Scientific American*, 299 (July): 78–83.

Brynie, F.H. (2009) *Brain Sense: The Science of the Senses and How We Process the World Around Us*, New York: AMACOM.

Cameron, O.G. (2001) "Interoception: The Inside Story—A Model for Psychosomatic Process," *Psychosomatic Medicine*, 63: 697–710.

Canadian Broadcasting Corp. (1983) "Anybody's Son Will Do," Kent, OH: PTV Publication.

Carney, D.R., Cuddy, A.J.C., and Yap, A.J. (2010) "Power Posing: Brief Nonverbal Displays Affect Neuroendocrine Levels and Risk Tolerance," *Psychological Science*, 21 (10): 1363–1368.

Carpenter, E. (1970) *They Became What They Beheld*, New York: Outerbridge & Dienstfrey/Ballantine.

Cassirer, E. (1961) *The Myth of the State*, New Haven, CT: Yale University Press.

Castiglione, B. (1981) *The Book of the Courtier*, New York: Penguin Books (first published 1528).

Chace, M. (1975) "Our Real Lives Are Lived in Rhythm and Movement," in H. Chaiklin (Ed.) *Marian Chace: Her Papers*: 169–174. New York: American Dance Therapy Association.

Chekhov, M. (1991) *On the Technique of Acting*, New York: HarperCollins.

Christ, P.A. and Schwartzman, R. (1999) "Medical Orgone Therapy," in N. Allison (Ed.) *The Illustrated Encyclopedia of Body–Mind Disciplines*: 405–409. New York: Rosen Publishing Group.

Condon, W.S. (1982) "Cultural Microrhythms," in M. Davis (Ed.) *Interaction Rhythms*: 53–76, New York: Human Sciences Press.

Copeland, A. (1941) *Our New Music*, New York: McGraw-Hill.

Cunningham, M. (1985) *The Dancer and the Dance*, New York: Marion Boyars/ Scribner.

Damasio, A.R. (1994) *Descartes' Error: Emotion, Reason and the Human Brain*, London: Papermac.

Darwin, C. (1998) *The Expression of Emotions in Man and Animals*, 3rd ed.: New York: Oxford University Press (first published, London, 1872).

Davis, F. (1973) *Inside Intuition: What We Know about Nonverbal Communication*, New York: Signet.

Davis, M. (1975) *Towards Understanding the Intrinsic in Body Movement*, New York: Arno Press.

Deutsch, D., Henthorn, T., and Dolson, M. (2004) "Absolute Pitch, Speech, and Tone Language," *Music Perception*, 21: 339–356.

Dobbs, D. (2006) "A Revealing Reflection: Mirror Neurons Seen to Effect Everything from How We Learn to Speak to How We Build Culture," *Scientific American Mind* (May/June), New York: Scientific American. Online. Available www.david dobbs.net/page2/page4/mirrorneurons.html (accessed October 20, 2010).

Doerr, E. (2008) *Rudolf Laban: The Dancer of the Crystal*, Lanham, MD: Scarecrow Press.

Doidge, N. (2007) *The Brain that Changes Itself*, New York: Penguin Books.

Dubos, R. (1972) *A God Within*, New York: Charles Scribner's Sons.

—— (1981) *Celebrations of Life*, New York: McGraw-Hill, 1981.

Dyer, G. (1985) *War*, New York: Crown Publishers.

Easty, E.D. (1978) *On Method Acting*, Orlando, FL: House of Collectibles.

Edholm, O.G. (1967) *The Biology of Work*, New York: McGraw-Hill.

Eibl-Eibesfeldt, I. (1972) "Similarities and Differences between Cultures in Expressive Movements," in R.A. Hinde (Ed.) *Nonverbal Communication*: 297–312. Cambridge: Cambridge University Press.

Eiseley, L. (1957) *The Immense Journey*, New York: Vintage Books.

Ekman, P. (1985) *Telling Lies*, New York: W.W. Norton.

—— (1998) "Afterword: Universality of Emotional Expression? A Personal History of the Dispute," in Charles Darwin, *The Expression of the Emotions in Man and Animals*, 3rd ed.: 363–393. Oxford: Oxford University Press.

Eliade, M. (1959) *The Sacred and the Profane*, New York: Harcourt Brace & World.

Eshkol, N. and Wachman, A. (1958) *Movement Notation*, London: Weidenfeld & Nicolson.

Ewen, D. (Ed.) (1933) *From Bach to Stravinsky: History of Music by Its Foremost Critics*, New York: W.W. Norton.

Feldenkrais, M. (1973) *Body and Mature Behavior*, New York: International Universities Press.

Feuillet, R.A. (1968) *Chorégraphie, ou l'art de décrire la dance* (facsimile), New York: Broude Brothers (first published, Paris, 1700).

Freedman, R. (Ed.) (1962) *Marx on Economics*, New York: Penguin Books.

Freeman, W.J. (2000) "Perception of Time and Causation through Kinesthesia of Intentional Action," *Cognitive Processing*, 1: 18–34.

Fry, R. (1926) *Transformations*, New York: Brentano's.

Gage, J. (1999) *Color and Culture*, Berkeley, CA: University of California Press.

Gallese, V. (2001) "The 'Shared Manifold' Hypothesis: From Mirror Neurons to Empathy," *Journal of Consciousness Studies*, 8 (5–7): 33–50.

Gibson, E. and Pick, A. (2000) *An Ecological Approach to Perceptual Learning and Development*, Oxford: Oxford University Press.

Gilbreth, F.B. (1953) "Motion Study," in W.R. Spriegel and C.E. Myers (Eds.) *The Writings of the Gilbreths*: 139–206. Homewood, IL: Richard D. Irwin.

Gladwell, M. (2005) *Blink*, New York: Little, Brown & Company.

Goffman, E. (1979) *Gender Advertisements*, New York: Harper Colophon Books.

Gombrich, E.H. (1963) "On Physiognomic Perception," in *Meditations on a Hobby Horse*: 45–55. London: Phaidon Publishers.

Green, M. (1986) *Mountain of Truth: The Counterculture Begins Ascona, 1900–1920*, Hanover, NH: University Press of New England.

Gregory, R.L. (1972) *Eye and Brain*, London: World University Library.

Guerrero, L.K., DeVito, J.A., and Hecht, M.L. (Eds.) (1999) *The Nonverbal Communication Reader*, 2nd ed., Prospect Heights, IL: Waveland Press.

Guest, A.H. (1983) *Your Move: A New Approach to the Study of Movement and Dance*, New York: Gordon & Breach.

—— (2005) *Labanotation*, 4th ed., New York: Routledge.

Guttmann, A. (1978) *From Ritual to Record*, New York: Columbia University Press.

Hackney, P. (1998) *Making Connections: Total Body Integration through Bartenieff Fundamentals*, Amsterdam: Overseas Publishers Association/Gordon & Breach.

Hall, E.T. (1959) *The Silent Language*, Garden City, NY: Doubleday.

—— (1969) *The Hidden Dimension*, Garden City, NY: Anchor Books.

—— (1976) *Beyond Culture*, Garden City, NY: Anchor Books.

—— (1983) *The Dance of Life*, New York: Anchor Press/Doubleday.

Halprin, A. (2000) *Dance as a Healing Art*, Mendocino, CA: Life Rhythm.

Hammond, R.A. (2009) *Respecting Babies*, Washington, DC: Zero to Three.

Hanna, T. (1995) "What is Somatics?" in D.H. Johnson (Ed.) *Bone, Breath, and Gesture: Practices of Embodiment*: 341–352. Berkeley, CA: North Atlantic Books.

Hartley, L. (1995) *Wisdom of the Body Moving*, Berkeley, CA: North Atlantic Books.

Hayakawa, S.I. (1978) *Language in Thought and Action*, 4th ed., San Diego, CA: Harcourt, Brace, Jovanovich.

Heeger, D. (2006) "Perception Lecture Notes: Visual Movement Perception," New York: New York University. Online. Available www.cns.nyu.edu/david/courses/perception/lecturenotes/motion/motion.html⟩ (accessed November 30, 2010).

Henley, N. (1977) *Body Politics*, Englewood Cliffs, NJ: Prentice-Hall.

Highwater, J. (1985) *Dance: Rituals of Experience*, New York: Alfred van der Marck.

Hodgson, J. (2001) *Mastering Movement: The Life and Work of Rudolf Laban*, London: Methuen.

Hodgson, J. and Preston-Dunlop, V. (1990) *Rudolf Laban: An Introduction to His Work and Influence*, Plymouth, UK: Northcote House.

Holmes, N.P. and Spence, C. (2006) "Beyond the Body Schema," in G. Knoblich, I.M. Thornton, M. Grosjean, and M. Shiffrar (Eds.) *Human Body Perception from the Inside Out*: 15–64. Oxford: Oxford University Press.

Huizinga, J. (1955) *Homo Ludens,* Boston, MA: Beacon Press.

Humphrey, D. (1959) *The Art of Making Dances*, New York: Grove Press.

Hutchinson, A. (1970) *Labanotation*, 2nd ed., New York: Theatre Arts Books.

Huxley, A. (1932) *Text and Pretext*, London: Chatto & Windus.

—— (1962) "Education on the Nonverbal Level," *Daedalus* 91 (2): 279–293.

International Somatic Movement Education and Therapy Association (2010) "Scope of Practice," Holyoke, MA: Author. Online. Available www.ismeta.org/about.html (accessed December 30, 2010).

Itten, J. (1961) *The Art of Color*, trans. Ernst van Haagen, New York: John Wiley & Sons.

James, W. (1981) *The Principles of Psychology*, Cambridge, MA: Harvard University Press (first published, 1890).

Jaques-Dalcroze, É. (1921) *Rhythm, Music, and Education*, New York: G.P. Putnam's Sons.

Jarvie, G. (2000) *Sport, Culture and Society*, New York: Routledge.

Jerome, J. (1980) *The Sweet Spot in Time*, New York: Summit Book.

Johnson, D.H. and Grand, I.J. (Eds.) (1998) *The Body in Psychotherapy*, Berkeley, CA: North Atlantic Books.

Johnson, M. (1987) *The Body in the Mind: The Bodily Basis of Meaning, Imagination, and Reason*, Chicago, IL: University of Chicago Press.

—— (2007) *The Meaning of the Body: Aesthetics of Human Understanding*, Chicago, IL: University of Chicago Press.

Jordan, S. (2005) "Preface," in Guest, A.H., *Labanotation*, 4th ed.: xiii–xiv. New York: Routledge.

Jourdain, R. (2002) *Music, the Brain, and Ecstasy*, New York: Quill/HarperCollins.

Juhan, D. (1998) *Job's Body: A Handbook for Bodywork*, Barrytown, MA: Station Hill.

Kaes, A., Jay, M., and Dimendberg, E. (1994) "The Cult of the Body: *Lebensreform*, Sports,and Dance," in A. Kaes, M. Jay, and E. Dimendberg (Eds.) *The Weimar Republic Sourcebook*: 673–675. Berkeley, CA: University of California Press.

Kingdon, J. (1993) *Self-Made Man*, New York: John Wiley & Sons.

Kirstein, L. (1969) *Dance: A Short History of Classic Theatrical Dancing*, New York: Dance Horizons.

—— (1970) *Movement and Metaphor: Four Centuries of Ballet*, New York: Praeger Publishers.

Knoblich, G., Thornton, I.M., Grosjean, M., and Shiffrar, M. (2006) "Integrating Perspectives on Human Body Perception," in Knoblich, G, Thornton, I., Grosjean, M., and Shiffrar, M. (Eds.) *Human Body Perception from the Inside Out*: 3–8. Oxford: Oxford University Press.

Knust, A. (1979) *A Dictionary of Kinetography Laban (Labanotation)*, vols. 1 and 2, Plymouth, UK: Macdonald & Evans.

Koffka, K. (1922*)* "Perception: An Introduction to the Gestalt-Theorie," *Psychological Bulletin*, 19: 531–585.

Köhler, W. (1924) *Die Physischen Gestalten in Ruhe und im stationären Zustand: Eine Naturphilosophische Untersuchung*, Braunschweig (Ger.): Friedrich Vieweg und Sohn.

Korda, M. (1979) *Power: How to Get It, How to Use It*, New York: Random House.

Korzybski, A. (1933) *Science and Sanity*, Lancaster, PA: Science Press Printing Company.

Kozloff, M. (1968) *Renderings: Critical Essays on a Century of Modern Art*, New York: Simon & Schuster.

Laban, R. (1928) *Schrifttanz*, Vienna: Universal-Edition.

—— (1956) *Principles of Dance and Movement Notation*, London: Macdonald & Evans.

—— (1957) "The Objective Observation of Subjective Movement and Action," *Laban Art of Movement Guild Magazine*, 19 (November): 12–13.

—— (1971a) *The Mastery of Movement*, 3rd ed., Boston, MA: Plays, Inc. (first published, 1950).

—— (1971b) "The Rhythm of Effort and Recovery," in L. Ullmann (Ed.) *Rudolf Laban Speaks about Movement and Dance*: 44–55. Surrey, UK: Laban Art of Movement Centre.

—— (1971c) "The World of Rhythm and Harmony," in L. Ullmann (Ed.) *Rudolf Laban Speaks about Movement and Dance*: 40–43. Surrey, UK: Laban Art of Movement Centre.

—— (1974) *The Language of Movement*, Boston, MA: Plays, Inc.

—— (1975a) *A Life for Dance*, New York: Theatre Arts Books.

—— (1975b) *Laban's Principles of Dance and Movement Notation*, 2nd ed., Boston, MA: Plays Inc.

—— (1975c) *Modern Educational Dance,* 3rd ed., London: Macdonald & Evans (first published, 1948).

—— (1984) *A Vision of Dynamic Space*, London: Falmer Press.

—— (n.d.) "Hands," unpublished manuscript, Rudolf Laban Archive, Guildford, Surrey, UK: National Resource Centre for Dance, University of Surrey.

Laban, R. and Lawrence, F.C. (1974) *Effort*, London: Macdonald & Evans (first published, 1947).

La Barre, W. (1954) *The Human Animal*, Chicago, IL: University of Chicago Press.

Lakoff, G. (1987) *Women, Fire, and Dangerous Things,* Chicago, IL: University of Chicago Press.

Lakoff, G. and Johnson, M. (1980) *Metaphors We Live By*, Chicago, IL: University of Chicago Press.

Lamb, W. (1965) *Posture and Gesture*, London: Gerald Duckworth.

—— (1986) "The Laban Lecture: Movement as a Common Denominator," *Movement and Dance*, 75 (September): 7–14.

Lamb, W. and Turner, D. (1969) *Management Behaviour*, London: Gerald Duckworth.

Lamb, W. and Watson, E. (1979) *Body Code: The Meaning in Movement*, London: Routledge & Kegan Paul.

Lane, H.L. (1976) *The Wild Boy of Aveyron*, Cambridge, MA: Harvard University Press.

Langer, S.K. (1953) *Feeling and Form: A Theory of Art*, New York: Charles Scribner's Sons.

—— (1957) *Problems of Art*, New York: Charles Scribner's Sons.

—— (1976) *Philosophy in a New Key: A Study in the Symbolism of Reason, Rite, and Art*, 3rd ed., Cambridge, MA: Harvard University Press.

Lawrence, D.H. (1976) "New Mexico," in T. Hillerman (Ed.) *The Spell of New Mexico*: 29–36. Albuquerque, NM: University of New Mexico Press.

Lecoq, J. (2002) *The Moving Body*, New York: Routledge.

Leonard, G. (1978) *The Silent Pulse*, New York: Bantam Books.

Levin, D.M. (1999) "The Ontological Dimension of Embodiment," in D. Welton (Ed.) *The Body*: 122–149, Oxford: Blackwell.

Levine, R. (1997) *A Geography of Time*, New York: Basic Books.

Levitin, D.J. (2007) *This Is Your Brain on Music*, New York: Plume/Penguin.

Lomax, A. (1968) *Folk Song Style and Culture*, Washington, DC: American Association for the Advancement of Science.

—— (1982) "The Cross-Cultural Variation of Rhythmic Style," in M. Davis (Ed.) *Interaction Rhythms: Periodicity in Communicative Behavior*: 149–174. New York: Human Sciences Press.

Lonsdale, S. (1982) *Animals and the Origins of Dance*, New York: Thames & Hudson.

McDonaugh, D. (1970) *The Rise and Fall and Rise of Modern Dance*, New York: E.P. Dutton.

McLuhan, M. (1964) "Games: The Extensions of Man," in *Understanding Media: The Extensions of Man*: 235–245. New York: McGraw-Hill

McNeill, W.H. (1995) *Keeping Together in Time: Dance and Drill in Human History*, Cambridge, MA: Harvard University Press.

Maguire, J. A., Jarvie, G., Mansfield, L., and Bradley, J. (2002) *Sports Worlds: A Sociological Perspective*, Champaign, IL: Human Kinetics.

Maletic, V. (1987) *Body Space Expression*, Berlin: Mouton de Gruyter.

—— (2005) *Dance Dynamics: Effort and Phrasing*, Columbus, OH: Grade A Notes.

Manning, S.A. (1993) *Ecstasy and the Demon: Feminism and Nationalism in the Dances of Mary Wigman*, Berkeley, CA: University of California Press.

Marks, J.E. (1975) *The Mathers on Dancing*, Brooklyn, NY: Dance Horizons.

Martin, J. (1936) *America Dancing: The Background and Personalities of the Modern Dance*, New York: Dodge Publishing Co.

Maslow, A. (1970) "A Theory of Human Motivation," in V.H. Vroom and E.L. Deci (Eds.) *Management and Motivation*: 27–41. New York: Penguin Books.

Massad, C.E. (1979) "Time and Space in Space and Time," in K. Yamamoto (Ed.) *Children in Time and Space*: 1–20. New York: Teachers College Press.

Meerloo, J.A.M. (1960) *The Dance*, Philadelphia, PA: Chilton Company.

Merleau-Ponty, M. (1962) *Phenomenology of Perception*, trans. C. Smith, London: Routledge & Kegan Paul.

Mlakar, P. (1979) "Thoughts of a Choreographer on the Importance of Kinetography Laban," in A. Knust, *Dictionary of Kinetography Laban*, vol. 1: xvii–xxi. Estover, Plymouth, UK: Macdonald & Evans.

Molloy, J.T. (1975) *Dress for Success*, New York: P.H. Wyden.

Montessori, M. (1969) *The Absorbent Mind*, New York: Dell.

Moore, C.L. (2005) *Movement and Making Decisions*, New York: Dance & Movement Press/Rosen.

—— (2009) *The Harmonic Structure of Movement, Music, and Dance According to Rudolf Laban*, Lewiston, NY: Edwin Mellen Press.

Morris, D. (1977) *Manwatching*, New York: Harry N. Abrams.

—— (1994) *Bodytalk: The Meaning of Human Gestures*, New York: Crown.

Mumford, L. (1967) *Technics and Human Development*, New York: Harcourt Brace Jovanovich.

—— (1978) *The Transformation of Man*, Gloucester, MA: Peter Smith.

Murphy, M. (1992) *The Future of the Body*, New York: Jeremy P. Tarcher/Putnam Books.

Myrdal, G. (1969) *Objectivity in Social Science Research*, New York: Pantheon.

Nierenberg, G.I., Calero, H.H., and Grayson, G. (2010) *How to Read a Person Like a Book*, Garden City Park, NY: Square One Publishers.

North, M. (1975) *Personality Assessment through Movement*, Boston, MA: Plays, Inc.

Oakley, K.P. (1961) *Man the Tool-maker*, Chicago, IL: University of Chicago Press.

Orme, J.E. (1978) "Time: Psychological Aspects," in T. Carlstein, D. Parkes, and N. Thrift (Eds.) *Making Sense of Time*: 66–75. New York: John Wiley & Sons.

Ornstein, R.E. (1969) *On the Experience of Time*, New York: Penguin.

Ortega y Gasset, J. (1986) *Historical Reason*, New York: W.W. Norton.

Osterley, W.O.E. (1923) *The Sacred Dance*, Brooklyn, NY: Dance Horizons.

Pearce, C. (1980) *Magical Child*, New York: Bantam Books.

Pinto, J. (2006) "Developing Body Representation: A Review of Infants' Responses to Biological Motion Displays," in G. Knoblich, I.M. Thornton, M. Grosjean, and M. Shiffrar, M. (Eds.), *Human Body Perception from the Inside Out*: 305–322, New York: Oxford University Press.

Polanyi, M. (1962) *Personal Knowledge: Towards a Post-critical Philosophy*, Chicago, IL: University of Chicago Press.

—— (1966) *The Tacit Dimension*, Garden City, NY: Anchor Doubleday.

—— (1969) *Knowing and Being*, Chicago, IL: University of Chicago Press.

Preston-Dunlop, V. (1998a) *Looking at Dances: A Choreological Perspective on Choreography*, London: Verve Publishing.

—— (1998b) *Rudolf Laban: An Extraordinary Life*, London: Dance Books.

Prinz, W. (2006) "Representational Foundation of Intentional Action," in G. Knoblich, I.M. Thornton, M. Grosjean, and M. Shiffrar, M. (Eds.), *Human Body Perception from the Inside Out*: 393–411. New York: Oxford University Press.

Rabinbach, A. (1992) *The Human Motor*, Berkeley, CA: University of California Press.

Ramsden, P. (1973) *Top Team Planning*, London: Cassell/Associated Business Programmes.

Ricoeur, P. (1977) *The Rule of Metaphor: Multi-disciplinary Studies of the Creation of Meaning in Language*, trans. Robert Czerny, Toronto: University of Toronto Press.

Riesman, D. and Denney, R. (1972) "Football in America: A Study in Cultural Diffusion," in M.M. Hart (Ed.) *Sport in the Socio-Cultural Process*. Dubuque, IA: Wm. C. Brown.

Rizzolatti, G. and Craighero, L. (2004) "The Mirror Neuron System," *Annual Review of Neuroscience*, 27: 169–192.

Rizzolatti, G. and Destro, M.F. (2008) "Mirror Neurons," *Scholarpedia*, 3(1): 2055. Halifax, Canada: Scholarpedia. c/o Dalhousie University. Online. Available www.scholarpedia.org/Mirror_neurons (accessed October 20, 2010).

Rodenburg, P. (1992) *The Right to Speak*, New York: Routledge.

Rosenfeld, P. (1972) *Discoveries of a Music Critic*, New York: Vienna House.

Rosenthal, R., Hall, J.A., DiMatteo, M.R., Rogers, P.L., and Archer, D. (1979) *Sensitivity to Nonverbal Communication: The PONS Test*, Baltimore, MD: Johns Hopkins University Press.

Ross, M. (1973) "Football and Baseball in America," in J.T. Talamini and C.H. Page (Eds.) *Sport and Society*. Boston, MA: Little, Brown and Company.

Rostand, E. (1981) *Cyrano de Bergerac*, trans. Brian Hooker, New York: Bantam.

Sacks, O. (1984) *A Leg to Stand On*, New York: Summit Books.

Schechner, R. (1985) *Between Theatre and Anthropology*, Philadelphia, PA: University of Philadelphia Press.

Scheflen, A.E. (1972) *Body Language and Social Order*, Englewood Cliffs, NJ: Prentice-Hall.

—— (1973) *How Behavior Means*, New York: Gordon & Breach.

Schiesel, S. (2010) "Motion, Sensitive," *New York Times*, New York. Online. Available www.access2art.net/69121/motion-sensitive-seth-schieselnew-york-times/ (accessed December 22, 2010).

Schwartz, J.M. and Begley, S. (2002) *The Mind and the Brain: Neuroplasticity and the Power of Mental Force*, New York: ReganBooks/HarperCollins.

Segel, H.B. (1998) *Body Ascendant*, Baltimore, MD: Johns Hopkins University Press.

Sessions, R. (1971) *Questions about Music*, New York: W.W. Norton.

Sheets-Johnstone, M. (2009) *The Corporeal Turn: An Interdisciplinary Reader*, Charlottesville, VA: Imprint Academic.

Shiffrar, M. (2010) "People Watching: Visual, Motor, and Social Processes in the Perception of Human Movement." Newark, NJ: Rutgers University. Online. Available www.onlinelibrary.wiley.com/doi/10.1002/wcs.88/full (accessed December 8, 2010).

Siegel, M.B. (1972) *At the Vanishing Point: A Dance Critic Looks at Dance*, New York: Saturday Review Press.

—— (1985) *The Shapes of Change: Images of American Dance*, Berkeley, CA: University of California Press.

Sorell, W. (1986) *Dance in Its Time*, New York: Columbia University Press.

Stanton-Jones, K. (1992) *An Introduction to Dance Movement Therapy in Psychiatry*, London: Tavistock/Routledge.

Steiner, R. (1983) *Creative Eurythmy*, London: Rudolf Steiner Press.

Stravinsky, I. (1970) *Poetics of Music*, Cambridge, MA: Harvard University Press.

Szwed, J.F. (1975) "Race and the Embodiment of Culture," in J. Benthall and T. Polhemus (Eds.) *The Body as a Medium of Expression*: 253–270. New York: E.P. Dutton.

Taylor, F. W. (1971) "Scientific Management," in D.S. Pugh (Ed.) *Organization Theory*: 124–146. New York: Penguin Books.

Thomas, H. (2003) *The Body, Dance and Cultural Theory*, New York: Palgrave Macmillan.

Thornton, I.M. (2006a) "Biological Motion: Point-light Walkers and Beyond," in G. Knoblich, I.M. Thornton, M. Grosjean, and M. Shiffrar (Eds.), *Human Body Perception from the Inside Out*: 271–303. New York: Oxford University Press.

—— (2006b) "Of Bodies, Brains, and Models: Studying the Perception of Biological Movement," in G. Knoblich, I.M. Thornton, M. Grosjean, and M. Shiffrar (Eds.), *Human Body Perception from the Inside Out*: 261–270. New York: Oxford University Press.

Thornton, S. (1971) *A Movement Perspective of Rudolf Laban*, London: Macdonald & Evans.

Tocqueville, A. de (1945) *Democracy in America*, trans. F. Bowen, New York: Alfred Knopf, Vintage Books (first published, Paris 1835).

Todd, M.E. (1973) *The Thinking Body* (reprint), Brooklyn, NY: Dance Horizons (first published, 1937).

Tortora, S. (2006) *The Dancing Dialogue*, Baltimore, MD: Paul H. Brookes.

Toth, N. and Schick, K. (1993), "Early Stone Industries and Inferences regarding Language and Cognition," in K.R. Gibson and T. Ingold (Eds.) *Tools, Language and Cognition*: 346–362. Cambridge: Cambridge University Press.

Trippett, F. (1981) "Why So Much Is Beyond Words," *Time Magazine* (July 13): 71–72.

Tuan, Y-F. (1977) *Space and Place: The Perspective of Experience*, Minneapolis, MN: University of Minnesota Press.

—— (1978) "Space, Time, Place: A Humanistic Frame," in T. Carlstein, D. Parkes, and N. Thrift (Eds.) *Making Sense of Time* (vol. 1 of *Timing Space and Spacing Time*): 7–16. New York: John Wiley & Sons.

Turney-High, H.H. (1981) *The Military*, West Hanover, MA: Christopher Publishing House.

Udy, S.H. (1970) *Work in Traditional and Modern Society*, Englewood Cliffs, NJ: Prentice-Hall.

Umminger, W. (1963) *Supermen, Heroes, and Gods*, New York: McGraw-Hill.

UniSci (2001) "Brain Areas Critical to Human Time Sense Identified," Cape Coral, FL: UniScience News Net, Inc. Online. Available www.unisci.com/stories,20011/0227013.html (accessed November 7, 2010).

United States Association for Body Psychotherapy (2010) "A Brief Description of Body Psychotherapy," Silver Spring, MD: Author. Online. Available www.usabp.org (accessed December 30, 2010).

Van Zile, J. (2006) "Interpreting the Historical Record: Using Images of Korean Dance for Understanding the Past," in T.J. Buckland (Ed.) *Dancing from Past to Present*: 153–174. Madison, WI: University of Wisconsin Press.

Wainwright, G.R. (2003) *Teach Yourself Body Language*, London: Hodder & Stoughton.

Wertheimer, M. (1938) "Laws of Organization in Perceptual Forms," in W. Ellis (Ed.) *A Source Book of Gestalt Psychology*: 71–88. London: Routledge & Kegan Paul (the original paper published in 1923).

Wilson, E.O. (1986) *Biophilia*, Cambridge, MA: Harvard University Press.

Wolfgang, A. (1995) *Everybody's Guide to People Watching*, Yarmouth, ME: Intercultural Press.

Wosien, M. (1974) *Sacred Dance*, New York: Avon Books.

Yamamoto, K. (2007) *Too Clever for Our Own Good: Hidden Facets of Human Evolution*, Lanham, MD: University Press of America.

Yanagawa, M. (1973) *The First Japanese Mission to America* (reprint), Wilmington, DE: Scholarly Resources (originally, 1860).

Yarrow, K., Brown, P., and Krakauer, J.W. (2009) "Inside the Brain of an Elite Athlete: The Neural Processes that Support High Achievement in Sports," *Neuroscience*, 10: 585–597.

Index

abstraction 48–51, 57, 63, 100
attunement 30, 153–154, 156, 166
automatic processing 44–45

ballet 103, 117, 139
baseball 107–108
Berger, Peggy 177, 178–179, 210
Birdwhistell, Ray 71–72
body knowledge 50–52, 54–56, 58, 60, 62, 126, 127, 164, 165; in hunting and combat 100, 102, 103, 104
body, perception of 13, 47–48
body prejudice 52–53, 54–56, 58, 60, 62, 127, 164, 165
body psychotherapy 121, 123
body, use of 136–139
brain 12–13, 26, 27, 33–37, 56–57, 58, 214

Captain Cook 73–74
categorization 48–52, 57
child development 34–37, 42
Choreometrics 92, 160
cinematography 212–213
coding sheets 163, 168–173
combat 103; see also body knowledge
Condon, William 17, 121
conscious people watching 9, 10, 218
contest 89, 90, 99, 105; see also games, sports
context 71–78, 83, 216–217
culture, influence on perception 46–47; see also context

dance 6–7, 25, 41, 92, 106, 131, 138–139, 212–214; Christian Church and dance 118–120; primal sacred dance 120–121; secular social dance 112–113, 116–118; theatrical dance 117–118, 119, 213
dance/movement therapy 121–122
dance notation systems 131, 163, 212–214; Benesh 7, 163; Eshkol-Wachman 7, 163; Feuillet 7; Kinetography Laban 213; Labanotation 7, 131, 163, 213
Darwin, Charles 68–69, 71
Davis, Martha 160, 162
deception detection 113
dimensions 141–142, 143, 149
Doodling 30, 154
Dynamics 59, 63, 154
dynamics/dynamic energy see effort
duration of observation 156, 158–160, 165, 166, 167

Echoing 30, 154
economy of motion 96
effort 134, 143–148; effort combinations 147; effort sequences 147–148
effort analysis 97–98
empathy 9, 21, 27, 28, 47
energy, dynamic see effort
entrainment 17, 26, 60; see also synchrony of movement and speech

ergonomics 98–99
etiquette 112–113
evolution 65, 90–92; biological 27,
    32–37, 56–57; cultural 27, 37–39,
    47, 57; of language 41–42, 45
exertion/recuperation 133, 134
extension systems 37–39, 57, 65,
    100; body movement as 39–42,
    45, 56, 57, 65, 76–77, 127

flow effort 143, 144, 147
focal awareness 8–9, 150–151,
    210
focus 143, 144–146
football 107–108
functional magnetic resonance
    imaging 214

games 105–109
Gestalt psychologists 29
gesture 136–139, 149
gesture recognition 214
Gilbreths, Frank and Lillian 95–96,
    97
Graham, Martha 139
Guest, Ann Hutchinson 131

Hall, Edward T. 72, 76–77, 121
hearing 16–17, 26, 28, 30
"hierarchy of needs" 88–89
humane effort 134–135
human movement, perception of
    14–19, 26–27, 28, 30; sensitivity
    to 19–22, 27, 44–45
hunting 100–101, 105

industrialization 93–94
initiation of body movement
    138–139, 149
Instant Replay 60, 63, 154

Johansson point-light walker 19–20,
    22, 26, 96

Kestenberg Movement Profile
    164
kinesphere 140
kinesthesia 11, 14–15, 26, 28, 30
Knust, Albrecht 131

Laban Movement Analysis 2, 130,
    150, 160, 177–178, 211, 213;
    elements of 136–148; general
    principles 132–136
Laban, Rudolf ix, 63, 97, 98,
    130–132, 212
Lamb, Warren 98, 177, 191, 210
Lawrence, F.C. 97, 98
"Ladder of Abstraction" 48–49, 51,
    60, 63
Learn a Phrase 59, 63, 155

making sense of movement 47–56,
    57, 156, 164–166, 167, 211;
    see also movement metaphors
Marey, Étienne–Jules 96, 97, 212
Maslow, Abraham 88–89
McNeill, William H. 40, 41
memory 22, 28, 30
metaphor 65–67, 78–79, 82–83
military training, uses of movement
    in 102–104
Mirroring 30, 153
mirror neurons 19, 20–22, 27, 28,
    42, 44–47, 57
modern dance 131, 139, 159
motion capture 96, 214
motion factors 143, 144
movement analysis, examples of:
    aikido 178–191; cabinet-making
    191–198; creative dramatics
    class 204–209; staff meeting
    198–204
movement, awareness of 2, 28–31,
    42, 44, 57, 127
Movement Canon 30
movement/dance style 159, 160,
    213
movement elements 59, 60, 135, 136,
    148, 149; body 136–139;
    dynamics (effort) 143–148; space
    139–143; *see also* selection of
    movement parameters
movement, functions of 87–90; *see
    also* social life, sports, war, work,
    worship
movement, meaning of 216–219;
    see also making sense of
    movement

movement metaphors: language 67–78, 79, 80; visual art 80; music 80–82

Movement Pattern Analysis 98, 160, 164

movement study, challenges in 6–10, 215–217

Moving Sculpture 59, 63, 154

"muscular bonding" 40, 41, 42

music 7, 80–82, 212

nerves, sensory: exteroceptors 13, 14, 19, 26; interoceptors 13–14, 26; proprioceptors 13, 14–16, 19, 26

neuroplasticity 12–13, 26, 33–36, 58, 214

neuroscience ix, 11, 214

nonverbal behavior 9, 10; style and social affiliation 110

nonverbal communication 2, 5–6, 9, 10; role in child development 35–37, 42, 57; role in human evolution 39–42

observation process 152, 156, 157, 158, 166

Olympics 106, 107

perceptual learning 46–47

"physiognomic approach" 69–70, 71, 216

Picasso, Pablo 75

planes of motion, *see* dimensions

play 105

point of concentration 59, 154–155, 156, 166

Polanyi, Michael 8, 9, 150–151, 154

posture 136–139, 149

power embodiment 70–71

prejudice 9; *see also* body prejudice

pressure 143, 144, 146

Ramsden, Pamela 52

recording movement impressions 156, 162–164, 165, 166, 167, 168–176; *see also* cinematography, motion capture, video recording

recuperation 30–31, 155–156, 166

relaxation 30–31, 152–153, 156, 166

role of observer 156, 157–158, 165, 166, 167

Sacks, Oliver 44

Schick, Pam 177, 198–199, 210

Scientific Management 94–95

Seeing without Words 30, 31, 153

sense organs 12

selection of movement parameters 156, 160–162, 165, 166, 167

sensory–motor system 11–12

Silly Walks 59, 63, 154

soccer 108

social life, role of movement in 90, 109–114, 126

somatics 121, 123–125

space effort *see* focus

space, use of 139–143, 149

spatial locale 140, 143, 149

sports 105–109, 137, 151

stability/mobility 133

subsidiary awareness 8–9, 150–151, 154, 210

"sweet spots in time" 43

synchrony of motion and speech 17, 26

Taylor, Frederick Winslow 94–95, 96

theatre 7, 114–116, 212

thinking 47, 63, 67, 88, 100

time, perception of 22–25, 27, 80; circadian clock 23; cyclical time 23, 158; duration 23; linear time 24, 158; time and movement 24–25, 27, 158–160

Time and Motion Study 95–96

time effort 143, 144, 146–147

touch 14, 16, 26, 28, 30

trace-forms 141, 143, 149

True, Sharon 177, 204, 210

"tune out" 8, 28, 29

Two Entrances 59, 63, 155

verbal language 41–42, 79

vestibular apparatus 15–16, 18, 19